After Capitalism & Christianity

Liberal Utopia ... or Great Tribulation?

After Capitalism & Christianity

Liberal Utopia ... or Great Tribulation?

Thomas G. Reed

Laurus BOOKS

*Unless otherwise specified, all Scripture quotations are from the **King James Version** of the Holy Bible (KJV)*, *which is available in the Public Domain.*

After Capitalism & Christianity

Liberal Utopia ... or Great Tribulation?

By Thomas G. Reed

Copyright © 2012 by Thomas G. Reed

All rights reserved. This book is protected under the copyright laws of the United States of America. This book may not be copied or reprinted for commercial gain or profit. The use of short quotations or occasional page copying for personal or group study is permitted and encouraged. Permission will be granted on request.

Paperback Book: ISBN-13: 978-0-9847683-2-5

E-Book: ISBN-13: 978-0-9847683-3-2

Edited and designed by Nancy E. Williams
Cover illustration by Jennifer Cappoen

Published by LAURUS BOOKS
Printed in the United States of America

LAURUS BOOKS
P. O. Box 894
Locust Grove, GA 30248 USA
www.LaurusBooks.com

This book may be purchased in paperback or eBook from LaurusBooks.com, Amazon.com, and other retailers around the world.

Dedicated to

Mrs. Mary R. Harper

for her unwavering confidence in me.

Acknowledgements

I wish to express my appreciation to
Mr. Perry Ennis
who was kind enough
to put me in contact with
a godsend—
Mrs. Nancy E. Williams,
my wonderful editor and publisher.

TABLE OF CONTENTS

INTRODUCTION 9

SECTION I: THE END OF OLD AMERICA

    1. The New America 15

    2. The Second Revolution 35

    3. The Anointed One 47

    4. Democracy Gone Bad 57

    5. Revolution or Reformation? 67

SECTION II: THE END OF CAPITALISM

    6. The Babylon Whore 77

SECTION III: THE END OF CHRISTIANITY

    7. The Effect of Humanism 99

    8. The Effect of Capitalism 111

    9. The Effect of Worldliness 117

    10. Apostate Leaders 123

    11. Worship in the Flesh 131

SECTION IV: THE END OF TIME

    12. The Coming Tribulation 139

    13. Why Have a Tribulation 161

Section V: The End of Self

14. The Need for Holiness 167

15. Dead to Self (The Old Man) 175

16. Keeping the Old Man Dead 183

17. Separating from the World System 193

18. Coming Out of Babylon 201

19. Alive Unto God 213

Section VI: The End of Mediocrity

20. The Worst of Times 223

21. The Best of Times 235

Appendix A: The Post Tribulation Rapture 247

Appendix B: The End of Time 255

Bibliography 259

About The Author 263

INTRODUCTION

After Capitalism and Christianity is a discussion about the worst of times and the best of times. In many ways, it is a sad story because, in it, we explore some painful truths about the future of our beloved country, our economic model, and our founding faith. Many sense the essence of these truths but are unable or afraid to admit that the American Eagle is struggling to maintain her flight and will eventually fall from her perch of international power and prominence. There is more sad news. America's economic model (capitalism) will also fail, and as is obvious to many, it is well on the way to failure already. We explain why the free market mode of commerce is destined to disappear. All of this is complicated by the obvious apostasy of mainline Christianity, laden with numbers but so diluted with worldliness that it is relatively ineffective in the struggles against immorality in America.

The demise of America and her foundational institutions is not by accident or default. It is a planned program of the destruction of a country and her way of life by a movement that is anathema to all we as Christian conservatives hold dear. The movement is humanism, and its pervasive tentacles (e.g. socialism, communism, feminism, etc.) are determined to destroy or at least humble us into submission to their globalist goals.

After Capitalism and Christianity examines the death grip that humanism has on America, her mode of commerce, and her religious structures. Contrary to accepted wisdom, we delve into the taboo topics of religion and politics, for nowadays the two have become one—politics has become a religion—and we are all affected by the humanistic mix, so much so that the future of our country, our economy, our faith and freedoms are at stake. And they are all under attack by the same forces of evil—the pervasive powers of religious humanism. So we want to look at its impact on all three.

Our discussion on the land that we love will be lengthy, for her enemies are many, and over the years, they have silently waged a successful revolution against all that was the old America. Now, they hold the higher ground in the struggle for uncontested power, as we shall see.

America's economic model is viewed by those of the humanist persuasion as the cause of poverty and the world's disparities in the distribution of wealth. As a result, when those who think that way came into power in the last century, they handcuffed capitalism with an array of rules, regulations, and illegal taxations on its way to the gallows of total socialist strangulation. *After Capitalism and Christianity* takes a long look at capitalism, her synthesis with socialism, and her eventual fall. As even a casual observer of politics has seen, capitalism is well on its way to total submission to the wishes of liberal socialists. Her end is near.

Sadly, mainline Christianity in America has backslidden and entered a heightened state of apostasy. It remains churchy but manifests only a form of godliness instead of the actual structure of holiness itself. Because there is no power without purity, Laodicean churchgoers will, of necessity, deny the power of God that accompanies godliness. So, two things—the church in America is unholy, and it is powerless.

As matters of state are ultimately impacted by matters of the heart, *After Capitalism and Christianity* devotes most of its space to the apostate church and how we, as its members, can rise to the heights of holiness. We will try to uncover the reason America's founding faith has failed to stem the tide of immorality and, in our opinion, lost the culture war. The church, its leaders, its powerless worship, the effects of humanism and capitalism—all are explored in great detail.

But we believe there is hope, if not for our nation's return to sanity, then at least for individuals in pursuit of sanctity. For those of us who choose holiness, these can be the best of times. Holiness—that is our goal and, yes, our only hope in these troubled times and what we believe is the prelude to the Great Tribulation, the end of time, and the return of Jesus Christ.

Granted, no man knows the day and hour Christ will return (we sure do not). Whether it is soon or many years away, we and those who follow us should live in awareness of the times and know what to expect when the end and that which precedes the end does occur. More importantly, it is that knowledge of the possibility of His return that should (if nothing else does) propel us to a holy walk with God (2 Peter 3:11). As Christ said, *"... be ye also ready: for in such an hour as ye think not the Son of Man cometh"* (Matthew 24:44).

We present our beliefs and opinions on how we should live as the end-time approaches but in no way pretend to have all the answers. There is no magic formula for the model walk before God. Each of us must work out our own salvation as we press toward the mark of Christlikeness. Of course, the Bible is the ultimate guide and source of all our beliefs. We just hope to help by collecting and categorizing end-time topics in a way that presents (in our opinion) model walk requirements as well as individual, corporate, and national consequences of turning our backs on God.

Unfolding events convince us that the end of time is near (see Appendix B). We therefore feel an urgency in knowing what we should expect, how we should prepare, and the rewards (the best of times) of our preparations, both in the here and now and afterward.

Before the end, we believe that Christians will experience a time of refinement (at God's hand) and severe persecution, even death (at Satan's hand). That means we believe the Rapture (First Resurrection) will occur at the end of the seven-year Tribulation but right before God's wrath is unleashed on a wicked, unrepentant world. We will attempt, with great detail, to explain the foundations of this belief in Appendix A.

If we are here in the Tribulation, we will be confronted with choices—take the mark of the Beast and worship his image, or be killed. If not killed outright, starvation would likely be our fate. No mark ... no buy or sell. Expect it! Also, expect the Beast's deceivableness, and know that the mark is not just another of this modern world's "harmless" identity markings.

Sad to say, the deceitfulness of Antichrist is already with us, in a big way. It seems a trademark of how things get done in America. Truthfulness is just another obstacle in the humanist's march toward total domination of the American landscape (the worst of times). So, let's begin with a comprehensive look at humanism in America and its effects on our morals, our politics, and our future.

Section I

THE END OF OLD AMERICA

1
THE NEW AMERICA

*A*merica has always been considered a Christian nation, not that all Americans are or ever were Christians. But a vein of biblically-based thought has run throughout our country since its birth. For nearly 150 years, the salt of Christian belief and behavior has mingled in our society, impacting favorably on every aspect of our lives. Our government, our educational system, our world view, and our culture, all reflected the traditions and teachings of God's Holy Word. Certainly, America had her problems with sin and periods of spiritual declension, but, as a rule, morality prevailed and, with it, freedom and liberty triumphed.

But now this can no longer be said. In spite of the nation's godly heritage, the Christian consensus over the past seventy-five years or so has lost its evangelical grip on the social and cultural aspects of American life. The old America has quietly disappeared. In the new America, Christian morals are no longer accepted and taught. Evil is called good; right is called wrong. "What is" determines what ought to be. Situational ethics supersede the unchanging, Holy Ghost-inspired absolutes found in God's Word.

In the new America, *truth has fallen in the street, and justice lies by her side*. Deception is on steroids. An apathetic self, lacking love, has become our god. The good are despised and maligned. The bad are often worshiped as heroes. Sin is accepted as everyday behavior. Blame is laid at the feet of society or poverty or discrimination.

Prosperity has spoiled us. We have borrowed recklessly with little or no concern for the future just to maintain a lifestyle we cannot afford. We are proud. We have plenty. We are lovers of pleasure compounded (entertainment non-stop). Hollywood turns out mind-numbing filth by the truckload—the depths of depravity are without limits.

We mass murder millions of innocent babies, then import (legally and illegally) foreign workers, especially from our southern neighbor, to do our menial jobs that we are too lazy or too burdened with debt to do. The church is in a state of apostasy, powerless but unaware of its ineffectiveness, too absorbed with doctrines of self emulation, self-improvement, and prosperity. Even so, Biblical Christians in the new America are hated, scoffed at, and portrayed as idiots.

In the new America, taking responsibility for one's own success has faded as individual and group rights have risen; not only have they risen, but they ride roughshod over the freedoms of those unable or unwilling to claim special rights. Typical of the rights movements are civil rights, women's rights, children's rights, animal rights, homosexual rights, labor rights, health care rights, security rights, litigation rights, etc. Yet, gone are the rights of the unborn who cannot speak and cannot vote but have fallen victim to the self lovers who glory in their right to choose death for the helpless baby. The babies who do make it grow up to harbor disdain, even disgust for their parents. Disobedience hardly describes the depths of their disrespect.

In the new America, the sin of homosexuality is blessed as just an alternate approach, devoid of natural affection, yet bursting with political clout. Our government officials and politicians bow and cater to their open, boastful, and often militant demands for special rights, as if they are somehow an oppressed people. They clamor for respect while they display rampant disrespect of and disdain for Christians and Biblical values.

The new America has (for the most part) turned her back on God and seems destined to continue to do so because our institutional infrastructures are powerful, pervasive, and godless. For this ethically challenged generation, traditional Judeo-Christian values have long since vanished from the public square, just like God's Word. With the Word banned publicly, we have lost our only true guide, for it contains unchangeable absolutes and laws to rightly govern the affairs of man—nothing else will.

Lost, too, is God's unseen hedge of protection around America. Much of the world hates us. Our enemies blackmail us with oil and threats of nuclear attacks. Others fly our own planes into skyscrapers killing thousands. Terrorist plots and homegrown cells put us under siege. Our borders are porous, hardly a barrier to determined America haters who threaten our annihilation.

Why, in such a short time, have basic Christian truths lost their influence over our once-godly nation? Why do we as a people bear so little resemblance to the brave souls who birthed us? Why has America been reduced to a second-rate nation, seemingly defenseless against a raging torrent of socialist insurgents, incurable diseases, and international terrorism? What happened to the old America?

For the apparent answer, we need look no further than humanism, the deadly cancer that has all but destroyed the Judeo-Christian infrastructure upon which this country was founded. Over the last eight decades, humanism, or the New Age Movement as it has been called, has dumped its killer germs into the mainstream of American political, educational, economic, and religious thought. Through an assortment of radical sub-movements—environmentalists, globalism, socialism, feminism, civil rights, gay rights, abortion rights, children's rights, liberalism, the green movement, progressivism, the peace movement, etc.—humanism has infected the very lifeblood of this country's existence.

Throughout this book, we will use the word "humanism," but let it be known that the word "liberalism" or "progressivism" could be used interchangeably with "humanism," for it is our opinion that liberals and progressives in America toe the humanist line in their anti-American, anti-capitalist, anti-Christian positions, rulings, and laws. When we look at America's future, we will include our thoughts on liberals and how their destructive policies, as humanism's ambassadors, contribute to the American eagle's fall from her perch of economic and military prowess.

For those who want to know the doctrines of humanism, look to the Bible. Every tenet of humanism is antithetical to the Word of God, just as Satan is the antithesis of God. If the Bible says yes, humanists say no. If the Bible says no, humanists say yes. *The Humanist Manifesto* is the Devil's bible, and humanists are his disciples. Humanism and Christianity are direct opposites and cannot long coexist in the heart of man or in the nation in which he lives. They are two entirely opposite world views as seen in the point-by-point comparison on the next page.

BIBLE (Word of God)	HUMANISM (Oracles of Satan)
There is one true God	There is no God (says the fool)
There is a Heaven and a Hell	There is no afterlife, no Heaven or Hell, imagine if you can
There are eternal consequences of sin	There are no eternal consequences for sin
Homosexuality is a sin	Homosexuality is natural
Endorses private ownership of property	Wants socialistic state ownership of production and property
God divided man at Tower of Babel by confusing their languages	Wants world community void of nationalism
God gave man dominion over the earth and the animals, etc.	Man is to worship the earth, promote animal rights
Self is to be abased, Esteem others better than self	Self is worshiped, promoted to godlike status
There are absolutes—values are fixed	The situation determines the action, values are fluid, no absolutes
Thou shalt not kill	Killing babies and old people is okay
Spare the rod and spoil the child	Children's rights / Animal rights
Women under subjection to their husbands	Men the butt of jokes, minimized and ridiculed, especially White males
Judaism and Christianity are distinct	There is good in all religions, but they must be massaged
Train up a child in the way it should go	Brainwash a child, practically from birth
God created all that is	Everything evolved
Man is born with a sinful nature	Man is inherently good
Liberty for all	All are slaves to the State
If a man does not work, neither shall he eat	If a lazy man does not vote (and vote often) neither shall he eat
Honor thy father and mother	Stick 'em in a rest home

In a nutshell, we might say that, as atheists, humanists are quick to affirm the supremacy of man and to deny the existence of God. Accordingly, they teach that everything evolved into its present state totally by chance without a special creative act of God Almighty. Since there is no god, they place man at the center of all things, as the measure of all things. As his own god, man began from himself with no knowledge except what he himself can discover.

Since there is no God, there are no standards outside of man, no absolutes to regulate his behavior. But then none are needed, for man is inherently good, in no need of salvation, without an eternal soul. There was no Fall; consequently, there is no sin nature, no right, no wrong. Man alone is responsible for his actions. He can love himself and find wholeness by being himself.

Since man is the essence of reality, he is self-sufficient, autonomous, independent, and in full control of his own future. All he needs is education and training to realize his most selfish fantasies and to actualize his unlimited human potential and intellectual awareness.

IMPACT ON AMERICA

The phenomenal spread of this cancerous filth into every facet of American life can be attributed to a massive, though sometimes nebulous, organization. Agencies like the American Humanist Association, the Aspen Institute for Humanistic Studies, the United Nations, and the ACLU are but the visible tip of the humanist iceberg. Through sophisticated networks, humanists have linked thousands of other organizations into an invisible tapestry, camouflaged so as to be imperceptible to the naked eye.

Then, with careful planning and dogged determination, they have planted members of these clandestine clubs in strategic policy-making positions throughout the country. In the twentieth century, as the humanist movement became more organized, it infiltrated every aspect of our society—the halls of academia, the entertainment industry, the informational media, the political process, and on and on. Now, they virtually control America's corporate business developments, her education process, her press, her government, her entertainment business and most of organized religion. As a result, humanism is legalized by her courts, legislated by her Congress, idolized by her schools, and sanctified by her churches.

Sure, there are vestiges of Christian behavior in the new America, and the majority of our citizens claim to be Christians, but humanists set the tone and are definitely in charge of our country. Their religion is the state religion. They control the preponderance of American behavior. We are definitely a changed people from even a few decades ago. Sure, old Americans survive, but the old America is gone. We now live in a new America, hardly recognizable to the older set who have fond memories of the way it used to be. The American eagle no longer proudly soars over a people of honor, integrity, and truthfulness.

So broad based is the New Age Movement, so engrained in all facets of our lives, and so effective are its disciples that humanism has actually become a way of life in America, and for good reason. New Agers so integrate every aspect of society that humanism seems like normal everyday living, and those who oppose it seem out of step. New Agers themselves admit that the movement moves toward integration and invisibility through the growth of familiarity and acceptance.

Sadly, some we would call new Americans have received humanism as the familiar and acceptable norm, not that they necessarily wanted to deny their Christian heritage, but because their mental composition has been progressively and systematically altered.

The wide scale mental transformation is being orchestrated by dedicated professionals with practices that are clearly antithetical to established Biblical procedure. Preaching values clarification, behavior modification, and situational ethics, these latter-day evangels do indeed alter the consciousness of all who open their minds to this insidious madness. In the reconditioning process, they defuse the conscience and leave their victims opposed to any direction from a God-authored source. When they are finished with the mutant, only the shell remains intact; the inner man has been transformed into a child of darkness. The self has been enthroned, and God has been eliminated from his heart altogether.

Through their invisible tapestry of networks, humanists have created armies of these mutants who love themselves, who view God as a mythical crutch for the ignorant and the weak of mind, who are tolerant of every religion in the world except Christianity, who vote as they are programmed to do, who shun and ridicule patriotic Americans with conservative values, who don't love their country but fashion themselves as citizens of the world.

ONE WORLD COMMUNITY

Beyond their stated objective of actualizing the self, humanists are driven by a compulsive desire to bring all nations together into a unified "world community." This transnational one-world conglomerate would, of course, be governed by international socialism: "A socialized and cooperative economic order must be established to the end that the equitable distribution of the means of life be possible."[1] It would be characterized by the "peaceful adjudication of differences"[2] and by the abolition of all nationalistic disputes, all destructive ideological distinctives, all inflexible puritanical restraints. And it would be disarmed. All men of all nations could then peacefully coexist in a golden age of brotherhood, total oneness and unequivocal unity—a liberal Utopia, if you will..

This, the New Ager's millennium, would also be noted for its spiritual experiences, experiences that would transcend the sacred and merge the whole of human experience into a continuum of religious thought and activity. In its final stages, the New Age Movement would be a religion, the religion of humanism. So said H. G. Wells, celebrated writer for the Movement: "It will have become a great world movement as widespread and evident as socialism or communism. It will largely have taken the place of these movements. It will be more; it will be a world religion. The large loose assimilatory mass of groups and societies will be definitely and obviously attempting to swallow up the entire population of the world and become the new human community."[3]

To arrive at this universal religious community, humanists must successfully synthesize all of man's divergent faiths into a comprehensive and apostate world religion under the control of a one-world Socialist government. Claire Chambers, a critic of humanism, observes: "It is the intent of the humanist hierarchy to mold all people of the world into an apostate religion under the control of a one-world Socialist government."[4]

For that to happen, America must fall from her place of prominence and power in the world. Likewise, capitalism must be eliminated or at least humbled into submission by saddling her with the burden of supporting financially the socialistic reallocation of privately produced resources and wealth. And to fold into a global religious structure, Christianity must be converted from its traditional beliefs and doctrines, those upon which America was founded, into a less offensive, less dogmatic and more humanist-friendly form. True Christians must be marginalized to minimize their impact on a changing world, mocked for their obsolete beliefs and behaviors, and then martyred to make way for the world's total acquiescence to the state religion of humanism.

We will look at the mechanisms, merger, and eventual fall of capitalism in Chapter Six. The blending and backsliding of mainline Christianity is so complex and so complete that we devote five chapters in Section Three to unravel it all. But for now, we want to look a little deeper into the fall of the American eagle—who is behind it, why they want the eagle to fall, and how they accomplish the fall of the land we love.

As with most Americans, we hold strong opinions as to the eagle's fate, especially in light of our recent elections. We believe that the demise of America and her foundational institutions is not by accident or default. It is a planned program of destruction of a country's history, its values, and its way of life by a movement that is anathema to all that we as Christian traditionalists hold dear. That movement is humanism, manifested politically as liberalism, and it is determined to create a new America filled with fully converted new Americans.

Sure, some old school patriotic Americans still live here and love their country, but for a large part of the population, the conversion is complete on two levels. One group represents the humanist clone who is totally brainwashed and manifests fully the ideas and ideals of his maker. The second group is the ignorant masses (the clowns) who do not have a clue what is going on, much less why, but they obey their masters for the handouts they get. The handouts serve a two-fold purpose—to cripple capitalism and, more importantly, to buy enough support for humanists to put their master plan into play.

Together, the clone and the clown make up a conglomerate colossal voting machine, which we shall call the "new Americans." The clones obviously think they are superior beings, and in their eyes, they tower intellectually above the rest of us, even their balloting brethren in the clown subset, the ignorant thugs they likely despise but nonetheless partner with to transform America according to the wishes of both their masters.

The new American has been conditioned by the liberal humanist machine to look like this: He hates his country. After all, what is in a country, a glob of dirt with trees and grass and lots of weeds? You can get that anywhere on the globe. Keep your flag to yourself; just show me the money. Sadly, new Americans don't care what happens to their country so long as the checks keep coming. Your country for a bowl of soup. Therefore, the new American strengthens the world at the expense of America. He brags on Castro and Hugo Chavez. He apologizes incessantly for his country's imperialistic behavior. He supports the anti-American United Nations. He sends billions in foreign aid to countries that hate us and to international money distributors who do the same. He allows millions of illegal aliens to enter and stay (and vote) in America.

The new Americans care not for our heritage and Christian traditions, much less the dogmas of the Christian faith. They legalize baby murder, homosexual marriages, banning prayer in public schools. The family unit is an unnecessary, often harmful, anachronism to them. Population control excites them. That is one reason feminism and homosexuality get such fanfare. That is one reason they have such hatred for males—the instigators of the mess in the first place. That is one reason they have killed an entire generation of our babies who could have supplied labor, teachers, doctors, soldiers, more honest politicians (closing in on an oxymoron).

The new American has been robbed of his responsibility, accountability, and freedom. Everything is planned for him by a corps of government central planners. He votes for legislators who pass anti-American, capitalist-killing legislation, plus laws and rulings promoting or leading to Marxist ideals, illegitimate births, abortion on demand, broken homes, feminism, increased crime rates, homosexual special rights, environmental militants, and unilateral disarmament. He votes to regulate prices and profits, for pork barrel spending, for unread and hastily passed legislation, for robbing the "rich" and redistributing to the "underprivileged," for cradle-to-grave mothering by the state.

The new American would replace the "barbarism" of unrestricted individual freedom and enterprise with the "sophistication" of state collectivism. He would wed individual interests to those of the state. He would have social planners mold society according to their will and not the will of the people. He demands uniformity of thought and action.

Equality is his operational principle, his mantra if you will. With religious fervor, he pursues economic and social uniformity. He is determined to make the unequal equal even if that necessitates individual surrender and subordination to the state, resulting in a kinder, gentler form of tyranny. Maybe not so kind or gentle anymore, but tyranny nonetheless.

But tyranny only tells part of the story as new Americans now live in a radically new America. The great American, Christian experiment in freedom and liberty for all has silently become an oppressive socialistic regime of repressive rules, regulations, and burdensome taxation without suitable representation. America is on the verge of a complete socialist takeover. Capitalism, the economic engine of America's past prosperity, is wounded and destined to die. Corporations and banks are being nationalized, life savings and retirement accounts wiped out. This is not without design, for humanist strategists and their liberal allies in government seem determined to destroy not only capitalism but every form and fabric of the old America. Freedom itself is under attack. Property rights and gun ownership are in their sights, for a reason.

Liberals would have all of us unarmed and unable to take up arms to resist a tyrannical government—theirs—when all the pieces are in place and they demand full compliance from the populace.

An extension of this concept of personal disarmament, liberals would have the new America itself militarily compromised if not downright defenseless. Because of our sin, God has allowed His unseen wall of protection around America to be torn down brick by brick by anti-American liberals. America's sovereignty has been sacrificed for "global" citizenship. Her interest subsumed to the global regulatory architecture. Time after time, they enact laws and rulings that are detrimental to America's health. As if America is an eternal entity, no matter what, they willingly expose her to her enemies through unilateral disarmament, cuts in defense spending, weakening the CIA, allowing her enemies to own an unhealthy portion of our debt, our businesses, and our properties, on and on.

The new America is bankrupt and on the verge of collapse. Trillions in debt with more on the way. Liberals hastened the downward spiral with their massive welfare handouts, national and international giveaway programs, deficit spending, borrowing, and printing until the presses melt. Already, the present value of all entitlement programs exceeds fifty trillion dollars. There is no way we will ever pay for that, and our liberal leaders probably don't intend to as they go on spending and digging the debt hole even deeper.

So successful are liberals at directing our lives with our own money that the new America is a welfare state. In their conceit and unparalleled arrogance, they believe most American citizens are retarded and must be directed into proper action. In their concept of freedom, men who want for anything are not free, so they set out to free them with handouts. They call them "entitlements," as if the recipients are somehow entitled to feed at the public trough because of their color, marital status, ethnicity, or geographic location. So dedicated are liberal redistributionists that those who refuse their attempts to guarantee happiness would be coerced into acceptance. They do this with nary a tinge of guilt and obviously feel justified about doing all this good for us even if it kills us because they feel their heart is in the right place.

The deliberate devaluation of all that was America makes for a sad story with an even sadder ending. It is painful to look into our future, especially with seeming helplessness to turn this mighty ship of state around so that she manifests even a semblance of the vision our founding fathers had for this great nation. It is so bad that they, men of integrity and in love with liberty, would have revolted long ago against this tyrannical mess. At the very least, they would have left for a land where people are actually still free. I believe many today would do the same if there were such a place. No doubt the Pilgrims and Puritans would not even consider making a landing here today, especially in a place like Massachusetts.

Sure, the world hates us and would love to dance on our graves. Communists hate our prosperity. Muslims hate our immoral lifestyles and allegiances to Israel. Iran considers us the great Satan and feels they must destroy us before their Messiah can come. Most of us can accept the hatred directed at us from our envious enemies, but it is sure hard to swallow that it seems some of us hate us, too. I speak of liberals, the enemies within our borders who follow lockstep the humanist's roadmap for the world's future, as well as our own. Why in the world do so many inside our country seem to want us to fail? Patriotic Americans cannot figure out why leftists and liberals are anti-American and want our nation to lose wars, our economic stature, our military capabilities, and defense systems. Why would they unilaterally disarm us?

For years, I have struggled with liberal's apparent and aggressive attempts to destroy the very fabric of America. Why would they want to take the greatest experiment in human governance, personal freedoms, and economic achievements and completely pervert or destroy all that is good about America, ideals that made her the greatest country ever to exist on this planet—bar none and none even close? Why?

Their efforts are so focused and unyielding that there has to be motivation and organization with a purpose to debilitate this once mighty nation that served as a beacon of hope and a shining city on a hill for so many of the world's oppressed. There must be a reason, or reasons, they want America to fall.

Comparing humanist writings with the way things have been going over the past several decades and on a decidedly faster track in the last few years, we have by deduction come up with some possible reasons they might want America to fall. Naturally, there are more, and maybe one day liberals will actually share them with us, openly and honestly (if it is within them). Here is what we think: We think liberals and progressives are warmed over humanists. Their beliefs match those as outlined in *Humanist Manifesto I* and *II*. So, we will use the labels interchangeably and look to these *Manifestos* for explanations as to their anti-American beliefs and actions.

Religion and economics are important to humanists (as we will see), but the hinge pin of their argument is building a unified world void of national boundaries. They believe that "the best option is to ... move toward the building of a world community ... we look to development of a system of world law and a world order based upon transnational federal government ... we believe in the peaceful adjudication of differences by international courts ... war is obsolete."[5] Furthermore, they "deplore the division of humankind on nationalistic grounds."[6] That is pretty plain.

Prerequisite to a one-world community of nations governed by international Socialism, the mighty eagle that is America must be wounded so as to blend with all the other nondescript fowls in the humanist/liberal flock of nations. On the way to their Utopia, their millennial Heaven on earth (since they do not believe in the hereafter), national superpowers have to go. They have no place in the New World Order. Neither does the patriot.

En route to the humanist world community, America the beautiful must be completely transformed into a globalist-minded citizenry whose focus is on: Peace, not freedom; collectivism, not individuality; rights, not righteousness; choice, not life; community, not family; unity, not distinctiveness; disarmament, not security; cooperation, not competition. The global citizen must think and act beyond his national borders. He is a member of the world community, no longer bound by national loyalties or inspired by a strong, independent, nationalistic spirit. Love for America has to be supplanted by the universal brotherhood of man. The global New World Order becomes his new home.

To the liberal, America is just a place to live and enjoy the fruit of someone else's blood, sweat, and tears. America's blessings are to be extorted and exported around the world (his new home) until there is nothing left to give away. So what if we go bankrupt in the process and blend into the emptiness of amalgamated nothingness nations with no personality, no mission, no beacon of hope for the world's estranged to escape to. Something to look forward to, huh? The concrete coldness of Soviet style rigidity, black markets, and even more corrupt officials and politicians (if you can believe it).

None of this matters to the liberal—only ideology. I suppose the theory and reasoning behind the globalist mindset is that the world has shrunk and so, too, must we. Accordingly, we must now think in terms of a global village with a transnational federal government, world law administered by international courts and global banking routed through the United Nations. Forget the local. Forget the national. Mismanaged economies and disparities in wealth within and among nations demand a global solution. America must be sacrificed for the good of the world.

Oh, liberals say they love America, but if they do, it is the new America, an America as they fashion it. They want to live in and control a nation that espouses, promotes, and abides by the rules of their religion. To us, America is the America of our forefathers; it is not the one liberals wish they didn't have to share with us rabble from the right. They want to control who lives and who dies; the old America outlawed that, and they hate it.

Because they don't love their country, liberals and their legions of blind followers want the America we knew and loved to fall. And it has, it is, and it will—I believe the die is cast. Scripture implies that it will occur before the end of time. How do we know? Because all nations are gathered with the Antichrist against Israel before the battle of Armageddon. That would require a paradigm shift in our thinking because Israel is our friend now—

albeit a shaky friendship. Secondly, we would not follow a world dictator unless we were reduced to the role of a follower. We must be followers for the logical next step.

Since all vital institutions are already globally situated, the next logical step would be to enthrone a global world leader to head it all up. After all, to the worldly minded, only a global world leader can "fix" all the world's problems. Naturally, a global leader could end all wars because nation states and nationalistic pride would cease to exist, or at best be forced underground. A world leader could obviously end all economic disparities by running a global financial system through the United Nations, which would have the knowledge of national inequities and the power to dispel them as they redistribute monies worldwide. This coming world leader, void of any nationalistic allegiance, will be Antichrist.

At present, America stands in the way of the New World Order. But globalists are powerful and, we believe, unstoppable at this late point in history. America will be destroyed or strategically marginalized. The eagle will fall from her perch of power, position, and prominence in the world. Even now, many conditions and unfolding events are at work to precipitate the fall of our once good and powerful nation and her merger into a global entity. The world's last national superpower is about to be no more. Our recent elections only hasten the race toward a global governmental order, with America just one more puppet on the Antichrist's string of enslaved nations. The new America presents a pretty façade of a strong, healthy nation, but inside there is the slow death and decay of immorality, extravagance, waste, and deficits that can never be repaid. America has not been officially declared bankrupt, but it is just a matter of time before the shell collapses around us and we become a member of the global corporation.

CAPITALISM

Since liberals hate our country, at least the version that we love, anything that made or keeps America strong becomes their enemy as well. Case in point, the free market model that transformed America into an economic powerhouse—capitalism.

We cannot say that liberals want America to fall because of her economic model, or that, for America to fall, capitalism has to be tamed or subdued as well. It could be some of both—actually a win-win set-up for liberals—because humanists are not bashful about publicizing their disdain for the free market and the idea of taking profits for one's efforts:

> "The humanists are firmly convinced that existing acquisitive and profit-motivated society has shown itself to be inadequate and that a radical change in methods, control, and motives must be instituted. A socialized and cooperative economic order must be established to the end that the equitable distribution of the means of life be possible. The goal of humanism is a free and universal society in which people voluntarily and intelligently cooperate for the common good. Humanists demand a shared life in a shared world."[7]

> "It is the moral obligation of the developed nations to provide ... massive technical, agricultural, medical, and economic assistance ... to the developing portions of the globe. World poverty must cease. Hence extreme disproportions in wealth, income, and economic growth should be reduced on a worldwide basis."[8]

Their disdain for capitalism translates into dilution through the process of synthesis with their own economic model—Socialism. As we will see in Chapter Six, the process is well underway and will eventually end with the destruction of capitalism, their ultimate goal. Until then, liberals will use their opponent to advance their own global agenda.

In the liberal's new America, capitalism is allowed to survive, weds itself to a "cooperative economic order" (i.e., Socialism) and partakes in the massive redistribution of wealth. No matter how unfair, unjust, or damaging is this "equitable distribution" of productive resources, the liberal would remove "disproportions in wealth" even if it kills the golden goose of capitalism in the process. And it will eventually do just that, sooner than later, if our Marxist President has his way and is allowed to continue his Sherman march through the defenseless fields of the free marketplace.

In their intellectual superiority, liberals insist that universal Socialism, without the profit-driven vices of capitalism, makes for their utopian paradise of a "shared life in a shared world." Without capitalism, long the mainstay of America's claim to financial superiority over the entire world, America would not be so high and mighty. It seems it is that meteoric rise in America's prosperity, leaving the world behind, that has destined capitalism to its demise. Have you heard the terms "exploitation" and "colonialism" before? Have you been made to feel guilty because we are too rich while the world is full of starving poor people?

From the beating liberals have given capitalism, you would think they hate the market-driven system as much as they do the old America. But maybe it is just that the subservient process must take on the appearance of hatred to accomplish the deed; one does not normally devise the downfall of person or thing if they hold affection for them. Hatred or not, capitalism has become another of the victims of liberal globalist's attempts to subdue America by harnessing her profit-taking machine and upgrade the world's standard of living in the process. Two birds with one stone routine, you know.

Whether they truly feel this way or just devise excuses to justify their dismantling of capitalism, liberals claim that capitalists exploit the poor, that America has grown rich as the expense of poorer nations and that the gulf between the rich and poor only widens. And since the poorer nations are traditionally those of people of color, liberals also hate white males whom they accuse of being "angry white men" who want to protect their unfair privilege gained at the expense of people of color. All this dates back to our founding fathers (all white) who drew this all up (in the liberal's mind) to favor persons of position who, in many cases, owned slaves to gain those positions, power, and of course, prosperity.

CHRISTIANITY

That leads us to the next crowd that has to go, either as preparation for the fall of America or as part of the fall, and that is the exclusionary, high-minded bigotry of Christianity. As a birthing partner with America in the great experiment with freedom of religion, Biblical Christianity is an enemy of the new state religion, humanism. Everyone knows there is a wall of separation between true religion and the one promoted by the state (I speak sarcastically). And since the humanist state is an all powerful god, it is not hard to figure who is going to be forced to the austere side of the now impenetrable wall. The fictitious wall liberals used to remove Christianity from the legislative process and insert theirs there instead will remain to keep the narrow-minded, fundamentalist idiots forever locked outside the camp. Come to think of it, that is not a bad place to be, as we will see in chapter nineteen.

Why do liberal humanists hate traditional Christianity so much? A few verses from their bible sheds some light on why God's teachings are anathema to theirs:

> "The distinction between the sacred and the secular can no longer be maintained."[9]
>
> "False 'theologies of hope' and messianic ideologies, substituting new dogmas for old, cannot cope with existing world realities. They separate rather than unite peoples."[10]
>
> "We begin with humans not God, nature not deity."[11]
>
> "We can discover no divine purpose or providence for the human species."[12]
>
> "No deity will save us; we must save ourselves."[13]
>
> "The human species is an emergence from natural evolutionary forces."[14]

In its dogmatic, hell-fire and brimstone form, there is no place in the New World Order for Christianity, but in a diluted form, humanism might be able to use it. They call it "reconstituted" or "reinterpreted" so as to update Biblical teachings to conform to humanist ideology in this enlightened, progressive world of ours. In their words:

> "Certainly, religious institutions, their ritualistic forms, ecclesiastical methods, and communal activities must be reconstituted as rapidly as experience allows, in order to function effectively in the modern world."[15]
>
> "We should reinterpret traditional religions and reinvest them with meanings appropriate to the current situation."[16]

It is working. America's founding faith is being decimated from within by the concerted efforts of disciples of the humanist faith. We are not saying all Christians have fallen prey to the "modernization" of Christianity, but we feel that most have because many of the institutions purporting to proclaim the gospel of Christ do not. Instead, they ramble on about social justice or rant and rave about liberation of the world's oppressed. Humanists could not be happier or more proud of themselves with what they have done to one of their primary doctrinaire adversaries and weakened America in the process. The two-edged sword of liberal discipline cuts deep and leaves a permanent scar, yet its blow often goes unnoticed by the victim until it is too late.

The liberal's sabotage and saddling of America's two foundational institutions—capitalism and Christianity—is pretty much a closed case. Oh, sure, compromised forms of either might be acceptable as useful idiots until such time as their elimination could occur without public dissent, and probably with their consent. Chapter Seven gives a detailed look at humanism's impact on Christianity.

MORE LIBERAL HATRED

Along with capitalism and Christianity, liberals hate the Constitution, (which they feel must be rewritten) and our "bigoted" founding fathers (whom they ignore, remove from history books, or defame as adulterers and scandalous slave owners). They hate the free market where the intelligent, the creative, the hard-working are allowed to excel and prosper above the slothful, determined to be ignorant, vote my paycheck crowd that is decimating America from the inside. They hate private property rights, for it is property that has traditionally been the vehicle by which its owner has gained advantage over the property-less. They hate traditional values, the way America was, unrestrained individual freedom, competition, profits, the truth, and patriots.

They have already won the culture wars, so now they would disassemble civil society piece by piece to rid their country of all who maintain traditional values and institutions, all who stand as obstacles to their dream world. In their glorified new America, gone is the embarrassing wild-and- free cowboy image of freedom-loving rednecks who threatened the world's stability. Gone is the ignorant NASCAR riffraff who were bound to have mental problems. Add to the missing the redneck country music crowd who did not have enough sense to realize that the country and its music have changed, that they were out of step with the times and in the way of progress.

These all frustrate the liberal's quest for Utopia, whatever that is. Can anyone honestly say what their dream world looks like, what exactly is their ultimate goal, when and under what conditions the Second Revolution would end? Do they even believe that an end is achievable, or will they forever press for "change we can believe in" until we are all transformed into programmable clones of our elitist masters eternally altered by them as all of mankind evolves into godhood throughout eternity and beyond.

The next four chapters try to explain how liberals actually took over America and what, if anything, we can do to take it back. They conquered the old America with nothing less than an all out revolution against all that was the way we were. Traditions and traditionalists were attacked methodically and mercilessly—no prisoners with them.

An important part of their battle plan has been the subversion of our republic into a democracy, then denigrating that governance model into mob rule where the manipulated masses determine the course of all our lives. They, in their numerical superiority, ensure that traditional Americans are humbled into submitting to the ultimate dissing—taxation without representation. Working Americans helplessly watch as their earnings are confiscated by their government, then shipped off to who knows where and to who knows whom.

Democracy gone bad comes with more side effects, even more serious than unrepresented taxation. The way things are shaping up, America is looking at one party rule, real soon. And with it comes a one party ruler, a dictator of sorts. We call him the Anointed One, and in Chapter Three, we take a hard look at some of his nefarious motives and deeds.

2
THE SECOND REVOLUTION

"The true revolution is occurring and can continue in countless nonviolent adjustments."[17]

Over the last century, liberals have launched a well planned, systematic, and all out war against the spiritual descendents of the very patriots who fought the British for our freedom in the first place. This, the second American revolution, has been directed not against a foreign foe but within to her own citizens, their core beliefs and behaviors, their faith and patriotism, their finances, and their history.

This somewhat silent but successful struggle purposes to dismantle or destroy every vestige of Christianity, every aspect of the free market, every memory of who we really are and where we came from. To a large extent and for a major portion of our population, liberals have won the culture wars and in the process created a new America in which traditionalists are now trapped inside an alien culture with no place to go except the corners of their minds for memories of days gone by.

The liberal's revolution is against the original America, her faith, her free enterprise system, her founding fathers. They attack not with guns and bombs but with the silent killers of government rules, regulations, taxation, policies, so-called reform. They march out an army of lawmakers, lawyers, judges, professors, social workers, journalists, union members, community organizers (e.g., ACORN). No segment of our society is untouched or untarnished by these foot soldiers from Hell.

The second revolution has been a bloodless affair, not by the use of force but by ideologies (for now) introducing us to a soft tyranny of sorts. It has been a decades long process of re-creating America in its own image—godless, secular, socialist and anti-Christian. Liberals have gradually, and successfully, built a new America while tearing down the old, and most of her citizens never even noticed. They don't even know they live in a new America, much less who the enemy is.

Of course, many Americans are now sensing that something is inexplicably different about us, but they can't quite figure out what or why. They know many people now act strange, as if possessed by an uncaring spirit of apathy and self absorption. Look into their eyes. You see coldness and indifference. They stare right through you while ignoring you. Sure, there are exceptions, but the humanist mutants do indeed possess the land.

Liberals admire the Bolshevik revolution but, in America, had to opt for a kinder and gentler "progressive" overthrow of our government and every element of society contrary to theirs. Whether by violence or by subtlety and treasonous subterfuge, the Marxist liberals' goal remains the same—a total transformation of America. To them anything is better than the status quo. America must be changed at any cost, by any means—en route to their own Camelot-style kingdom of Heaven on earth.

The goal of the second revolution is universal socialism, absent any nationalistic allegiances, and void of any evidence of Christianity. Liberals would use capitalism to finance their giveaway programs, then completely remove private corporations by nationalization. They would destroy every symbol, tradition, and Biblically-sound doctrine of Christianity and anyone who reveres or believes in them.

They would use international pronouncements of our "sins" and backwardness to make us question and doubt our institutions of faith, family, and patriotism as outdated and in need of modification or replacement.

Liberals would defame the old America as racist and run by "angry white men" who exploited the poor, especially people of color, so we would question our honorable heritage and fall out of love with our own country. They would rewrite our history to remove or denigrate our founding fathers, our traditions, our triumphs. They would disparage and criminalize our heroic forefathers to whom we owe so much. To the liberal, history and accumulated knowledge, our traditions, truths, and concepts of freedom are merely dead weights and must give way to the theory that there is no single meaning, there are no absolutes and no arguments, that history is an unfolding evolutionary process driven by the state, of course.

Liberals would dumb down America (the student body and the work force) so as to make us more susceptible to their propaganda, more easily led as sheep to the slaughter, and coincidentally, less competitive in the global marketplace. Through affirmative action, quotas, and reverse discrimination, they would force the acceptance (into schools), hiring and promotion of the less qualified while rejecting and demoralizing the qualified. Who could be surprised when American productivity falls?

What they would do, they have done quite successfully. The old America is gone, slowly and silently killed by liberal fascism through an assortment of well planned attacks on every infrastructure institution of the country we love. They employ every method and any means, with no regard for traditional morals, to overwhelm the old guard. They acquire and keep power so they can transform America into an idyllic bastion of peace, harmony, and global-mindedness. They launch a blitz of misinformation and lies attacking conservatives, fundamental Christians, and freedom-loving patriots. They unleash such an onslaught of radical changes to our faith and our traditions that we feel completely surrounded by the enemy, and we don't know whom or what to fight first, if at all.

Their forces are so many and sometimes so hard to actually identify that we wonder if it is possible to defeat them. They simply overwhelm us with debilitating regulations, open-ended legislation, scurrilous lawsuits, Marxist professors, biased media lies, bigots flashing the race card, PC thought police, taxes and more taxes, crises that aren't, global warming that isn't, and relentless attacks on the family, marriage, fatherhood, and white men.

What follows is a closer look at some (certainly not all) of the tactics liberals deploy in their revolution against old school Americans.

LIARS FOR JUSTICE

Liberals are unaccountable, slanderous liars whose only ethics are situational, whose unquenchable lust is for power. And power they must have in order to implement all their statist programs. To get there, they make their own truth and decide their own morality. They are "liars for justice." To impose their will on the people, they lie at will. To the liberal, truth and lies hold similar value when pushing their ideas into the world of reality. There are no boundaries—they do whatever they want. To them, self-love is never having to tell the truth or say they're sorry for it. Remember, as humanists, ethics are fluid depending on the needs of the situation. Consequently, tradition and truth are dissolved, justice and honor dismissed. "It's the results, stupid—power, control, remaking America."

And power they now have, for their organization of mis-information and outright lies is gargantuan and growing. They have no code of ethics, no Biblical set of absolutes to govern their lives. They lie with impunity, when it suits them, for they are accountable to no one since the press, which they practically own, has their back. Their brothers in the media always cover for them, so they go on lying to us to get their way.

PROJECTION

Liberals are masters of psychological warfare, even if some of their tricks are little more than the use of child psychology on a dumbed-down populace. Take, for example, the devious ploy of projecting their "sins" and schemes onto the opposition, falsely accusing them of the very things they are guilty of. Liberals always blame conservatives for what is wrong and place labels on them, like fascist. As a cover, they pretend and promote the false promise that fascism will rise out of the political right. All the while, fascism in America has birthed and matured in the vast liberal, humanist movement. They even redefine terms and names (e.g., patriot = fascist) so as to exacerbate the effects of projection.

They are masters at diverting blame or cushioning blows by saying their opponents do the same thing as they. Usually, if that is true, and sometimes it is, it is a mountain to a molehill comparison. Liberals are never wrong; conservatives are never right. And when they are caught in something, which is unusual since the media refuses to expose them, they have always got an example, no matter how weak or irrelevant, of conservative misbehavior or bad policy (e.g., Bush's initial TARP bailout, No Child Left Behind, Medicare prescription drug benefits) to deflect or dampen their own oversized illegal, unconstitutional, or bankrupting policies.

They blame conservatives for every bad thing that happens (and the media carries it) even if it is they who caused the problem (e.g., the sub price housing collapse). They never take responsibility for their evil deeds. They go so far as to claim victimhood while they victimize their foes. In the midst of hurling stones filled with hatred and lies, they hide behind hollow claims of shameless mistreatment at the hands of the vast right wing conspiracy or the Republican Attack Machine. Of course, neither of these exists, but the clone is amused with the game, and the clown is amazed that anyone could be so mean to their masters.

CRISES

A valuable weapon in the liberal's second revolution has been, and continues to be, the creation and exacerbation of crises. They can take any form so long as they allow liberals to further their purposes. Typical crises include: War, Global Warming, The Housing Collapse, Health Care Crisis, Poverty, Racism, Executive Greed and Corruption, you get the picture.

Crises, in the manipulative hands of liberals, work wonders, for:

- They heighten a sense of emergency, making it easier for liberals to bypass conventional rules and legislate from the bottom of the deck. The fabricated sense of urgency releases the liberal from all constitutional constraints in his quest for absolute power.
- They allow liberals to short-circuit debate and deliberation; to by-pass conventional rules; to mobilize the masses, making them easier to manage and manipulate; to force their will upon the people—the greater the crisis the more freedom and individualism people are willing to give up.
- They are used by liberals to impose social changes they long for; to smash the old order; to expand government control over the economy; to bring a focus to public over private; to polarize society; to further strangulate capitalism and spread the wealth to their loyal constituents; to lead to collectivism and central planning. As an example: liberals fabricate global warming and climate change so as to stifle the free market with the green movement—green being the new red as a campaign to rid the earth of "greedy capitalists."

Is it any wonder liberals take every opportunity to create crises and instill fear in the American people? Fear is a very strong motivator and has been used masterfully by liberal change agents to fashion a new America with the crisis still booming or mutated into an even bigger problem. Leave it to liberals to foul everything up on their way to fixing us.

PC MOVEMENT

Warriors of the second revolution have deployed an amazingly effective weapon to actually silence their opposition. Having been around for several decades now, this insidious thought and speech control apparatus is affectionately known as the Politically Correct (PC) movement. An indoctrination mechanism, it is designed to mold us all into uniformity of thought and action, and they mean to get it by force, regulations, or social pressure. All this translates into fear.

Because of the PC movement, people are now afraid of offending one of the precious and protected subgroups in America, of appearing ignorant and behind the times, or worse yet, bigoted. Probably the greatest fear is that of saying the wrong thing and being called a racist, Nazi, or fascist (one of their projected catch words).

Isn't it the ultimate shameful irony that, in the "home of the brave," we are actually afraid to talk openly anymore? Especially harmful is how the "PC police" have silenced Christians from speaking their convictions against sin and sinful lifestyles lest they be labeled prejudiced, or one of their pet propaganda adjectives.

Safe to say, Americans of the old guard have surely been told to shut up and never say an unkind word about one of the liberals' protected species groups. Sad to say, it is working.

WHITE HATRED

Liberals hate the old America so much that anyone who reminds them of the way it was or who looks like and thinks like our forefathers is hated, too, with a passion. That would be whites—specifically, conservative white males.

One way they show their hatred is by promoting diversity and multiculturalism to diminish respect and proper recognition for descendants of the white founders of this country and enhance that of their "disadvantaged victims." They manufacture and peddle white guilt as a springboard to the passage of laws to redistribute the earnings of honest, hard-working citizens to a growing glut of non-producing, non-descendants who have no interest in advancing and who are totally unconcerned for the waste all around them. They sport "identity" politics to promote the stature of their interest groups, e.g., feminists, blacks, Hispanics, homosexuals, etc. They push for special rights for their people to alienate traditional Americans who are not entitled because of their privileged birth as heirs of the founding aristocracy, yet are determined to protect their unfair privilege.

In this war on conservative white males, liberals have an ace in the hole—the race card. And they are not afraid to play it. If you are a conservative, you are automatically a racist. If you are against government-run healthcare, you are a racist. If you oppose Obama's policies, you are a racist. If you resist welfare programs or racial preferences aimed at minorities (considered by some as overdue reparations for slavery) you are considered a racist.

Naturally, many whites who would not normally do so have succumbed to the public pressure and sided with liberals in their war against "angry white men" (i.e., the ones who want to preserve the America our forefathers envisioned). They don't want to be associated with the retrofitted Bible-thumping rabble who always look backward. Instead, they want to appear sophisticated as part of the progressive avant-garde society crowd. All they really are is "useful idiots" to the vast left wing conspiracy. Funny, they think they are so smart.

DEMONIZE THE ENEMY

Liberal ideas for remaking America are many, but their arguments for change are weak, and they know it. So, rather than debate the issues, they attack the messenger, not the message. They go for the person, not his positions; they kill his influence; they assassinate his character in the hope that his message will die along with his reputation. They marginalize him to silence him into useless oblivion. They berate and intimidate him in smug holier-than-thou tones, glaring down their pious noses at the backward, Bible-thumping, mental case who dared to question their infallibility. In short, they demonize him because it is easier to destroy him than his beliefs in personal freedom, lower taxes, and less government.

Is this fair? We don't think so, but, as humanists, the "religious" left has no code of ethics holding them back from demoralizing, diminishing, or even destroying anyone who disagrees with them and stands in the way of "progress." Void of guilt, they can hate their opponents because they view them as dehumanized symbols of ideas and interests and not as people.

Since they are mere symbols of outdated ideas, the poor soul who opposes liberals finds himself the target of their venomous, vitriolic, and relentless attacks on his beliefs, even his personal and family life. Liberals play to win. They play dirty, no holds barred with them. All is fair in their war for the heart and soul of our beloved country.

To destroy their enemies so their positions are neutralized, or worse, liberals invent derogatory names, catch phrases, and sinister-sounding labels (e.g., Right-winger, homophobe, religious right, sexist, racist, fascist, Nazi, Christianist), then plaster them on the backs of their foes. Their robotic corp of media propagandists then tattoo the false claims on the public brain with mind-numbing repetition. If you agree with them, the liberal media will let you get away with anything short of murder (oops, forgot about Vince Foster). However, if you disagree with them, they smear, slander, and even lie about you—whatever it takes to render you and your worn out views meaningless in the public square.

Obviously, demonization is working and has cleverly worked conservatives into a trap. If they reject state intervention and entitlement programs (mostly aimed at minorities), it proves they are bigots and hate those whom the state proposes to help. So most conservatives give in and vote for government-run programs. President George W. Bush even touted his "compassionate conservatism" to garner favor with liberal constituents, but it only proved him a stoolie of the liberal establishment while alienating true conservatives. It gained him nothing because liberal-crats are faithful to their masters, and Bush certainly was not that, especially after the press got through demonizing him.

For enemies of the liberal, reputations mean nothing. A person's name and integrity mean nothing. The pain they inflict on families and loved ones mean nothing. Their agenda is all that matters, much like Stalin's, as millions of dissidents were thrust into eternity so that his "plan," along with them, could be executed. Individuals are expendable—only the "people" are worthy. Those expendable misfits who stand in the way of the divinely ordained collective are routinely attacked and, if necessary, done away with.

Killing the opposition sometimes becomes a necessity if they are considered incorrigible, unnecessary, or are seen as impact players for the opposition. I have no doubt that doctrinaire liberal Marxists are actually advocates of the discipline of the sword. Anyone who would unjustifiably assassinate a person's character, destroying their careers, fortunes, and family lives, would ultimately kill the person themselves if they resist all efforts to synthesize them into the program. We feel that Antichrist will fulfill this, the liberal dream, of physically destroying all who oppose their progressive plots, especially Biblical Christians.

THE STATE AS GOD

Coinciding with the liberals' decades-long war on Christianity is their equally aggressive campaign to enthrone the state as god. By their own proclamations that God is dead and Christianity is a rotting corpse, liberals are quick to offer up another god for us to worship—the eternal state. The state, as a benevolent god, will take care of us all. The state guarantees happiness and meaning in life. Our needs will be met and our wants fulfilled if we worship the state and forget about a God that, at best, is dead and probably never existed at all.

To get to the point of godhood for the state, liberals had a lot of work to do. No matter what these liars say, America was born a Christian nation and has always been a Christian nation, with God enshrined on her currency, her architecture, and in our hearts. Embedded in her laws, customs, holidays, and the like were the influences of Christian thought.

Those who wanted to destroy the old America knew that a corrupted or collapsed Christianity would advance the process, for it was Biblical Christianity, its fundamental adherents, and its traditional value system that contributed to America's uniqueness and greatness in the world. Its operating principles served as a bellwether for national behavior for nearly two hundred years. And we prospered. were safe within our borders, and were respected in the world.

But now, thanks to liberal humanists, all that remains is the shell; the substance is gone. The name lingers on; the essence has long since departed. America is clearly no longer a practicing Christian nation but, clearly, a nation whose god is the almighty state.

Our "one nation under God" is now essentially many nations, with each hosting its own hyphenated anti-Americans struggling for dominion over the classical set of plain old patriotic Americans. Our allowance of subsets and acquiescence to all their demands for special rights and veiled reparations (through redistribution) has completely disintegrated our "one nation" into the angry, amalgamated mess we have today.

It is a tragic twist that the one true religion upon which this country was founded and prospered is now the scourge and scapegoat of the humanist, conglomerated majority. Biblical Christianity, for now, is relegated to the back seat of the bus, but soon, it will be mercilessly thrown under the bus as America slides into communist-like controls with one party rule and a deceitful dictatorial style ruler like the one emerging today.

The colonists came to America for freedom, to get away from the all-encompassing purposes of monarchs and clergy. They risked life and limb to be free from church and state planners. They wanted to be free to worship as they pleased, to make their own plans, to make their own choices. Freedom—they got it, and for centuries, they kept it.

But now, after decades of liberal humanists' intrusion into our lives, "we the people" are no longer truly free. The new America more resembles that of the European monarchy or the fascist/communist dictatorships, with all the constraints placed on the individual's right to plan out his own life or distribute his excess resources as he sees fit to help the less fortunate. Instead, the liberals in both parties do our planning for us after confiscating our earnings, then giving to others we know nothing about. In the new America, the state has become the benefactor and the decision maker, taking on god-like status and robbing us of our power to freely choose the allocation of all our resources as we please.

When the state steps in and does our planning, personal accountability and responsibility are lost. Responsibility and freedom go hand in hand. If man is not free to choose between good and evil, then he is not responsible for his actions. Liberals divert blame to circumstances or society. Hence, man is not free nor is he free to choose. He must be cared for cradle to grave—socially, financially, and spiritually. The liberals' socialism fills the bill by planning everything from above for him, taking away all his choices, his responsibility, and most of all, his freedom.

The role of government should be to protect and preserve its people and to secure peace and property of all its citizens. Instead, government in the liberals' America works to destroy the individual's natural proclivity to improve his circumstances, to compete and take risks, to achieve a better life, to achieve success by following his hunches, his ingenuity, inventiveness, and genius. Forget all that, liberals prefer to enslave us all to the drab and dumbed down world of dependence, conformity, and ignorance.

Liberals also prefer to break us financially, and their welfare state works wonders because of the carefree mindset it instills. When under perpetual government care, gone is the individual's incentive to avoid waste. They, like the state, are unaccountable for the money trail. Someone else is footing the bill, so who cares? It is easy to blow another person's money. Honest, hard-working Americans might like a shot at it sometime. No, they are too honorable to do unto others what is done to them every day of their lives by their own government extortionist. Thank God, some Christian morality still lives on.

That notwithstanding, the humanist worldview has silently overwhelmed the Christian worldview. Humanist liberals have created a new America while systematically destroying the old. Biblical Christians and conservatives cling to the old America in a futile attempt to preserve institutions and traditions upon which this nation was founded and prospered for over two hundred years. That America is gone. The age of innocence, kindness, and respect for others is gone.

The culture wars have, for all intents and purposes, been lost. Too late we failed to recognize the enemy and his pernicious ways. Now, we seem too weak spiritually to defend our values and traditions against the white hot fervor of these liberal zealots who use any means to attain their goals. Relentless are they to the point of wearing out the opposition; many have just given up the fight when it seems futile to resist any longer.

America's founding faith has faltered and failed to counteract the omnipresent influences of humanism and its exhortations to ignore or violate the commands of God. To liberals, God stands in the way of the state. If God is dead and truth is slain with Him, then there is only power—the power wielded by the state so that the state becomes god. It cares for the needy, and we succumb to its code of ethics or anti-ethics if you will.

The ethics—more specifically, the morals of Christianity—just don't suit liberals. In fact, nothing about Biblical Christianity or its dramatic impact on society suits them. Solution? Liberals want to go back to pre-Christian paganism and start over. They insist that man has chosen the wrong path, made the wrong turn. They want to take us back and make the right choice this time.

Lord only knows where they would take us—an "enlightened" Dark Ages maybe; somewhere in the B.C., I suppose—and pretend that Christ was never born, never died a sacrificial death, never rose from the dead by the power of Almighty God. They would pretend that millions never died for their belief in Christ, that countless lives were not changed for the better by the same power that resurrected Christ, that America was not a shining city on a hill for so many immigrants because of our Christian heritage. Liberals are determined to create a better America through their own devices without God, His Son, or His army of blood-bought followers. There is no need for the Christian's God; the state will take care of us all.

We conclude this section with a brief look at the liberals' most successful attack on Christianity—the erection of a fictionalized wall of separation between church (Christianity) and state (everything public). They have effectively wielded this imaginary weapon to banish Christians to the voiceless side of the invisible wall, to evict the Christian's God and secularize our entire nation.

Gone is the Christian voice in the policy debate, in our schools, in entertainment, and on and on. Gone are his sacred symbols, his supernatural "myths," his revered personages from the public domain.

Rushing in to fill the void, the all-caring state. Divorced from all elements of Christianity, our culture is now a culture of death and hatred, bigotry and biases, deception and demonizing, class warfare and reverse discrimination, PC hogwash and endless law suits. Hiding behind the imaginary wall, liberals force every tenet of their religious manifesto into every aspect of our lives. The hypocrisy of this double standard staggers the fair minded while it escapes altogether the close-minded followers of this folly.

3

THE ANOINTED ONE

John Adams rightfully said, "Our constitution is made only for a moral and religious people. It is wholly inadequate to the government of any other." America is no longer a moral and religious people, so what has become of our Constitution?

Our Constitution has been maligned and distorted by liberal judges who make false interpretations and prejudiced misapplications, considering it an outdated document that must evolve with the changing times, and subject to the interpretations of those in power. Roe versus Wade, the most damaging ruling to the moral health of America, typifies what we mean.

Such a unique and magnificent document has in many ways been wasted on the immoral mob that clamors for its protection but rewrites it to further their leftist agenda. Dissolution of the fabric of society, the disintegration of our morals has paved the way for the immoral majority to capture our country at the voting booth. And when they did, activist liberal judges were not far behind. Soon to follow, the beginning of tyranny and the end of freedom.

Freedom coexists with moral behavior and individual constraints. Self rule only works for those with self under subjection. An unholy people ultimately only respond to a dictatorship. Absent the Christian code of ethics and its inherent limits on behavior, humanist relativism takes over, eventually followed by anarchy. Their remedy—the tyrannical rule of a dictator accompanied by the brute force of his ego unleashed on all who stand in his way.

Absent the moral code, America is ripe for a dictatorship where the ignorant masses are manipulated by their "organizers" to accept enslavement to the all-knowing one. This, their Anointed One, will meet all their needs as if the means to do so are just created (by him) and not extorted from the "evil ones" who actually work for a living, trying to save a little and help the less fortunate along the way.

Barack Obama is the Anointed One. He entered the political scene from out of nowhere and has been wildly successful almost beyond belief. It is as if he has been supernaturally empowered by "The Force"—the forces of darkness and deception from the prince of the power of the air, Satan himself.

Obama embodies the spirit of Antichrist—deceitful eloquence with a lust for power, hatred for his enemies, and the use of any means to achieve his goals. He is always right and has all the answers. Everything bad is somebody else's fault, and only he can fix the mess they made. He is repulsed by criticism. He demands to have his way much like a spoiled child. All who oppose him must be silenced. He holds no national allegiance or certification of birth—the world is his stage, his playground if you will, his entourage of cult worshipers.

Obama masks his Antichrist spirit with a façade of the faithful. He claims to be a Christian but pushes an anti-Christian, Marxist agenda. Marx was no Christian, nor did he care for Christianity or believe in its God. Obama's mentors, associations, and advisors are Marxists. His tactics are radical (à la Saul Alinsky), so antithetical to those of Christ. Above all, he is a liar, and a clever one at that. The way he twists and tortures the truth with that straight face of his staggers the mind of those who have the stomach to listen to him.

As a doctrinaire Marxist, he shares the international left's disdain for America, no matter what he might say to the contrary. His executive orders and hastily passed legislation only accelerate the demise of America, a point at which we will be, at least, no more than par with other countries. Our modern day FDR, with all his Marxist heritage and deceptive eloquence, will bankrupt America, with that as his apparent goal. He is just using this fair land, what is left of our prosperity, to further the causes of Marx and internationalism.

Marx would be so proud of the way Obama nationalizes vital American industries or brings his union buddies in as partner-owners with him. He fires "greedy" capitalist CEOs at will with hardly a whimper of protest from the state-run propaganda machine.

He boasts an army of slavish foot soldiers and an array of Czar coordinators to fight the revolution in the trenches while he directs everything from his white house. He can depend on undying support from the ranks of ACORN, organized labor (a Marxist tool), peaceniks, feminists, civil rights groups, environmentalists, and especially, the press and media.

Almost every informational and entertainment outlet in America covers for him and exalts him as their Anointed One. He is their mouthpiece, their hammer and sickle for radical change and for mowing down the opposition. The media elected Obama and will keep him in power, regardless of how much damage he does to America. To the media, his policies are not damaging but the necessary pain of metamorphosis into their fairytale land of global mechanisms ushering in universal peace and levelized prosperity without the scrutiny of a fabricated deity with all his superimposed dos and do nots to cloud the conscience and inhibit growth to full human potential.

The press surely protects him, but he also hides behind a smokescreen of innocuous sounding words like "social justice" (code for communism), "equality" (who could deny people of that?) and "security" (secure from want). But to get to his utopian paradise free from want and class distinction, he would abolish private enterprise and the private ownership of the means of production. The taking of "evil" profits has to go. He must question why anyone should be rewarded for their creativity, inventiveness, and investment of capital.

Obama sees a "planned economy" as the only way to achieve his redistributive ends, and that, in and of itself, calls for a government that is oppressive and tyrannical, with a leader that is necessarily dictatorial. The Anointed One must surely think that he is the one and his army of foot soldiers and unaccountable czars, counselors, and advisors will force his agenda on the American people.

What is his agenda? Given the power and the necessary platoons of brown shirts, what would Obama do?

He would render us defenseless in a world that hates us, that's loading up on weapons and figures to use them on us. He speaks of peace while the world is poised to destroy us. He advocates unilateral disarmament, nuclear arms reduction, abandoning missile defense sites in Eastern Europe, negotiating with terrorists and rogue states, releasing captured enemy combatants so they can kill more of our soldiers.

At the same time, he and his slugs strong-arm Israel to forget about defending themselves from the same people he offers an olive branch with a fat check rolled around it. He has basically thrown Israel on the chopping block by siding with her enemies regarding even more Israeli land in exchange for "peace" and forbidding Israel to build more settlements on her own land.

He would disarm us individually so we cannot resist our own government when he assumes total control and clamps down on rebels like us. With all the regulations, insurance requirements, and registrations his people can throw at gun owners, it is not as inconceivable as we would like to think that he could disarm us. It is his intention. Beware!

He would sacrifice our vaunted health care system on the altar of government-controlled misery for all. He lies and says non-citizens are not included in the plan, but look beyond his rhetoric—he wants their votes, and his friends at ACORN will make sure he gets them. Let's face it, universal government-run health coverage is the finest hour for Marxist redistribution and Darwin's survival of the fittest. Obama's so called disadvantaged will receive free care at the expense of taxpaying Americans, especially small business (one of his main enemies). Under his plan, the unfit will be phased out of the system and into another existence. People are not his concern; power is. Healing the healthcare system is not his focus; nationalizing it is.

He would kill babies even after they are born, all in the name of choice. As if partial birth killing were not bad enough, here comes the Anointed One and takes it a step forward—after birth killing. That is the point of no return. We are all at risk if he deems us unworthy to live any longer because we are not contributory to society. His universal health care collective would offer a bureaucratic vehicle to cut out some of our nation's nonproductive, too-expensive-to-care-for old folks. Just look at it as partial death abortion.

He would increase all our energy costs by capping emissions and taxing corporate offenders, which translates into higher costs for end users. His focus is on "greening" the economy, not saving the planet. His tact of environmental blackmail is to further "redden" our country, not save us money or preserve our freedoms.

Obama would cripple capitalism in his Marxist quest for redistributed wealth and government-run business. Capitalism just does not work with heavy weights like that strapped on its back. Does he care if there is unrestricted legal action against corporate America? Does he care if his union buddies stifle competition, slash productivity, and drive up costs for us all? I don't think so.

His disdain for competition and profits is so intense and the possibilities of them so alien to his constituents that he would bankrupt America to rid winners of the mechanism to excel and earn more money than their less motivated or less capable neighbors. He is determined that there be equality, at any cost. And what a cost it will be to the individual's incentive to improve his and his nation's ability to beat the competition.

In spite of his hatred for capitalism, he would reform the keepable aspects (i.e., those that work with him, like the "socially minded corporations"), then bend them to serve the common good. He would form "strategic partnerships" with corporate America just so they can implement the state's social agenda for him. In essence, business just becomes government by proxy with paid health care, free day care, and the like.

In return for big business bowing to a complicit alliance with The Anointed One, Obama would do his part to crush their small business competitors. He must despise small business the most because of their voting patterns, their independent spirit, and focus on frugality. He would place additional burdens on the little business guys with his government health care initiatives. He groups them in with the rich (greater than $250,000 annual income), thereby stacking additional taxes on them.

As one who pours it all into your business, what could be worse than working day and night, only to see much of your money going to support the growing class of lazy bums who never work? What could be worse than to have the fruit of your labor taken from you and fed to others, many of whom are too sorry to work for their own? Then to make sure you don't grow any more fruit, Obama would cut down the tree.

Obama would not only exploit a crisis to thrust his ideals and ideologies on the American people, he and his people (ACORN and the like) actually employ tactics to cause crises in order to get their way. He as a major player in the socialist mandates of the "Community Reinvestment Act" very much contributed to the housing meltdown and subsequent financial crash of 2008. By forcing banks into affirmative action, sub-prime, uncollateralized, no-down-payment lending, Obama very much contributed to the collapse. Probably by design, the collapse helped get him elected and paved the way for the gargantuan deficit spending he has inflicted on us and our descendants since his corrupt crowd of voter-cheaters put him in the White House.

Obama would, if he could, trash our Constitution and write another altogether from scratch. I've often wondered what in the world a liberal Marxist's constitution would look like. Answer to self—if Obama has his way, we will soon find out.

His first step was to appoint a leftist judge to the Supreme Court who decrees by empathy rather than established law so she can assist with rewriting an evolving constitution. This is exactly as Obama would have it, for he believes the document is outdated and definitely not written for our modern times and for this multi-amalgamated mass of diverse peoples.

THE NEW SLAVE CLASS

Obama befriends avowed communists, Marxist professors and anti-American radicals for good reason—they have similar beliefs. He hires anti-white racists, socialists, and homosexual activists to his cadre of advisors for good reason—they have similar beliefs. He sits under the tutelage of a black liberation, white-hating, Jew-hating, theologian for twenty years for good reason—they have similar beliefs.

Is Obama a black racist? You decide for yourself. One thing we do know—he is creating a new slave class, and for the most part, they don't look like the ones brought over on boats a few centuries back. Ironical isn't it? Roles have reversed. Obama is the new slaveholder, the new Master of a whole group of "cotton picking" taxpayers who though not in jail are still not free.

The walls of Obama's serfdom are invisible, yet nonetheless imprison his subjects with the ball and chain of repressive laws, regulations, and unrepresented taxation, from which there is no escape. There is no place to go (except to jail). There is no one to turn to who can actually dissuade the Master of his tyrannical ways and, more importantly, his motives to enslave the spiritual descendants of the original slaveholders.

The new slave class are actually paying reparations to the "disadvantaged" heirs of African slaves to even the score. According to Master Obama, a one-time reparations dole out to slave heirs would not be enough. In his view, there must be an ongoing, never-ending process of sharing the wealth. He sees repayment in perpetuity in the form of taxation on society's producers, supposedly descendants (or, as we will call them, spiritual heirs) of the original slaveholders, then redistribute confiscated earnings to the disadvantaged.

The new slave class, which includes most small business owners, have no real voice but are taxed mercilessly to support the no good, non-producers who by virtue of their mass voting power get their way. This is especially true now with a liberal Marxist in the White House and with his ilk polluting both houses of Congress with superior numbers but vastly inferior intelligence and even less concern for the fate of honest, hard-working Americans.

As if unconstitutional taxation is not enough, Obama and his slave drivers in Congress have a lot more flogs to lay on the backs of their unpurchased possessions. To further level the playing field supposedly skewed by whites who got an early start, Obama and people who think like him have inflicted the founder's spiritual prodigy with a litany of inflamed wounds that one day could kill them. Maybe that is the underlying objective of these programs:

- Affirmative Action
- Quotas
- Housing Grants
- Community Redevelopment
- Racial Preferences
- Wasting trillions on Welfare
- Federal and State Relief Programs
- Food Stamps
- Government-run Health Care
- Minimum Wage Increases *ad infinitum*
- Sub-prime Loans to people who could never repay

On the surface, these might be considered noble causes, if they were done with liberals' money alone and not confiscated funds, and if they only impacted the liberals' world. But we have to consider the harmful effects on the morale and take home pay of the non-liberal working class. Furthermore, these and other similar programs have severely undermined America's competitiveness in the global marketplace. Whatever happened to filling positions with the most qualified and pay being commensurate with a person's contribution to the product?

An example of a far-from-noble move by liberals to spread the wealth is their silent assent to fascist-style street violence in low-rent districts. Liberals view this senseless destruction as necessary acts of mistreated victims of slavery and segregation. But, in reality, it allows street thugs to destroy their own neighborhoods so the government (taxpayers) can rebuild them with confiscated earnings from the "guilty" class of working Americans.

ONE PARTY RULE

To make all his Marxist dreams come true, Obama would have America governed by only one party—his. He would do everything he can get away with to guarantee a Democratic dictatorship in which the shrinking class of producers support the swelling mob of bus-me-to-the-polls, non-producers. Here is how the Anointed One plans to repress the Republican Party and enthrone himself:

- He would stuff the ballot boxes with many more union members (part of his voting wedge) by denying workers the right to a secret ballot. It doesn't bother Obama to unionize by force. Remember—means to an end—the end being absolute power with him at the throttle.
- He would politicize the census by moving it to the White House. Fox in the hen house? We think so.
- He would direct stimulus money to his constituent-dominated counties.
- He would ensure health care for illegal aliens, as they are a wellspring of votes and potential votes
- He would pull a bait and switch with political candidates. That is, run moderate democrats in conservative districts and states to get them elected, then pressure the newly elected to vote his way, which is to the left of many communist dictators in other countries.

- He would illegally enroll illegal immigrants, the unknown, the well known, the dead, and particularly the ignorant, easily-swayed masses. Overwhelm the system; they can't catch every infraction. They don't; the crooks, in effect, elect themselves and, by the same devious below-board tactics, proceed to make our lives miserable and ruin our country in the process.
- As a thin-skinned cry baby, Obama would silence the voice of all opposition, especially conservative talk radio and the Fox cable channel. He would kill free speech with the so-called Fairness Doctrine or some backdoor approach to the same effect of controlling the media. It works for his comrades in Cuba and Venezuela—why not in America?

No matter how much Obama masks his evil intentions with a fake smile and a bagful of lies, underneath lurks an impetuous, impatient, egomaniac bent on subjugating conservatives (especially whites), dismantling capitalism (after he has drained it dry), and disarming America (so his global admirers are happy). It is as if it is his destiny as the Anointed One to destroy the old America and, with it, all the spiritual descendants of the founding fathers.

4
DEMOCRACY GONE BAD

*S*trange as it might seem, the interim government of choice for Obama and his liberal, humanist friends is democracy. Sure has a nice ring to it, doesn't it—*of the people, by the people, for the people*—but the question is, which people is the government of, by, and for? It sounds good to say that the powers react only to the "will of the people," but is it the will of all the people?

The answer is no. So why do liberals advocate "political democracy" and boast that "many kinds of humanism exist ... 'democratic,' 'religious,' and 'Marxist' humanism ..."[18] Because it is the perfect form of government for their silent revolution, and for good reason—democracy purports to represent the will of the people, but properly manipulated, it morphs into the will of its liberal manipulators. You might say that liberals love democracy because it sounds like such a noble experiment while it serves their many ignoble purposes.

THE DARK SIDE OF DEMOCRACY

The way liberals abuse the honorable intentions of the mechanisms of government to accomplish their own purposes highlights the dark side of democracy. The unseemly side effects of democracy gone bad manifest themselves as liberals exploit the system to:

- Supplant the will of God with the will of man
- Rewrite the Constitution
- Steal elections
- Secure one party rule
- Usher in a dictatorship
- Spread the wealth
- Tax their opposition while denying them representation
- Enslave capitalism and enthrone socialism
- Allow democracy to fail when it is no longer needed

America was founded as a Republic, but there arose a compromise that allowed for religious pluralism that did not stress a nation under the divine jurisdiction of the one and only true God. Consequently, our nation has, in the name of religious pluralism, abandoned its safe haven "under God" and rejected the vision our Pilgrim and Puritan founders had for their new home.

As our republic grew less righteous, it became more democratic, reaching the point today of almost pure democracy, where everyone votes regardless of their stake in our nation's survival. Sadly, so many who vote today care only about the return on their invested trip to the polls, what their country can do for them, what is in it for them.

You know democracy has gone bad when the majority cares more for their own selfish "rights" and wallets than for the good of their country as a whole. With the loss of traditional Judeo-Christian values of humility and love for others, the restraints on immoral majority voting power are gone.

Humanists had to first convert America to an immoral people to get democracy to work best for them. They have, and it is. Ours is now an unrighteous, humanist democracy married to religious pluralism, headed for tyranny, then dictatorship. Any system of governance is only as good as the people being governed. Self rule only works when the self does not rule. Democracy only works for a moral people. We are not that.

Liberals have advanced a mild and peaceable revolution via the democratic ballot box. They have built a government of, by, and for the ignorant clowns and ideological humanist clones to form a majority that cares only for their own agenda. Granted, each has its own reasons for following lockstep behind their masters—the clowns follow for material gain, the clones have bought into the humanist, Marxist worldview.

An integral part of the liberals' second revolution is their silent "democratic revolution" in which a consortium of various humanist factions have united and deceived enough of the ignorant masses to form a syndicated immoral majority. The majority then democratically elects leaders of the humanist persuasion who proceed to legislate anti-Christian dogmas and to thrust America toward a one-world government under world law. They proceed to confiscate and redistribute individual wealth (and, in many cases, individual means of earning a living) within America and to brazenly dispense our extorted monies to nations around the globe to reduce disproportions in wealth worldwide.

One reason humanists love a democracy is that it exalts the individual self, giving even the most ignorant and least contributory voters a voice in the allocation of our nation's wealth and the legislation of immorality. As such, they assume godlike status, an understood objective of the humanist hierarchy.

If fifty-one percent of the people vote to legalize immorality, then it is right in the eyes of the law. That goes for abortion, homosexual marriages, etc. God says these vices are wrong, but when the majority makes them the law of the land, then the voice of the people, by default, becomes the voice of God. The dark side of democracy shows up full force as the will of God is supplanted by the will of an immoral majority who does what is right in its own eyes, even though God's Word clearly and definitively says it is sin.

But then, we must remember that liberals do not believe in sin and the Biblical view of right and wrong. So, they don't care if they trample on God's Word en route to remaking our Christian America into a humanist stronghold via the dark side of the democratic model. Get the votes by whatever means necessary to run out of office the honest, patriotic politicians. They are a dying breed, and this is why.

In a pure democracy, there is nothing to check the majority from ganging up on the minority, sacrificing the weaker party to the omnipotence of numbers, the totalitarian poisons of popular rule. Simply put, democracy is a lethal weapon in the wrong hands. This is painfully true as democracies by design allow the majority to easily exploit the more prosperous minority.

The most numerous in any society will necessarily be the poorest, the most ignorant, and the most gullible to the professional politician who waters and nurtures them to remain in power. Since the upper classes are always the minority, democracy taken to its full end will consequently place the whole of our country's property and resources in the hands of the poor and their elitist redistribution masters.

When that happens, democracy is finished. A temporary form of government, it serves its purpose on the way to a totalitarian regime and then is gone. Democracy self-destructs when morals collapse and self lovers vote themselves generous gifts from the public treasury. The well runs dry, chaos ensues, and a dictator arises to restore order. But in the process, freedom is lost, and there simply will not be any more "will of the people" or "one man, one vote." You will do whatever the dictator says.

Another reason liberals love democracy is the ease with which they are able to steal elections. At election time, they have brigades of foot soldiers from ACORN, the unions, the NEA, and the like at their beck and call to register throngs (alive and dead) of potential voters to overwhelm the system and sneak multitudes pass scrutiny at the polls. Furthermore, their armies of faithful brown shirts mass bus their rubber stamps to the polls as part of their "get out the (guaranteed) vote." They intimidate legitimate voters and flat out force their will and their way on God-fearing patriots.

The art of winning and accumulating votes is the key to stealing elections. How liberals do this under cover of the darkness of corrupted democracy is sickening to the lover of justice and fairness. Some of the tricks include: bribery, intimidation, lying about and demonizing the opposition, pushing class jealousy and prejudices, doling out dollars, setting the many against the few, motor voter campaigns, false accusations, ridiculing opponents, aggravated grievances, inciting racial and ethnic divisions, and universal suffrage.

Whether it just worked out that way or was by design, democratization of our political process and lowering suffrage over the last one hundred years or so has been the secret formula for liberals to steal elections. In so doing, they have adeptly disabled our economy and degraded our traditional value system down to the humanists' anti-Christian standards. Now we are headed for universal suffrage where even illegal non-citizens can vote (we all know who they will vote for). Amnesty may very well leave America with no illegal non-citizens, making this issue a moot point and guaranteeing millions more votes for liberals.

The consequences of universal suffrage have always been the beginning of the end of democracy. Lowering the suffrage proves to be a slippery slope with no safe place to stop. An integral part of the democratization of our republic and a collapse into mob-induced socialism has been the progressive lowering of standards for voting. We are now down to the ignorant masses that have no stake in the future viability of our nation. What is worse, liberals have abused the democratic process so much that we now have what we might call, democracy plus. That is where dead people vote, alive people vote more than once, Mickey Mouse has a say in who goes to D.C., and much more.

The logical end of the universal suffrage slippery slope is one party rule. That party will then seat a dictatorial style fascist figure who will rule everyone's life and ruin the lives of many. With their myriad of connections and contemptible practices, liberals are closing in on single party rule—the machinery is already in place for them to take over the rulership of our nation. What a wonderful tool democracy has proven to be for liberals to peaceably hijack our government and convert it to mob rule and then a dictatorship, paving the way for Antichrist on a global scale.

It seems many in America (in both political parties) are determined to hasten global rule (many perhaps unknowingly) by pushing the idea of nation building and democratizing their people. We have no business doing this! Who made America the world's master builder? We have no right or mandate to democratize the world even though that seems to be the battle-cry of the humanistic west. Seems America has been elected to carry out the process, even to fight unnecessary wars to "democratize" the world—maybe that's part of the plan to weaken us in the process.

It seems to be an obsession—democracy for everyone whether they want it or not. The word is thrown around as if it is the silver bullet that would fix everything that is wrong in the world. If only the people could govern of, by, and for themselves, they would rule themselves appropriately. The majority must know what is best. Right!

Anyway, why should we want to democratize the world when our own system is turning into a failure? Its two hundred year shelf life is past its expiration date and is unraveling fast. But before it fails—and contributing to its failure is another costly reason liberals love democracy—they can tax the unrepresented members of the productive class mercilessly.

TAXATION WITHOUT REPRESENTATION

"The economic side of the democratic ideal ... is in fact socialism, itself."[19]

We have already concluded that democracy is the political system chosen by humanist liberals, for it allows them to clandestinely overwhelm the opposition as they accomplish their stated goals, probably the main one of which is controlling the economy. This they do with decentralized economic decision making: "... we must extend participatory democracy in its true sense to the economy."[20]

In so doing, liberals open the door to socialism, "... the economic side of the democratic ideal,"[21] and close the door to capitalism, the economic slave of the democratic machine. Working through the democratic process, liberals have strategically and quite successfully strapped capitalism with the obligation to care for the world, as socialists see fit, and to whom they see fit. They would eventually hang the golden goose or rebrand it with a government label, leaving just enough slack in the noose for her to lay an occasional brick of fool's gold. The free market, they say, produces unjust results and creates classes that separate society, so the government has to step in and level the playing field to ensure "economic justice" and equality for all.

If a liberal had to give you one phrase that defined his very existence, it would have to be "spread the wealth." Obsessed with equalizing disproportions in wealth, liberals redistribute with a vengeance. Of course, it is not their money they spread around. Their socialist system produces no wealth, so they naturally turn to the economic model that does in order to fuel their compulsion to give money away.

Compound that with the insatiable appetite of those taking the money that is given away. The Bible is clear that covetousness is a sin, which means that it is a sin even to contemplate the seizure of another's possessions for our own use. How much worse to actually vote to confiscate his goods (particularly his money) knowing they will be doled back out to you. In a very real sense, it is not a stretch to assume that the recipients of redistribution actually covet the goods of those being extorted.

Democracy in the hands of these covetous self lovers will inevitably weaken and eventually destroy capitalism when the population is sufficiently captivated. As a team, humanists and democracy confiscate from the more prosperous minority and dispose to the majority and, in the process, dispose of all incentive to excel, degrading the profit-driven apparatus to a mere support mechanism until it is finally dissolved by the state.

Capitalism is destined to fall in a democracy when morals disintegrate and the self gods vote themselves a paycheck extorting money from entrepreneurs and the productive working class instead of working hard for it themselves. This exploitation of the dark side of democracy kills the incentive to succeed of those with a natural desire to improve and to reap the rewards of their superior talent, energy, and skill.

Call it what you will—highway robbery, economic justice, extortion with a smile—we liken it to veiled confiscation when one class imposes taxes (through the ballot box) and another class pays them. Ever felt helpless, with no say in the amount you pay at tax time? With good reason. You have been silently disenfranchised from the political process. So said William Edward Hartpole Lecky, "The inevitable result is to give one class the power of voting taxes which another class almost exclusively pays, and the chief taxpayers, being completely swamped, are for all practical purposes completely disenfranchised."[22]

The voice of many in our democracy has been surreptitiously silenced by way of the subterfuge of taxation exacted by the representation of others. The taxed, for all intents and purposes, have not representation. The forty percent of Americans who do not pay income taxes plus the liberal coalitions easily elect enough higher tax representatives to overwhelm productive patriots. Taxpayers who vote for representatives of the lower-tax, smaller-government persuasion are mired in the minority and really do not have a voice in whether or not they are extorted of their earnings.

What we have devolved into in America is a classic case of taxation without representation. Those who pay no longer chiefly control where their pay goes. Taxation no longer matches representation. But representation is the mouthpiece of consent, and our consent is the only means by which we should be taxed. Therefore, no representation equates to no consent, a fundamental impetus for the first American Revolution.

Furthermore, we should receive just compensation for the confiscation of our hard-earned money. According to the Fifth Amendment to the Constitution dealing with due process, it says, "... nor shall private property be taken for public use, without just compensation." Property, according to

James Madison, includes a man's land, merchandise, and money. Point being—our money is our private property, and we definitely do not receive just compensation from our taxed dollars.

So, in today's liberal spend-and-tax freefall into the abyss of inescapable bankruptcy, two things are purposefully missing from the poor taxpayers' state-managed life—consent to and compensation for the confiscation of his money. In an earlier time, when men were men and freedom and fairness were the essence of life itself, being taxed without consent and "just compensation" was enough for taxpayers to rise up in revolt against the heavy hand of the extortioner. Ask King George next time you see him; mention this to the Anointed One if you ever see him.

Did you ever wonder how we got where we are today with a tax structure designed to soak the more productive and give their money to those who, for whatever reason, cannot compete in the free market? You probably already know that the progressive income tax (the rate progresses upward the more money you make) is from Karl Marx's *Communist Manifesto* whose objective is, as you might expect, to soak the rich and spread their wealth. And it does. It works wonderfully for liberal, spiritual heirs of Marx.

The Income Tax amendment was passed in 1912, and since then there have been no constitutional limits on the progressive rape of personal and corporate income earners. It is so bad now that we have no immunity from the manipulative micro-managers in Washington, D.C., who brazenly extort money from the productive and profitable in our country and dole it out to the non-productive and non-profitable. Granted, some have no choice in their financial standing and do sincerely need our help, but we all know many more are just milking the system.

A flat tax might be okay, especially if our money was used only for protection, meritorious purposes, and the common good, but it is not—not even close. The progressive tax has become a marvelous vehicle for redistributing wealth from the voiceless minority who see their income, savings, and wealth confiscated by the majority who do have a voice because they have more representatives. The minority, in effect, has no effective representation, yet it must bear the burden of supporting a self-serving and immoral people who care nothing about the injustice they inflict on the smaller group nor of the damage they are doing to our nation. Taxation without representation epitomizes democracy gone bad and is probably the main reason this form of "representative" government eventually fails, and will fail in America.

CONCLUSION

We have to decide, as a people, if we are going to be governed by the ignorant masses and the intellectual humanist elite who manipulate them or by the honest patriots who love the old America and would revive and preserve the traditions of self-reliance and strong moral basis that made us the greatest nation ever to populate the earth. Will we choose freedom lovers who would defend us from our enemies, who would seek justice and tell us the truth, who would fight for the life and rights of our unborn citizens, who would rule for public service and not party ideologies, who were chosen for merit not money or the promise thereof?

I fear that as long as humanism is our state religion, "we the people" will not have the desire or the knowledge to reject the dark side of democracy and elect officials who are worthy to speak for all the people, all the time and who will govern the nation and not the vocal, oftentimes well-heeled groups.

I am also afraid that only a grassroots reformation or a taxpayers' revolt of some kind against the unrepresented taxation and forced compliance with unconscionable rules and regulations and Supreme Court rulings will return this nation to favor with God who will then rebuild the invisible hedge of safety that long kept every enemy from our shores. We will look closer at our options in the next chapter.

5

REVOLUTION OR REFORMATION?

The same humanist force that aggravates and exalts our own sinful natures also orchestrates the demise of America. It is a grand scheme, well thought out, and painfully successful. An outline of their strategy for creating a new America that is fit for the liberal Utopia of religious tolerance, socialist good will, and global allegiances would go something like this:

- Sabotage the church, rendering it not only useless in the culture wars, but causing it to act as an actual advocate of humanism. Then berate, ridicule, and demonize Biblical Christians to mute their message.
- Take control of corporate America and cause capitalism to merge with and provide all the material support for socialism's entitlement and redistribution efforts.
- Turn our Republic into a democracy, then subvert democracy into mob rule, providing the perfect vehicle for "spreading the wealth," for stealing elections, for establishing one-party rule, and creating a new class of slaves.
- Infiltrate and take over nearly every infrastructural institution in the United States, including education, entertainment, and information. Most importantly, they would "own" the press who would cover for all the illegal acts of their comrades in government, especially their President.

- Take over our government and then enact laws and regulations to weaken and eventually cause us to be defeated by our many enemies, or force us to submit to global governance with global economic capabilities and international law. Additionally, they would defame America, bankrupt us, destroy our intelligence capabilities, and defund the military, leaving us virtually defenseless in an increasingly dangerous and nuclear armed world.

The strategy is working. We now have a new America dominated by liberal elites and ignorant, self-serving masses who ask only what their country can do for them.

Sure, remnants of the old America survive, but they are enslaved and encapsulated within the invisible walls of the liberal's fortress. In other words, there are now two Americas. One is in power, and the other, the older, is harmlessly and, for the most part silently, tucked inside.

Sadly, the America that liberals have created is set up for failure, probably by design. The new America will fall because of the following:

- God has forsaken America because of our sins, allowing her wall of protection to fall.
- Her liberal leaders want her to fall into the abyss of global oneness, stripped of her national identity, patriotic zeal, and nationalistic pride.
- She is disarmed or lacks the desire or resolve to fight.
- She is bankrupt, and her lover lenders have called in their notes.
- She is hated by the world for her sins (some supposed) of nation-building, democratizing, world meddling, commercial exploitation, and a holier-than-thou attitude, while sporting a lavish and blatantly immoral lifestyle.
- She has been convinced that only globalism will save her and the rest of the world from wars, terrorism, global warming, and economic disparities.

Since all nations will gather with Antichrist in Israel for the Battle of Armageddon, it is clear that America will either cease to exist as a national entity, be weakened into submission, or willingly join the global synthesis of nations. Given that America will fall or fold, how might we surmise that her demise will take place?

Will it be from within as the likes of Obama, Reid, and Pelosi disarm us while driving us to the poorhouse with their massive and wasteful giveaway programs? Will there be a complete financial meltdown on Wall Street as the market senses the futility of struggling any longer with the liberal's ball and chain molded to their every move? Will the Chinese call in their loans, forcing America to declare bankruptcy, and making it a cold hard statement of fact, not just a set of economic stats we choose to ignore while we borrow more to maintain lifestyles we certainly don't deserve?

Could our fall come from a successful terrorist attack or a series of the same? Will North Korea, Iran, China, or Russia launch a nuclear attack against a defenseless America? Or will a nuclear enemy simply blackmail us into submission because our Marxist leaders lack the resources, resolve, or desire to see us survive as an independent nation?

We certainly do not know how the fall will occur or to what degree we are brought down. We suspect it is the culmination of processes already in motion in which we surrender our sovereignty without a single shot and just slip into subjugation, deceived by our leaders into thinking it is the only way to go. It is also certainly possible we could be attacked and not even be a viable player in the One World Community.

How we go down probably depends on how much we, the old school Americans, resist a synthesis into the global unit. It could very well depend on how we, as a people, respond to the sin in our own lives and the saturation of corporate sins throughout our nation.

So, how do we resist the liberal fascist's domination of our nation's power structures? How do we effectively deal with the sins that have rendered us personally powerless and nationally cowering to a handful of herdsmen half a world away? What can we do to save our nation and ourselves? How do we take our country back? Can we? How do we prepare our souls for the darker days ahead? Will we?

We don't know under which scenario America will be humbled before being folded into the Antichrist regime. But we do know that the old American eagle has fallen, at least for now. Can she be revived, or is the die cast? How we answer this last question will likely determine what we do from here on out.

If we assume that the die is cast, we might just sit back, do nothing, hope for the best, and watch the total collapse of America. We might play the game, keep the mouth shut, take the handouts, and hide our faith under a basket, smother the flickering flame of our fight against the forces of liberal fascism. Or we might acknowledge the inevitable, prepare ourselves spiritually, get ready to be persecuted (even killed), and lead as many as we can to the truth of what is coming and how to prepare for it.

If we assume that the old eagle could be revived, many would likely try to take their country back or, by some natural means, secure a portion of it where men are still free. Some of the measures they might consider taking include:

- **Waging a war of ideas with the liberal ideologues and their flock.** Conservative ideas far surpass those of the liberals, but with the mass media firmly ensconced in the liberals' pocket, it is unlikely that conservatives can win this war.
- **Electing more conservatives to office.** Conservatives will win some elections, to be sure, but the way liberals are stacking the electoral deck, I for one doubt the country can be won back that way. Conservatives, who are less likely to buy votes or push out hordes of ACORN and union vote peddlers, will find it hard to win another national election. The mobs and elitist snobs simply outnumber freedom-loving traditionalists. Entitlements and immigration, legal or otherwise, will likely ensure liberal empowerment indefinitely. We are past the point of electing enough honest, patriotic politicians because liberals have hijacked the process with all their interest groups melded together into a self-serving mass of me-first, country-last voting blocs.
- **Seceding from the unholy union state by state and govern themselves as they see fit.** After all, power should rest in the hands of the states whose consent made possible the original federal government in the first place. Secessionists could then see their taxes go for purposes they deem worthy instead of supporting the over-represented class of lazy bums who have learned how to beat the system. Let them live in their own state(s) with their liberal masters and see who then pays their bills for them. Maybe they will all go to work, and we can send the illegal aliens back home, finally and for good.
- **Revolting against an oppressive government that hates America**

and anyone in the country who loves their homeland. These modern-day Minutemen would take up arms like their eighteenth century forefathers against a tyrannical force bent on enslaving its own people, then selling them to a vastly larger global entity when the time is right. These revolutionaries would rather go down fighting, surrendering their freedom only after a live-free-or-die kind of effort.

We do not advocate another revolution, but a successful overthrow would surely put power back in the hands of those who produce wealth, own property, provide employment, and who have a vested interest in the continuance of our nation as an independent entity. Of the options, revolution seems the most likely to unseat the corrupt professional actors running our country today.

It is our opinion, however, that all aforementioned efforts to take our country back would fail. The conservative's war of ideas, their ballot box battles, another try at secession, or a revolution with force all seem but futile efforts of a determined but loosely organized minority. There is not the ideological cohesiveness and dogged determination to offset the tsunami of liberal fascist attacks from multiple sources and from every direction. They hold the power. They hold the higher ground.

As stated, we believe that physical and philosophical attempts to uproot liberal power bases in America would likely fail. That includes a militia-style uprising from good ole boys with shotguns and pistols but lacking any form of training or strategy-minded leadership. But, there is hope—all is not lost; no need to give up in despair.

Since humanists, embodied in the form of liberal fascists, got us in the fix we are in today, it makes sense that the only effective weapon against them would be the antithesis of humanism—a return to Biblical Christianity. The watered down mess we have today is no match for the extremely organized, disciplined and determined forces of evil drowning the world in their socialistic filth. A voice here and there crying in the wilderness will not do it this time. America must have a sea change—a paradigm shift in our mood and morals, a transforming national reformation, if you will.

A national reformation would of necessity begin with individual reform. If the die is cast for America's future, our only hope is our own spiritual revolution, our internal overthrow of immorality and anything that smacks of humanism. The revolution must start within ourselves in the form of a revolt against sin and the effects of progressive, liberal humanism on our hearts and lives.

We are in a war for our souls and the soul of America. It may be too late for America to be "saved," but we can win the fight against humanism, liberalism, and relativism in our own lives. It is not too late, but time is running out. Our quest for holiness must be sought with the same passion our enemies exercise against us.

And this we will do once we are convinced that holiness is the only antidote to the forces arrayed against us and our country. This we will do once we are convinced that holiness is our only real hope in a world overwhelmed by humanism. Holiness will no longer be stigmatized as a dirty word; instead, it will be sought after for its cleansing effects on the heart contaminated by humanist filth for so many years.

Now, what of America? How closely are we tied to her fate? Is it too late for her to be reformed on a national level? Only God knows. But not knowing does not preclude our struggle to save our nation from the liberal fascists who hold it hostage to their global intents. We should all keep one thing in mind: we will not change America by our statements of faith and doctrines of works or by imposing our will in the political arena. Rather, we impact the world around us by our behavior and mannerisms, our outward manifestations of a holy heart inside.

America will fold or fall before Armageddon; in what manner we do not know. But note, a reformed America can fall, too. It could well be after true Christians are killed, shortly after mid-Tribulation when only secular humanists are left (see Section Four: The End of Time). Perhaps a national reformation could save America only to see the axe of Antichrist erase her Christian population, rendering her not only susceptible to but a willing participant in the global menagerie.

Revolution or reformation—that is the question. If things get much worse, some may indeed revolt against a corrupt government that cares not one whit for their welfare or for their safety. That is their choice.

Even so, and no matter what course others may take in winning back their country, as for us we choose to fight the underlying cause of our demise (humanism) with the only effective weapon formed against it—holiness. We choose to reform ourselves and do what we can, especially by example, to influence a reformation that will have eternal benefits no matter what happens to America. Let's do all we can to impact our nation for good, but above all, let's prepare our own souls for eternity.

Section Five of this book gives our views on pursuing a life marked by holiness, the trademark of our own personal reformation, the necessary corporate quest for the true transformation of our great country. We have already seen where America stands heading into the end of time, but we want to take a closer look at the fate of capitalism, the hollowness of apostate Christendom, and the perils of the Tribulation before we take a ride on the highway of holiness in Section Five.

Section II

THE END OF CAPITALISM

6
THE BABYLON WHORE
(CAPITALISM)

Babylon is given much space in Scripture, including two and one-half chapters in the Book of Revelation. It is important. It is always representative of evil. Christians are commanded to leave it. So what is Babylon?

John the Revelator saw Babylon as a lavishly dressed Harlot riding on the back of a seven-headed beast!

> ... I saw a woman sit upon a scarlet coloured beast, full of names of blasphemy, having seven heads and ten horns.
>
> And the woman was arrayed in purple and scarlet colour, and decked with gold and precious stones and pearls, having a golden cup in her hand full of abominations and filthiness of her fornication:
>
> And upon her forehead was a name written, MYSTERY, BABYLON THE GREAT, THE MOTHER OF HARLOTS AND ABOMINATIONS OF THE EARTH. (Revelation 17:3-5)

In keeping with the Revelation tradition, John does not tell us who the Harlot is. Bible scholars, confounded by the symbolism, are at a loss when they attempt to identify her. Few even try. Those brave souls who do try seldom agree. Some say that Babylon is Catholicism or apostate Christendom. Others think she is the United States. Many feel that the "great Harlot" represents the entire world system, the epitome of lust and pride

(1 John 2:15-16). Still others hold to a literal interpretation of a city built at the original Mid-East site in modern-day Iraq.

Is Babylon's identity a supernatural secret, another thorn in the flesh riddle where each of us comes up with his own interpretation? No! Babylon's sin and her sudden fall in the last days compel end-time saints, more than any others, to identify and separate lest they, too, partake of her sins and receive of her plagues (Revelation 18:4).

Babylon's association with the seven-headed, ten-horned beast makes her a prominent historical and end-time figure, for the beast upon which the Harlot rides represents earthly kingdoms, the last of which is that of Antichrist (see Revelation 13). The ten horns symbolize ten end-time kings who *"... shall give their power and strength unto the beast"* (Revelation 17:13).

Babylon's influence is worldwide—*"... all nations have drunk of the wine of the wrath of her fornication, and the kings of the earth have committed fornication with her ..."* (Revelation 18:3).

Because Babylon's adulterous deeds have affected the entire world of nations throughout history, many feel that the mother of harlots represents false religion and its known impact on peoples and governments. Granted, spiritual matters do transcend time and national boundaries, and the seductive powers of false religion do overwhelm the mind. But Scripture, when referring to great trade cities such as Babylon, liken their business transactions to adultery. The prophet Isaiah, in a denouncement of Tyre, linked her commerce to spiritual fornication—*"... she shall turn to her hire, and shall commit fornication with all the kingdoms of the world ..."* (Isaiah 23:17). And John the Revelator emphasized Babylon's commercial activities rather than her religious affairs with his frequent references to merchants and riches.

John said of Babylon, *"... thy merchants were the great men of the earth ..."* (Revelation 18:23). Today, business magnates from the free world wield unprecedented power and command universal respect. No political system, not even Communism, hinders their movement around the world. Hardly a nation escapes their warlike quest for larger markets, cheaper labor, and scarcer natural resources.

John further alludes to Babylon as an economically-based process in which *"... the merchants of the earth are waxed rich through the abundance of her delicacies"* (Revelation 18:3). In Babylon, merchants grow rich because they have the freedom to employ their skills and their possessions to accumulate more wealth—*"... that great city, wherein were made rich all that had ships in the sea ..."* (Revelation 18:19).

The financial freedom enjoyed by Babylon's merchants matches that same flexibility and opportunity allowed under capitalism. While we cannot say with certainty that Babylon is none other than the capitalistic economic system, the parallelism is too strong to ignore. Since nothing else (e.g., Catholicism, the United States, or the city itself) comes close to matching Babylon's worldwide power to generate wealth like capitalism, we are comfortable with our conclusions. Anyway, what but a system of this magnitude could God command all Christians to separate from? He certainly would not ask us to leave the United States. But He could command us to walk away from an economic model if it manifested ungodly principles. It does, and He does.

CAPITALISM – HISTORY AND PHILOSOPHY

Capitalism is an economic model in which all or most of the production and distribution capabilities are privately or stockholder corporately (not state) owned. It is based on the premise that man will pursue a path that enhances his own self interest. It is fueled by ambition, enterprise, invention, and self sacrifice. It capitalizes on man's natural desire to improve and to reap the rewards of superior talent, energy, or skills.

The reward of his efforts comes in the form of profits—the main reason capitalists provide goods and services, the main reason most privately-held or stockholder institutions exist at all. Down through history, whenever business has had the freedom to take in more than it spent, usually, it has done just that.

Though hardly the complex system we have today, the use of commerce to freely expand markets and accumulate wealth has existed for thousands of years. An ancient form of capitalism began in Egypt and then spread to Mesopotamia. It would later pervade the other five world empires, but with the demise of the Roman Empire in A.D. 476, free enterprise also subsided as world trade ceased. Through the ensuing Dark Ages and for the next thousand years, the standard of living was severely disabled as capitalism gave way to feudalism with its hereditary landlords, nobility, and strict social classes.

However, the medieval feudal system was destined to die, its death precipitated in part by the resurrection of private enterprise. Contributing to capitalism's renewal after hundreds of years of dormant silence were the Christian Crusades and the discovery of America. The Crusades helped initiate a revival of international trade, and Columbus' 1492 findings brought new trade routes and staggering amounts of New World gold and silver to Western Europe. There they would later be used to help finance the Industrial Revolution. This era of phenomenal industrial growth saw huge inputs of capital transformed into extraordinary outputs of merchandise. Production for personal use gave way to production for sale, and modern capitalism was born.

Until the 18th century, most industrial production was small, privately-owned workshops. The Industrial Revolution changed this with the concentration of production in the hands of a few wealthy capitalists, the independent factory owners. At the same time, powerful landlords were driving small farmers out of business and into town where they became a source of abundant, and cheap, labor. Workers with no land or no means of production were forced to sell their labor in order to survive. Capitalists, with heavy investments in equipment and human labor, merged the two into a profit-producing marriage of man and machine.

During the early years of modern capitalism, governments adopted a "hands off," laissez-faire policy. Private enterprise was characterized by unobstructed competition among independent and unsubsidized firms. They operated under the premise that competition would bring success to the most efficient producers. Governments, at that time, agreed.

America furnished the gold, and the Industrial Revolution provided the machinery, but two other historic events produced the mindset needed to accept and promote capitalistic principles for generations to come. Influencing the development of modern capitalism as much as anything was the revolution in ideas born in the Renaissance and the Protestant Reformation.

The Renaissance was characterized by humanist thought that regarded life as an end in itself. This contrasted the medieval belief that life was but a short testing period determining whether the soul would be saved or damned after death. Contrary to Biblical precepts, this humanist outlook stressed the desirability of material advancement and improved living conditions.

The Protestant Reformation introduced, amid predominant sound doctrine, several ideas that complemented humanism's fleshly appeal that was so prevalent during the Renaissance. Most noted were teachings of John Calvin. He "legalized" the collection of interest on loaned money, encouraged savings and stimulated a materialistic drive among Protestants by interpreting "predestination" in such a way that made business success appear to be a mark of God's favor.

By Calvin's standards, God blessed 18th and 19th century capitalists. Owners of business often grew rich, and those who sold their labor to growing companies also prospered as the standard of living in industrialized countries generally increased during the period. Financial institutions and investment bankers with international affiliations likewise blossomed in response to insatiable appetites for new capital. Corporations evolved and continued to grow as the beginning of the 20th century ushered in a period of peace and prosperity.

But in October, 1929, the bubble burst. The stock market crashed, and the Great Depression which followed dropped capitalism to its knees. When it struggled back to its feet after eleven years of despair, private enterprise was forever altered to alleviate the misery of its "victims." Capitalism was saddled with the responsibility of securing both the present and prospective needs of every member of society, whether they belonged to the economic structure or not. Social, or state-managed, capitalism evolved and swept over the world of heretofore free economies. Recent economic crises have greatly accelerated the demise of capitalism at the hands of its arch enemy—Socialism.

SOCIALISM – HISTORY AND PHILOSOPHY

Concurrent with and contributing to the dramatic change in capitalism was the rise and spread of socialism in its varied forms, the most coercive of which is Communism. Primarily responsible for the man-centered philosophies of socialism (and communism) was the 19th century German economist, Karl Marx. His writings, little read during his lifetime, gained popularity after his death and exploded into the 20th century's most catastrophic phenomenon.

Marx's ideas clashed with the predominant capitalistic order, but depending on the type of government (authoritarian or democratic), confrontations would either be violently disruptive and quick or peacefully subtle and gradual. Countries ruled by monarchs or dictators would experience brutal communist-style revolutions. In democracies, socialists would press for revolutionary changes through education, legislation, and trade union negotiation.

Socialists take advantage of democratic freedoms to peacefully transfer capitalism's blessings to the politically active masses through a "democratic revolution." Marx argued that democratic republics would be transformed into "dictatorships of the proletariat" by the numerical superiority of the working class. Workers would wrest political control from capitalists, thereby transforming the state into socialism. Political freedom and tolerance of civil liberties could still characterize the socialistic state but without the economic individualism enjoyed under capitalism.

In exchange for freedom, the state would offer security and economic equality. Since wealth belongs to everyone in society more or less equally, benefits would be offered to all, regardless of their job status. Ideally, the state-supported system would evolve upward until the nation experienced utopian bliss; blessings would be accorded to one and all with absolutely no help from the Christians' God.

Marx had no problem with a preeminent state or a deified man because, to him, there was no God in whom man could trust or to whom he should be subservient. Marx was convinced that man projected his ideals onto supernatural beings; he actually created gods in his mind. Marx felt that unfulfilled human desires for humane, just, and loving relationships among men materialized as characteristics of the gods, perceived as independent beings. This he believed would be corrected by creating conditions in which these desires could be fulfilled. As it was, human needs are made subservient to the imaginary gods of religion or the financial institutions of capitalism. The man-made product, be it God or money, assumed ascendancy over man.

This was possible because, to Marx, man does not act as a free agent but responds only to external stimuli. Man is a product of his environment, particularly his economic environment. The evils of the world are not the result of man's sinful nature but are products of institutions whose removal would bring happiness. The primary institution of evil, to Marx and his successors, was private enterprise as it exists under capitalism.

Paradoxically, Marx viewed capitalism as evil but necessary in the evolutionary process. He was appreciative of the production capabilities of private enterprise for they would be used to enhance the equal development of humans as society was transformed into the next evolutionary stage—socialism. Capitalism's powerful forces of production would be turned into vehicles of social reform as they financed socialistic human development projects and allowed man the leisure to develop his own creative potential.

However, the benefits derived from capitalism could not be fully realized as long as production and distribution capabilities were privately owned. Marx argued that workers never received in wages the equivalent of the value of the commodity because the unproductive capitalist always creamed off the surplus (profit) while driving workers to greater levels of productivity. He contended that owners stole the profits from workers. For that reason, he wanted workers of the world to unite and resist capitalists' efforts to overwork and underpay them. But, more than that, Marx wanted to remove the profits motive altogether, thinking that the inherent evils with capitalism would then disappear. To do that, he would end private ownership of business and replace it with public (social) ownership. Of course, "public" should be translated "government" as, in socialism, the state assumes ownership or control of previously privately-owned institutions.

ENEMIES UNITE – NOT BY CHOICE

Our Western European friends are a showcase for Marx's state-controlled economies. Following years of infiltration, most of Europe is now dominated by socialist policies and governments.

Although Europe has fallen, America has not yet experienced a total conversion to socialism, even after decades of relentless socialist attacks. However, she has adopted, through the democratic process, enough of Marx's theories that countless demands have been placed on her once-free economic process, Social Security taxes, minimum wage standards, unemployment compensation, employee quotas, and other benefit packages have helped convert private enterprise into an unwilling sponsor of socialism. With great success, socialists have legislated their arch rival into a rather effective ally. Our recent elections with Marxist-inspired leaders have greatly accelerated the process.

Along with legislation has come taxation. By taxing producers and donating the proceeds to non-producers, the state, as an errand boy for socialism, redistributes huge chunks of this country's corporate (and personal) wealth. In just four decades, the government's war on poverty has cost American taxpayers trillions.

Honest Americans are saddened and sickened by the exorbitant cost of their government's social programs. Even more disheartening is the political ineptitude and reluctance of elected officials to make changes, even though studies show their pet projects to be wasteful, ineffective (even harmful to participants) or destined for bankruptcy.

One such program is the social security system, a commendable idea, but nonetheless an expensive and inequitable pyramid scheme whose true character will eventually surface. When its fraudulent nature appears, the system will collapse, and latecomers will lose. But before that happens, payroll deductions will continue to escalate as the ratio of workers to recipients steadily declines. And, as the number of retirees (and with them, costs) goes up, rivalry between the generations will increase, creating further social divisiveness.

Another example of misguided government intervention is minimum wage laws. Contrived to help workers on the low-end of the pay scale, they actually have a negative effect on workers with less marketable skills. To compensate for resultant cost increases, employers raise prices, increase productivity levels, and often fire or refuse to hire workers in the minimum wage category. In addition, minimum wage laws decrease competition that higher skilled workers face from the lower-skilled, creating a situation of unfair advantage to the skilled worker. The unskilled remain unemployed and the skilled grow steadily more affluent.

Yet another case in point is massive tax transfers to the poor in the form of food stamps and assistance for medical treatment and housing. The quality of life of America's impoverished is worse than before the advent of welfare because of the disabling, binding, and perpetuating character of government handouts. Welfare in the U.S. is clearly counterproductive because recipients have changed their behavior patterns to comply with the new rules. Naturally, the incentive to work diminishes when the unemployed receive as much or more not to work as their employed neighbors. Naturally, illegitimate births rise when unmarried women who become pregnant are paid to remain unmarried.

Though obviously injurious, fraudulent, and unjust, the political sacred cows will remain unchanged by our government. Liberals in Congress will never allow the drains to be plugged; they profit too much by trading on the misery of the poor. As the Communists use the proletariat, political poverty pimps use the poor as a device to assume and retain power.

Since anti-poverty programs in the U.S. have actually increased poverty, left-leaning politicians have an even broader base of support for their merger of capitalism and socialism. Sad to say, the die is cast. Until the end, American economics is destined an unholy mixture of philosophies espousing material blessings on the one hand and altruistic welfare on the other.

In spite of, and maybe partially because of, the Great Depression and ensuing social reforms, capitalism in the late 20th century boasted of unprecedented wealth, sharing (perhaps involuntarily) its blessings with more people than ever before. In spite of profit-robbing legislation and taxation, capitalism, ironically, became even more profitable in the second half of the 20th century.

Attribute much of her success to greater managerial efficiency, ingenuity and aggressiveness. Giant corporations, with widely distributed ownerships, are now managed by highly-trained professionals rather than owners. Automation of work functions has resulted in significantly higher levels of productivity. Rapid advances in computer-based technology offer even greater potential for mechanization of manual efforts. Aggressive financial services, here and abroad, generate fortunes in interest dollars for capital-rich investment firms.

Additionally, capitalists indeed capitalized on socialist redistribution efforts; the integration of economic thought has turned out to be nothing less than federal subsidization of corporate growth. Increased wages, benefits, and welfare packages aided business by pumping billions of dollars back into a capitalist economy. Consumers had more money and, as is the case with most Americans, they spent it. The law of supply and demand drove prices up and business prospered. Prices climbed after trade unions extracted increased wage and benefit packages from reluctant profit-conscious corporations. The never-ending spiral of increased costs followed by higher prices generally favored the corporation. In essence, capitalism has shared enough of its bounty with the working class to buy them off while it rebounded from a near collapse into the most prosperous haven of private enterprise ever.

As long as corporations and workers remained prosperous, at least by their own reckoning, ownership would remain in private hands. Until there is a fundamental shift toward government ownership, (as we are now experiencing) capitalism will survive. That means the system will likely remain in tact until the end, or nearly so. Until then, she will manifest a spirit as troublesome to the Spirit of God as the Marx-inspired, Satanic filth flooding the world today.

In spite of the hatred and the ideological struggles between capitalism and socialism, the two manage to intermingle in most twenty-first century societies. The world's opposing economic systems clash violently in the philosophical area but, for now, blend grudgingly in the practical world of reality. With the recent financial meltdown, all of that is about to change, and ownership of much that is private is about to become state-owned.

WHAT'S WRONG WITH CAPITALISM?

Of course, Marx was wrong; not all privately-owned enterprises are capitalistic in nature, nor do all corporations harbor the Babylon spirit. Neither is the concept of private enterprise inherently evil, for God has always advocated man's economic freedom and individual responsibility. This must certainly include his right to own property, to enter into voluntary exchange with whomever he chooses, to select the vocation of his choice, to provide goods and services in order to make enough money to provide for his family, to help the needy, and to put enough aside for a rainy day.

This writer is a firm believer in free enterprise and the concept behind pure capitalism, but something within the capitalist system—the misuse of its freedoms—must defy God's laws relative to making money. These abuses of privileges distinguish mere private ownership from capitalism. The introduction of these abuses into an individually-owned business signals the departure of God's sanction and the entrance of the Babylon spirit to administer its economic affairs.

So, from this point forward, when we use the word "capitalism," we do not mean the free enterprise system *per se* but the willful perversion of those freedoms into a competitive, ever-expanding monster, incapable of expressing even the slightest measure of human compassion. By capitalism we mean the merger of equipment and human labor into a profit-producing machine incapable of looking beyond its own voracious appetite for larger markets, cheaper labor, and scarcer natural resources. By capitalism, we mean an attitude, or spirit, within an economic system that lends itself to the old man's natural desire for fun, fame, and fortune, that focuses on selfish desires as they seek gratification through the things of the world, that forsakes the right of others and perverts the love of God into a Laodicean craze for pleasure, possessions, and prestige.

Any business, regardless of its size, can be possessed by the Babylon spirit. Pride, covetousness, and the pursuit of pleasure can motivate even the smallest businessman, making him, like his corporate counterparts, yet another cog in capitalism's wheel of fortune and fame. For that reason, each enterprise, large or small, must be judged on its own merits and by the presence of the soul-damning Babylon spirit. Void of feelings for people it operates merely to make more and more money.

As with Marx's theories, the Babylon spirit originated in Hell. Isaiah pointed this out when he wove a description of Lucifer into that of Babylon's king. He asked the fallen angel:

> "How art thou fallen from Heaven, O Lucifer, son of the morning! How art thou cut down to the ground, which didst weaken the nations! For thou hast said in thine heart, I will ascend into heaven, I will exalt my throne above the stars of God ... I will be like the most High." (Isaiah 14:12-14)

Ezekiel did the same thing in his prophecy against the ruler of Tyre. He said of its prince, *"... thine heart is lifted up, and thou hast said, I am a God"* (Ezekiel 28:2). Then he switched to Satan, the real king of that prosperous trade city:

> "Thou hast been in Eden, the garden of God ... Thou art the anointed cherub ... Thou wast perfect in thy ways from the day that thou wast created, till iniquity was found in thee." (Ezekiel 28:13-15)

The Babylon spirit, also found in Tyre, is perpetuated by trade:

> "By thy great wisdom and by thy traffick [merchandise] hast thou increased thy riches, and thine heart is lifted up because of thy riches ... By the multitude of thy merchandise they have filled the midst of thee with violence, and thou has sinned ... Thou hast

defiled thy sanctuaries by the multitude of thine iniquities, by the iniquity of thy traffick [merchandise] ..." (Ezekiel 28:5, 16, 18) *[Bracketed words added for clarity.]*

Although the Babylon spirit grows out of the world's trading exploits, Babylon itself does not represent the entire world system boasting of political, military, and economic might and teeming with man-centered educational, religious, and entertainment structures. Rather, Babylon is only one aspect of the world system, the economic means to obtain the things of the world. Babylon provides the finances for us to enjoy *"... the lust of the flesh, and the lust of the eyes, and the pride of life ..."* (1 John 2:16). The Babylon spirit is an attitude within an economic system that lends itself to fallen man's natural desire for fun, fame, and fortune—the things of the world. Ancient Babylon catered to these Adamic impulses; Isaiah said of the city, *"... thou that art given to pleasures* [lust of the flesh]*, that dwellest carelessly, that sayest in thine heart, I am, and none else beside me* [pride of life]*"* (Isaiah 47:8). Jeremiah added, *"O thou that dwellest upon many waters, abundant in treasures, thine end is come, and the measure of thy covetousness* [lust of the eyes]*"* (Jeremiah 51:13).

In violation of God's greatest law, the law of love, the Babylon spirit focuses on selfish desires as it seeks gratification through the things of the world. Scarred by lust and pride, it mocks the idea of love for others while perfecting the art of self love. This is so because the lust of the flesh depicts self-centered appetites and pleasures. The lust of the eye (covetousness) describes a craving for "things" with little regard for the rights of others. And pride is a satanically-based desire to exalt oneself above another: *"I am, and none else beside me"* (Isaiah 47:8). In either case, the self is elevated or pampered, the rights of others forsaken, and the love commanded by God perverted into a Laodicean craze for pleasure, possessions, and prestige.

This self-serving attitude reached its zenith in Babylon, the city, but has existed in capitalism since its inception. Today, modern capitalism provides a perfect haven for the Babylon spirit. Granted, lust and pride germinate elsewhere, but America's economic structure provides the most fertile ground for these deadly sins.

Capitalism gives birth to our latent impulses to covet "things" and extol ourselves because the foundational principles upon which it operates are geared toward accumulation and self emulation. Absent the love of God, these principles often violate the rights of others, particularly the poor. This abusive nature of capitalism is now, more than ever, characteristic of America's greed-based, money making process. Using its freedoms to reap gain, often at another's expense, makes capitalism just as obnoxious to God as atheistic Communism. And it makes conforming to its self-centered tenets just as damnable to the soul as flatly denying the existence of God.

At the heart of capitalism, dominating its every precept and principle, is a competitive drive for higher profits. A business filled with the Babylon spirit is not content to merely cover costs and make a reasonable profit. It exists solely to make more money. Accordingly, its every act is directed at higher numbers on the bottom line of the financial report. Any technique that enhances the profit picture generally gains management approval. Even programs for employees are little more than morale boosters designed to increase production and maximize profits. In short, fairness to employee and consumer are forsaken, and both become pawns of the system, their value measured only in terms of their contribution to the business.

When the bottom line looms as the driving force behind nearly every management decision, those decisions eventually and inevitably lead to expansion. Marx rightly concluded that capitalism had no stopping place but was relentlessly driven by greed to innovate and increase output. To increase profits, companies lower production costs. This, in turn, requires increased scales of production resulting in centralization into fewer and larger corporations. Mergers, acquisitions, and takeovers concentrate most corporate wealth and power into the hands of a few major corporations.

This dangerous concentration takes a deadly toll on small businessmen, but the loss of human compassion and understanding is far more devastating. Our basic human need to feel wanted and loved suffers with the advancement of capitalistic expansion. Capitalism has outgrown the "small" idea of sharing, love for others, fairness when setting prices, consideration and high esteem for those building as well as buying its products. Instead, it opts for the high volume/high profit marketing concept that treats people as objects from which money must be extracted. With growth, compassion has steadily been replaced by greed, and love has given way to selfishness. This is far from the Christian ideal.

Bottom line management, characterized by unending expansion, is inextricably bound to another lust- and pride-induced principle—competition.

Central to capitalism, equality is nothing more than equal opportunity of all to compete freely for economic advantage.

With advantage must come, of necessity, disadvantage; invariably the weak suffer most in a fully competitive environment. Having adopted and applied to economic behavior Darwin's "survival of the fittest" philosophy, capitalists bless with religious fervor the competitive struggle for superiority among and within corporate structures. They smile as the strong grow more prosperous and the weak necessarily grow poorer. They have little compassion for losers but boast proudly of their affluent winners.

Although critics of capitalism fault the competitive, profit-oriented system for giving birth to deprivation and nurturing an ever-widening gap between the classes, capitalists adamantly oppose this line of reasoning. They contend that capitalism did not cause poverty; it only made poverty more visible by pulling the poor off their small plots of land from which they barely earned a living and into urban centers of manufacturing and commerce. They say that an industrialized society only created an awareness of poverty itself. To a degree, they are right. Most people did barely survive on their small plots of land in a pre-industrialized society but everyone, except wealthy land barons, was in about the same financial fix. Of course, poverty was less noticeable when everyone was poor. But with the prosperity of increased commercial growth, industrialists and workers alike rose to affluence, thereby driving a wedge between those inside and outside the capitalistic structure.

However innocently, capitalism does create a noticeable poverty, and an increasing price structure perpetuates the economic distinction between the upper (and middle) classes and the poor. Capitalism did not necessarily produce poverty by taking the poor man's money (although this is true to an extent in the price he must pay for necessities), but it did create a chasm which few will cross. Excepting a handful of "rags to riches" stories, those inside the economic order tend to maintain or improve their status while those on the outside get poorer as product prices continue to rise. This is true not only for America's impoverished but for the poor in the rest of the world as their economic standing continues to decline. Sixty percent of the world's population has an income at or below the level of bare subsistence. A century ago, per capita income in developed nations averaged two times that in less developed countries. Today, the difference has grown to five times as much. The disparity widens. Capitalism does create a world after its own image—those not competing, die.

So, to solve the poverty problem, advocates of capitalism feel that, rather than subdivide the pie into smaller and smaller parts, there ought to be a bigger pie. In other words, there ought to be more capitalism. Instead of offering money or non-cash items (food, medical assistance, etc.) to the poor, offer them the capitalistic process so they can compete with other capitalists, thereby creating their own wealth. Capitalists justify their selfish hoarding, while millions die of starvation, by explaining that wealth must be created before it can be donated, so what the poor really need is their own means of production, not handouts. Offer them competition and self-sufficiency, but money, never.

Of course, socialists in our government have forced capitalists to share some of their bounty with the less fortunate, but they soon got it back. Trillions destined to alleviate somewhat the plight of America's poor, has ended up, instead, in corporate cash registers. Inflation, resulting from increased costs (for welfare), followed by higher prices only serve to shift everyone in society proportionately upward. The poor remain at the bottom of the socio-economic ladder, worse off than before because they have no one to whom they can pass along price increases. As long as the competitive system survives, and in spite of social programs, government handouts, and foreign aid, the poor will remain, and the rich will get richer.

Capitalism (not private enterprise) would fail if everyone in America followed Christian precepts of love and self-denial. Competition's fleshly lure would lose its effectiveness because there would be no flesh to seduce; the old man with his affections would have been crucified with Christ. Likewise, love and high esteem for others would destroy the competitive, self-interest drive.

Capitalism will fail, but not because everyone in America suddenly adopts Christian values and applies them to their business life. Sadly, most Americans, including Christians, are determined to preserve or improve their current lifestyles and the economic system that ensures its preservation. Accordingly, the Babylon spirit will continue to spellbind and enslave all who abuse their economic freedoms and do so with little regard for the rights or feelings of others. That is, *until the end.*

THE DEATH OF CAPITALISM

In spite of her universal influence and the prominence and wealth of her partners in adultery, the Harlot will suddenly fall to her death at, or near, the end of this present age. When she falls, the world's purchasing power will likewise crumble: *"... the merchants of the earth shall weep and mourn over her; for no man buyeth their merchandise any more ..."* (Revelation 18:11).

Babylon will fall quickly: *"For in one hour so great riches is come to nought ..."* (Revelation 18:17). What but a financial collapse like that of 1929 could trigger the sudden loss of great riches and of merchants' wherewithal to accumulate more? Certainly not the fall of an apostate church or a city that has laid in waste for thousands of years. (Note: Even if we have reached the wrong conclusion that Babylon is capitalism, it seems obvious that capitalism will fail in the near future.)

Babylon's fall is precipitated by the ten nations who align themselves with Antichrist. They hate the Harlot and, with God's blessings, destroy her:

> "And the ten horns which thou sawest upon the beast, these shall hate the whore, and shall make her desolate and naked, and shall eat her flesh, and burn her with fire. For God hath put in their hearts to fulfill his will ..." (Revelation 17:16-17)

With the termination of the financial system which allows merchants to freely amass wealth, Antichrist and his ten puppets will institute a controlled, dictatorial order which only those with his mark or his name or his number (666) may participate:

> "And he causeth all, both small and great, rich and poor, free and bond, to receive a mark in their right hand, or in their foreheads: And that no man might buy or sell, save he that had the mark, or the name of the beast, or the number of his name." (Revelation 13:16-17)

Babylon sits atop the Beast peacefully now. Capitalism and socialism coexist today in a fascist style marriage of convenience, but in the end of this age, the Beast will devour the Harlot system. Socialism will totally envelop capitalism. The evolutionary process, begun in the early 1900s, will end with a final *coup de grâce*. Just as the Beast hates Babylon, socialists hate private enterprise and are determined that it must end. They are not content with a mixture. To remedy the world's ills, they feel that nothing less than the death of capitalism and complete redistribution of the world's wealth will correct the mammoth inequities in today's economic structures.

The stage is set for a final end-time clash between the world's two economic forces. Capitalism is already dying. It is even now being strangled to death by taxing, regulating, and litigating forces of governments dominated by socialists. Kept alive for now, capitalism is used to provide production capabilities and resources to fuel socialism's worldwide redistribution rampage. After all, isn't it the capitalists who finance, albeit unwillingly, the spreading of their wealth to the world's poor, the ones from whom they obtained their wealth?

Humanists view capitalism as an obstacle to human progress. To them, capitalism functions as a religion because it sacrifices individuals on the altar of utopian promises. To them, commercialization is a debasing force. To them, individuals are ground down by the weight of capitalism and must be rescued by the state. To them, when cyclical economic bubbles burst (as the recent housing debacle demonstrates), they always blame capitalism and use the crisis (as did FDR) to pass massive redistribution legislation.

With such hatred, ideological fervor, and overwhelming political clout, socialism (humanism) is bound to win the struggle. And they will, in a global manner. Somehow, the ten kings will precipitate the collapse of all remaining privately-owned institutions and replace them with public, international socialism. The ten kings of John's prophecy (Revelation 17) need but finalize a socialist takeover that was first introduced in the United States seventy-five years ago but that today is hopelessly engrained in the moral fiber of a materialistic, security-conscious people.

William Bowen, a noted authority on humanism and globalism, said, "The complete takeover will come through an economic catastrophe. Most likely, it will be the result of a bankruptcy of the United States government. That will trigger a devaluation of money and lead to a stock market crash. This will bring on a world depression—and a global government which will be thought necessary to solve all our problems."[23]

When the Harlot falls, Antichrist will be free to institute his worldwide socialistic state. Dictatorial powers will be his as he controls all buying and selling with the issuance of a mark in the hand or forehead. Gone forever are free trade and private enterprise as they exist in Babylon's seductive state—*"… Babylon … shall be found no more at all"* (Revelation 18:21).

When Antichrist and his associates take over, they will implement communist-like dictatorial controls. With some version of socialism either controlling or heavily influencing every major government, the machinery is already in place. All that is missing is a financial collapse and a powerful leader to organize confused, national economies into a universal system marked by the total absence of private ownership and personal liberties.

Such restraints characterize communist states today even though communist theory itself seems quite commendable and seemingly harmless. Communism, on paper, stresses community ownership of all property. It encourages cooperation, with each producing according to his ability and voluntarily sharing with others according to their need. To ensure fairness, intellectual elite (those who with their lofty ideals of a capitalist-free society incite the poor working class, the proletariat, to revolt against their exploitative bosses) take charge, then plan and control all phases of the economy. This they do, supposedly, until the ignorant masses are capable of governing themselves.

However, once the elite seize power, they doggedly cling to it. Proletariat dreams of community ownership, voluntary cooperation and equal participation in a democratic central government quickly deteriorate into communist nightmares. The means of production and distribution, theoretically owned by the community, are in reality owned by the state with workers receiving only bare subsistence in exchange for slave labor. Collectivization of agriculture and forced distribution of scarce commodities replace voluntary sharing. Democratic central governments become, instead, dictatorial states with no proletariat participation.

Those who oppose the state are generally crushed without question. The brutal murder of millions of dissidents in Russia, China, Vietnam, etc., attests to this grim fact. Loss of life means nothing to a Communist. The state must be preserved. The Communist Party must remain in power and unchallenged.

Such selfishness portrays the mastermind behind this hellish philosophy; Karl Marx was humane in his theories but arrogant and dictatorial in his style. He was domineering, with boundless self-confidence. Devoid of any belief in God, Marx and his friends were described as self-appointed gods. Marx even considered himself godlike and equal to the Creator, not unlike his deceptive predecessor, Satan, and his egomaniacal successor, Antichrist.

Is it any wonder that Marx's theories, when put into practice, produce governments that emulate the style of their creator? His philosophies, born in Hell and wrapped in deception, inevitably lead to dictatorial, atheistic states governed by self-appointed gods. They lead to totalitarian thought control and brutal measures to re-educate. They lead to loss of life and liberty, to the perfection of slavery and inhumanity, to concentration camps. They lead to monopolization of privilege and power by a small aristocracy. They lead to economic stagnation, collective poverty and tyranny. They lead to chaotic economic activity, inefficiencies and scarcity. Finally, they lead to Antichrist.

Section III

THE END OF CHRISTIANITY

7

THE EFFECT OF HUMANISM

(Although the rhetoric in this chapter is strong as we rail against the apostate church in general, we in no way believe that all Christians or even all organizations are guilty of the sins of Laodicea. We must all examine ourselves in light of God's Word.)

Capitalism has been wounded and will eventually fall. America is being weakened and will eventually fold. And, before there can be a universal religion deifying the self, Biblical Christianity, with its emphasis on salvation, sacrifice, and separation, would have to be watered down or even converted into a more palatable form.

Toward that end, humanists teach that there is good in every religion, that all are one in origin and only incidentally differ from each other. So, rather than dissolve organized religion, they would redefine and restructure it as a useful vehicle for the spreading and propagation of New Age doctrines: "Certainly religious institutions, their ritualistic forms, ecclesiastical methods, and communal activities must be reconstituted as rapidly as experience allows, in order to function effectively in the modern world."[24]

This merging and rearranging of all the world's religions is nearing completion, if not in fact then certainly in focus. Roland Gammon, a New Age activist, claims that "... all living religions today are trying to function as an integrated spiritual grid."[25] Soon, the synchronizing of all religions into an all-embracing faith, with every sect and creed united, will be fact and, when it is, Christianity will have, for the most part, fallen completely away from the foundational truths of God's Word.

In its subdued state, Christianity would no longer antagonize the self, nor would it condemn the society in which self lives. Since much of present-day Christendom is guilty of neither offense, it is obvious that the humanist conquest of the church is nearing completion, the prize almost wrapped and ready for delivery to the man of sin.

As has always been the case with Satan's change agents, the humanist assault on Christianity has taken two forms—forceful or involuntary dominion (laws, persecution, death, etc.) and cooperative surrender (infiltration, modification from within, etc.). Both are progressing at a frightening pace.

FORCE

At present, the more obvious move to forcefully overthrow true Christianity in America is being made in our courts and legislatures. Humanists are using their powerful legal arm, the ACLU, to strip away all Christian traditions, emblems, and practices that occupy or enter the public domain. Prayer has been banned in the classroom, but prayer is not all that is being removed from public view. Humanists also "oppose the use in any public school of any religious ceremony, pageant, monument, symbol, costume, textbook, or system of instruction which favors or promotes any religion."[26] Additionally, humanists advocate the abolition of tax exemptions for church property, opening prayers at governmental meetings and athletic games, "In God We Trust" from American currency, etc.

INFILTRATION

The less obvious, yet devastatingly more effective, attack on Christianity is being staged within the church itself. The infiltration is so entrenched that, in many churches, humanism is covertly preached under the name of Christianity.

Christianity has money, universal outreach, and evangelical zealots, all of which are being used of Satan (via humanism) to usher in his own kingdom with his very own messiah (Antichrist). How cunning of Lucifer to enter, as a Fifth Column, that which was ordained of God, restructure and pervert its purposes and precepts so that Christians actually work for him while thinking they do a great service for God. Satan gets his one great desire—a worldwide kingdom—while, at the same time, sending millions of so-called Christians to Hell for their self-worship and their blatant disobedience to God's Word.

Humanism has a host of silent partners working inconspicuously within the church. Numbered among these humanist undercover agents are the holders of doctrinal positions and denominational by-laws that allow the self to roam and reign freely in hearts and lives. By doing nothing to deny self, they obviously, though perhaps unknowingly, give muted assent to the self-emulating dogmas of the New Age.

On the other hand, certain members of the church actively advance the humanistic gospel of self. Again, many may be innocent of their openly heretical practices, but through them the New Age has nonetheless been carefully and deceitfully passed into the church. Humanism has, in effect, become the new gospel of those who claim to possess power over the universe of man's personal and societal circumstances, of all who would, through their own spiritual energy, conquer the material world of sickness, poverty, social divisiveness, and international strife. Like secular humanists, Christians in this "Human Potential" Movement would, through some inherent power of their own, preserve health, produce wealth, procure peace, and present the earth to Christ as they take dominion over every facet of the established world order. They would, in the final analysis, overcome (independently of God) all opposition and establish a one-world theocratic government with themselves (and their Christ) in charge.

MIND POWER

Obviously, since God has no intention of establishing a millennial-like kingdom before the Millennium, He is not the impetus behind this quest for peace, prosperity, and worldwide domination. If not God, then what (or who) is the source of this power? Satan, of course, but according to Christian humanists, the power originates in man's mental processes, his positive thinking, and his positive confessions, through his psychological superiority over the physical and spiritual aspects of the universe. Man's mind, they contend, when properly channeled in a positive direction, actually generates force with a measurable impact on the visible world.

The power of this force is discharged to anyone, saint or sinner, who knows and properly applies this "Universal Law" of mind control. The power is available to alter one's own private affairs as well as those of the collective world of all humanity. Positive/possibility thinking then becomes a means to a desired end with self still on the throne and sin still reigning in the heart.

SELF AS A GOD

This rationale has but one logical conclusion: the elevation of self to godhood with special restorative and creative powers and the uncanny ability to forestall prophesied judgments on a sin-cursed world. Self-reliance denies our need to rely on God. We can do for ourselves things that people of faith ask God to do. Such thinking taken to it logical end leads to the belief that the self is a kind of god. Some Christian humanists have become as bold as to declare that, created in God's image, man is actually a "little god."

As his own god, man has no compulsion to appease Jehovah God with such negative rituals as repentance, no need to burden his own soul with such negative concepts as sin, salvation, guilt, and eternal damnation. Repentance would only be an admission of guilt, an acknowledgment of a higher power and of a fearful judgment. Talk of sin would have only a negative impact on his self-esteem.

Since the cosmic energies are best activated when man maintains a positive self-image, New Age Christians rewrite the Word of God, discarding as legalistic bondage all so-called scriptural negatives. And since Christian humanists can only look upon the positive and never the punitive side of God, they trample under foot His many warnings to the ungodly. Evidently, they agree with card-carrying humanists that "... promises of immortal salvation or fear of eternal damnation are both illusory and harmful."[27] So, instead of a lake of fire, they promise life, and the sinner remains in his sin: *"... ye have ... strengthened the hands of the wicked, that he should not return from his wicked way, by promising him life"* (Ezekiel 13:22).

Positive thinkers seek not only life, but the *good life* in the here and now. To that end, God's Word is massaged and maligned when positive confessors openly encourage the aggressive pursuit of wealth and fame. Clearly, this teaching has humanistic origins: "the quest for the good life is still the central task for mankind."[28] But, it has penetrated the church and devoured a materialistic and security-conscious element of half-believers. More and more so-called Christians are attempting to harness the mind's potential power to promote their own material advancement and personal achievement. More and more believe they can "think and grow rich." More and more believe that God should be sought for His gifts. Through Him they can realize their dreams and aspirations and become affluent and successful as some celebrities and self-made individuals who happen to be Christians.

CHARISMATICS

While the masses in affluent Christendom (in America) readily accept humanism's quest for the good life, one faction in the church welcomes and more fully expresses the overall objectives of the New Age hierarchy. Humanists have been particularly successful in subverting Charismatics because of their emphasis on supernatural manifestations conjured up through some sort of hyper-faith, even when the conjurer maintains but a trace of personal holiness in his walk before God. William Kirk Kilpatrick elaborates on the deceptive relationship that can develop between emotional experiences and fraudulent imitations: "Because evangelical and charismatic Christians place such a great emphasis on the experience of faith, they are particularly susceptible to these imitations. That part of the world the Christian finds most attractive will often seem like Christianity itself. There will be much talk in it of brotherhood and love and the spirit. It will sound right. It will feel right. But it is wise to remind ourselves in the face of such temptation that the sacred can be drowned in a well of warm feelings just as surely as it can dry up in a secular desert."[29]

As a hunger for the supernatural gnaws at more and more souls, charismania reaches out farther and farther to satisfy it. As a result, the manifestation movement is, like humanism, spreading infectiously throughout the church. Even now, all of religion is moving into the realm of "power evangelism."

In light of the church's casualness toward God, one might well ask, "Why all the concern over signs and wonders?" For one thing, a secularized church that hardly believes in God will paradoxically believe in His miracles. Too, a frantic, fast-paced society demands a spiritual experience that is compatible with its physical: "Furthermore, the masses are easily excited by charismania, by an overemphasis on the spectacular, to the detriment of the ongoing works of charity. A generation whipped up to a frenzy by high-tech show biz may well demand charismatic Christianity and be bored with anything else."[30]

DOMINION

Not only do Charismatics join their non-tongues speaking brethren in confessing wealth, health, and happiness, but they are also enamored with visions of conquering the world for Christ. When viewed from a secular point of view, this parallels perfectly the humanist's goal of world domination and utopian bliss. To the humanist, there is no Heaven; earth is his home, so he intends to make this world into a kind of paradise, i.e., "a world in which peace, prosperity, freedom, and happiness are widely shared."[31]

This theme has been conveyed to earth-bound Christians by a growing number of Charismatic, Kingdom/Dominion preachers pledging to restore the earth to a state of perpetual peace, love, and brotherhood (a humanist dream). Those who have advanced to this higher level of heresy feel that, through their collective efforts, all elements of society will be subdued and made disciples of (or at least subservient to) their brand of Christianity. When they succeed in conquering and Christianizing the world, they will present their conquered foe to Christ upon His return. Until that time, he is being held in Heaven awaiting their overthrow of all Satan's strongholds.

Like everyone else in the Human Potential movement, "Kingdom" theologians sedate their followers to conceal the extent of this world's actual miseries. They're always smiling, always positive, always painting a rosy picture of revival. Their theology must espouse ever a movement higher and wider until the world is encompassed and suitable for a reigning Christ. In keeping with their ever-positive mentality, they never mention God's judgments on a wicked world. They never talk about the coming Tribulation. Its horror and its pain do not mesh very well with the up-tempo, keep-everything-positive dominion scenario.

Neither does the Rapture. Rather than teaching Rapture, dominioneers push New Age principles of ruling and reigning right here on earth. They don't want a sudden catching away to foil their plans. They want to establish with their own hands, then waltz right into the Kingdom of God, taking from Him His destined duty to *"… put down all rule and all authority and power"* (1 Corinthians 15:24).

UNITY

To enlarge the scope of Kingdom theology, its advocates are now promoting wholesale integration of the many divergent theological persuasions within Christianity. This proposed unification crosses all theological and denominational boundaries and differences. It accordingly stresses solidarity above diversity, unity above purity, toleration above separation. A.W. Tozer, who was a pastor and prolific writer, points outs that "a new Decalogue has been adopted by the neo-Christians of our day, the first word of which reads 'Thou shalt not disagree'; and a new set of Beatitudes, too, which begins 'Blessed are they that tolerate everything, for they shall not be made accountable for anything.' It is now the accepted thing to talk over religious differences in public with the understanding that no one will try to convert another or point out errors in his belief."[32] Within the unity movement, there is no conviction and no condemnation of sin—only compromise, conformity, and cooperation.

Toward that end, Charismatics work to merge historic Pentecostals with their younger, more flamboyant, tongues-speaking cousins. With the lowering of moral standards by traditional Pentecostals, a major obstacle to their union has been removed. Both now place more emphasis on experiences and spiritual manifestations than on sound doctrine. In the midst of rampant corruption and immorality, both are beginning to deny Paul's prophesied latter-day apostasy just so they can proclaim a widespread revival with a majority of the world converted to Christianity. Both are fulfilling a prophesy given during the famous Azusa Street revival in Los Angeles in 1906:

> "In the last days three things will happen in the Great Pentecostal Movement: 1) there will be an overemphasis on power, rather than on righteousness; 2) there will be an overemphasis on praise, to a God they no longer pray to; 3) there will be an overemphasis on the gifts of the Spirit—rather than on the Lordship of Christ."[33]

This union of compromising Pentecostals, as one phase of the unity movement, suits perfectly the tight network of New Age propagandists who are even now plotting the fusion of all religious thought into a one-world composite fit for nothing but the man of sin. Wholesale unification, as part of overall dominion theology is the final phase of the seduction of Christianity.

When the merger is complete, Antichrist will be revealed, and the Tribulation will be in full swing.

SICK CHURCH

The Tribulation must be upon us for organized religion has already succumbed to the overpowering spirit of Antichrist—the spirit of humanism. Whether by force or by seduction, Christianity has been sufficiently subdued so as to render it almost totally ineffective in its mandated war on sin. Those within the church with enough backbone to admit it must agree that the difference between New Testament Christianity and today's church is vast.

That which poses today as Christianity in no way resembles that of the apostolic fathers. Activity without purpose, practices without purity, worship without power—these are trademarks of New Age Christianity in America. Many claim salvation and serve God with their lips, but their hearts are far from Him. An appearance of religion, a façade over an empty life—these describe the average Christian in our affluent, humanistic society.

The so-called moral majority has fast become the immoral majority, lots of numbers, yes, but woefully unable to exert any moralistic muscle on a wicked American population. Millions strong, yes, but restore morality and godly convictions to hearts ripped apart by uncontrollable lust and pride—no, the church is too saturated with self for that. Light a flame that purges a nation of its sins and causes it to burn with passion for Christ—no, the church is too content in its own sins for that. Regardless of the pomp, parade, and position-building among God's people, the evidence points clearly to one sad conclusion: the salt has indeed lost its savor.

THE ENEMY WITHIN

As the church mingles and merges God's teachings with Satan's, it finds itself more confused than ever—extolling the virtues of humanism on the one hand, while offering token resistance to its vices on the other. As is always the case during periods of spiritual declination, and especially since humanism has penetrated its hallowed walls, the church itself is the problem.

In recent years, the church lights have almost gone out, dimmed into relative obscurity not only by humanism but by an even deadlier nemesis —sin! Detached from the light-producing Vine, Christians with sin in their lives have no resistance to humanism or to the many false doctrines born out of its unholy marriage with the church. Absent the presence of God, sinning saints are simply overwhelmed by a deluge of hell-bred deception and darkness, and they don't even know it.

Christians with sin in their lives do not have anything to offer a sin-cursed world either. They cannot manifest a Christ whom they do not know. Neither can they legislate morality; it must be learned, and right now, there are hardly any teachers (or role models) in America who can truthfully say, "I have no known sin in my life, but if I sin or if God reveals anything out of character with Himself, I'm willing to repent and turn from it with all my heart."

Because holiness is rejected as a relic of the unlearned past, the apostate church no longer condemns sin. Because there is no conviction, some Christians can now out-sin the wicked, without even blushing.

Not too many years ago, sinners refused salvation because they knew it meant they had to stop sinning. Today, no problem—the church condones sin, almost apologetically making reference to it. And sinners roam freely about the church, welcomed, and appeased with smooth words of love and grace. Where unrepentant sinners once feared to go to church, now they are respectable members. Many stand in the pulpit. Many even rail against the obvious intrusion of humanism upon the American landscape.

But until sin is purged from the church, we, its members, cannot thunder against the evils of society. It is hypocritical to tell the abortionists they have sinned (and try to pass laws to make them stop sinning) when we have sin in our own lives. Until we clean our own vessels, we cannot tell the world to "turn or burn," to "repent or rot in concentration camps."

That is where America is heading. God never changes, so His treatment of sin is completely predictable—it will always be punished; American's sins must inevitably call for her destruction. As with all peoples before us, our country's downfall is due not so much to humanism as its passion for pleasure and possessions, its lust for leisure and recreation, its obsession with sin. Sin opened the door to humanism, and sin keeps it open. As long as America bathes herself in sin, humanism will remain the nation's state religion, incurable diseases will claim millions of lives, and communism will push closer to our shores.

THE FLESH

The humanist cancer is man's more apparent spiritual enemy. Sin is his less obvious though more dangerous adversary. But deeper than both of these, the flesh is the root cause of all his personal and societal problems. Behind his endearment to humanism and behind his proclivity to sin is man's natural and sometimes subtle tendency to sit on the throne of his own selfhood and declare "I am," "I will," or "I did."

There lies within man the potential to chase after his many lusts. That sin-provoking potential within the heart of every man is his "self." It is the "house devil" in every man, the idol that would kill us all. Man's real enemy is, therefore, within; for it is his own flesh—his own lust, pride, and self-sufficiency—that is so easily swayed by Satan's humanist demons. Man's real enemy is, therefore, himself; for it is his own self-will that causes him to give in to the serpent's lies, taste the forbidden fruit, and sin.

So many Christians in our affluent society are, therefore, slaves to sin because they are, as Paul prophesied of end-time men, *"... lovers of their own selves ... proud ... heady, high-minded ... "* (2 Timothy 3:2, 4). Joining the rest of society, they smile on and openly encourage the self-confident, self-satisfying attitude that has its roots in humanism.

Although Paul said, *"... in lowliness of mind let each esteem other better than themselves"* (Philippians 2:3), Christians today primp, pamper, and praise themselves, hardly ever recognizing the needs and accomplishments of others. Although Paul said, *"Let no man seek his own, but every man another's wealth"* (1 Corinthians 10:24), Christians today push their own potential to the limit and explore their own capabilities to the extreme, giving hardly more than a passing thought to the struggles of their neighbor.

Although Christ said, *"... If any man will come after me, let him deny himself, and take up his cross, and follow me"* (Matthew 16:24), Christians today dress, doctor, and drool over their mounds of clay, striving for physical perfection while the soul lays waste, virtually neglected. Then, self-consciousness flares up and Christians, like the rest of a humanistic society, are saddled with the burden of continually protecting their precious self-image.

CLOSET HUMANISTS

The Christian population, desiring to maintain its proper image in the community, often dutifully attacks humanism through natural means, while the real enemy—the self—gains dominion over their lives. And, since humanism is selfishness carried to its ultimate, unabated end, most believers have actually become closet humanists without even realizing it. By elevating the self to godhood and refusing to renounce the flesh with its many lusts, "born again" but self-centered children of the Most High are really humanists at heart. What New Agers boldly declare, these worldly Christians cowardly concede by their actions—that there is no god but self, no time like the present, and no sins like poverty and pain.

The transition from Biblical to New Age Christianity has been a smooth one, for the same energy that drives New Agers also tempts each of us to follow the course of our own hearts. We are all born with selfish desires and visions of grandeur; humanism just capitalizes on these Adamic tendencies, pushing them to their undisturbed, unaltered, and logical conclusion—the deification of self. Man has an inherent bent toward selfishness, so he likely would have arrived at his present preoccupation with the self, even if left alone. However, humanism hastened the corruptive process by encouraging man to cast off all restraint, to seek the good life, to please himself, to forget outmoded Puritanical inhibitions.

Flesh has always sought expression and recognition, but never has there been such an outlet for its edification as with humanism. Humanism is an organized, disciplined and instructed means of self-emulation. In yesteryear, our failure to reckon with sin and self would only send us to Hell (as if that weren't bad enough). But today, this slackness makes us part of a worldwide movement destined to culminate in the reign of Antichrist. We cannot prevent his rise even if we conquer all our fleshly lusts and live righteously ever after. But we can avoid his humanistic influence on our lives.

8

THE EFFECT OF CAPITALISM

While Christians in Russia and other Communist countries suffer persecution for their faith, believers in the West blend comfortably into the socially accepted order, particularly the economic order. Christians in America know little of rejection, imprisonment, and torture because, rather than resist the evils of capitalism, they are an integral part of the process. Sad to say, they are some of capitalism's most active supporters.

Today, Babylon has respectability, a facade of Christian virtue. Believers in capitalist nations have been conditioned to accept the lie that Christianity is 100% compatible with capitalism. As we have already noted, the idea of private enterprise is not inherently evil, and, of course, God requires that we work—*"… if any would not work, neither should he eat"* (2 Thessalonians 3:10). But, by taking advantage of the so-called "Protestant work ethic" and Scriptures encouraging hard work, e.g., Romans 12:11, capitalists have won virtually unanimous Christian allegiance to a force which stands in stark contrast to values for which saints throughout the ages have given their lives.

However cozy she might be with latter-day saints, the Harlot has not always enjoyed close fellowship with the holy. The economic process promoting pride, possessions, and pleasure has clashed with saints down through the years. These confrontations between the greedy and the godly quite often resulted in the deaths of the latter. The rich of Babylon have always worn out the saints of God—*"And in her was found the blood of prophets, and of saints, and of all that were slain upon the earth"* (Revelation 18:24). Modern capitalism, catering to risk-takers and profit-makers, has the same spirit as its economic predecessors that, in yesteryear, killed the saints. The spirit of greed and gain, power and prestige, fame and fortune inevitably leads to the death of God's people. Saints of old resisted the seductive system and were killed; end-time believers unite with the Harlot and die spiritually.

Capitalism, though not a killer of men's bodies, is nonetheless a slayer of their spirits. The same demonic energy that once killed the saints now enslaves them by taking their souls captive, leaving them spiritually dead. The profit-oriented capitalistic system has evolved over the millennia into a well-conceived snare that today prompts millions of Christian souls to proudly rank their relationship with a company on a higher level than their relationship with God.

Not only is this relationship void of any redeeming value, but it is potentially damning to the soul as well. Christian involvement with companies that thrive on profits and prestige is nothing less than spiritual adultery, the most damaging aspect of which is the formation of a binding, psychosomatic union between the believer and Babylon. Uniting with the Harlot, therefore, binds Christians in a profound and mysterious way to capitalism, making them as one with the Harlot system, a mass-produced clone stamped out in the whore's image, her ways having become their ways. They take on her principles and characteristics, losing their own identity in the adulterous process. This change of identity is painfully evident in today's Christians, driven by a compulsive quest for money, prestige, power, self-expression, and leisure.

The transformation of a once-godly nation into a rebellious throng of self-serving, glory seekers did not occur overnight, nor was the change forced on us—we are free. Americans have freely chosen to fornicate with the Harlot economic process. Since we enjoy freedom from dictatorial demands (for now), coercion into transgressing God's laws has taken the more subtle form of seduction.

As entry into any adulterous relationship is voluntary, the Babylon Harlot seduces her victims by appealing to their carnal desire for riches, recognition, and recreation. She caters to the nebulous, and not so naughty, sins of covetousness, the pursuit of pleasure, and growing in individuality independent from God. The defiant Christian accordingly follows his selfish impulse for money and reputation into an unholy affair with the Harlot. His appetite for self-exultation swells into an addictive craving, and he is trapped in Babylon. Perverting his freedom by choosing the Harlot as a partner ironically leads to the loss of that freedom in Babylon's slave camp.

The free-will nature of man necessitates that choices, good or bad, reflect on the condition of his soul. So, abusing his freedoms to the extent of fornicating with the Harlot system endangers the soul of man. Likewise, the freedoms of private enterprise, when misapplied by selfish desires, become twisted to violate the freedoms of others. To prevent this, freedom must exist in relationship to God's moral law; Christian truths must prevail to temper freedoms with Biblical restraint, love, trust, and genuine compassion. Otherwise, the very freedoms that allow us to abuse our freedoms in the reckless pursuit of pleasure, popularity, and prosperity will eventually destroy us as individuals and, on a larger scale, as a nation.

COVETOUSNESS

Probably the most powerful seductive force thrown at Christians in affluent nations is covetousness. Many succumb to the urge to get ahead, fueled by an explosive and sometimes unquenchable lust of the eye. They are actually jealous when their neighbor gets something they don't have, and then push even harder to get it. Once the cycle begins, they acquire a taste for the finer things in life. Soon the luxuries of yesterday become the necessities of today.

To pay for these necessities, American families have, in many cases, mortgaged their home lives. Homes are shattered. Divorce courts are full. Kids, with little guidance at home, turn to drugs, sex, and violence for answers. In so many ways, fulfillment is not available from career-oriented parents.

The precedent for the enslaving power of covetousness was set in 586 B.C. when God sent Israel into Babylonian captivity for their idolatry and because *"... they covet fields, and take them by violence; and houses, and take them away: so they oppress a man and his house, even a man and his heritage"* (Micah 2:2). Isaiah added, *"For the iniquity of his covetousness was I wroth, and smote him ..."* (Isaiah 57:17). Jeremiah railed against the spirit of acquisition that had possessed God's chosen people, and then promised that God would take vengeance against them:

> "For among my people are found wicked men: they lay wait, as he that setteth snares; they set a trap, they catch men. As a cage is full of birds, so are their houses full of deceit: therefore they are become great, and waxen rich. They are waxen fat, they shine: yea, they overpass the deeds of the wicked: they judge not the cause, the cause of the fatherless, yet they prosper; and the right of the needy do they not judge. Shall I not visit for these things? saith the LORD: shall not my soul be avenged on such a nation as this?" (Jeremiah 5:26-29)

Prophecies aimed at backslidden Israel have even more relevance today for saints who slumber in self-gratification while the Bridegroom makes His final preparations for the wedding feast. Most Christians in America are like the pretenders who sat before Ezekiel. Outwardly, they appear as children of God, masking their adulterous relationship with an endless array of religious rituals, but inwardly they worship the golden calves of materialism and success (Ezekiel 33:31).

Many are taught that covetousness is merely a desire for something their neighbor has. It is all right if they want one *like* he has but not his. Such false teaching leaves the door wide open to the spirit of this age, for covetousness, a form of idolatry (Ephesians 5:5), is much more than that. It is serving the god of "things"—cars, houses, clothes, etc. It is preoccupation with and the pursuit of material possessions (whether your neighbor has them or not). It is always grasping for more, driven by a nagging discontentment with the status quo. It is accumulating and gathering beyond actual need, squandering everything for self. It is a craving, not just for one particular thing, but a reaching, Achan spirit that is not satisfied until it has one of everything (Joshua 7:1).

These cravings of the eye lure believers to capitalism. Their desire for things not really needed drives them to perpetual requests for more money. There is plenty in Babylon, so covetous Christians rush in grasping for all they can get. They figure if they keep scratching the itch will eventually go away, but it doesn't. It only itches more. Fat, overstuffed Christianity is bloated with materialism and still not satisfied.

Prosperity enables Christians to keep on stuffing their bellies and their bank accounts while diverting their attention from the things of God. Unprecedented abundance has led to rampant covetousness among God's people. Their lust for things has, in turn, contributed to the last-days apostasy, the "falling away" spoken of by the Apostle Paul (2 Thessalonians 2:3-12), the falling away paradoxically occurring in the midst of the latter rain outpouring of the Holy Spirit.

Prosperity-seeking, pleasure-loving saints will invariably have a form of godliness but deny the power of God's Spirit. Paul said, *"... in the last days perilous times shall come. For men shall be lovers of their own selves, covetous, ... proud ... Having a form of godliness, but denying the power thereof"* (2 Timothy 3:1-5). Possession-minded and proud Christians, serving God with their mouths, have a form of godliness but their real god is their appetite for material things. Paul said they were *"... enemies of the cross of Christ: Whose end is destruction, whose god is their belly, and whose glory is in their shame, who mind earthly things ..."* (Philippians 3:18-19). Covetous Christians are earthly minded, in love with the world. They talk of Christ, but their hearts are far from Him. They claim the risen Savior, but they don't know Him. They speak of salvation from sins past, but they deny the power of God to purify from sins present and future.

Without the purifying power of the Holy Spirit, the believer will forever be under the dominion of sin. His failure to deal with covetousness will lead to carelessness and compromise in other areas of his life—

> "But they that will be rich fall into temptation and a snare, and into many foolish and hurtful lusts, which drown men in destruction and perdition. For the love of money is the root of all evil: which while some coveted after, they have erred from the faith, and pierced themselves through with many sorrows" (1 Timothy 6:9-10).

Covetousness is the great sin upon which hang many others. Often, the lust of the flesh flourishes when the lust of the eye reigns uncontrolled in a person's life. And pride, with its companion independent spirit, generally follows the accumulation of things and money—*"... by thy traffick hast thou increased thy riches, and thine heart is lifted up because of thy riches"* (Ezekiel 28:5).

SELF-SUFFICIENCY

Christians are further seduced by capitalism's broad range of security packages made available to those who, through their own cunning and skill tap into the Harlot's vast storehouse of guaranteed protection against prospective financial shortcomings. Humans naturally crave security and guaranteed success; Christians are quite human in this respect. Not only do believers want Babylon's money but they want her security as well. With attention directed to self and its abilities, security-conscious Christians manipulate and allocate funds in the capitalistic process to secure their present lifestyles until they die.

Increased wages and benefits over the past seven decades have sent prices for goods and services skyrocketing. The resultant inflation further binds Christians to Babylon because they want her escalator clauses and her security blankets to maintain their standard of living, regardless of price increases and regardless of their employment status. The world system is so expensive that even children of God are afraid to trust Him for their medical, retirement, and other basic needs. One visit to the hospital and, without insurance, they are wiped out. No longer do Christians say, "The Lord is my helper," for savings, insurance, and retirement plans have practically replaced dependence on God. Consistent with the man-centered theology of New Age Christianity, God is seen as little more than a means to self-fulfillment. New Age Christians no longer need God, for their trust rests in their own abilities—"... *in the power of their hand*" (Micah 2:1)—and in security programs either furnished or financed by the world's wealthiest economic system.

9
THE EFFECT OF WORLDLINESS

Our society has become so enthralled with the world that its competitive, covetous, self-serving spirit has invaded the church of the living God. So flesh driven are we that most of our religious organizations are little more than theological extensions of the world system of big business, big money, power, and prestige. They have the same kind of pyramid structures, social clubs, and payment systems. They have the same kind of power-hungry hirelings posing as preachers but who are, in reality, little more than pious pimps for the great whore.

All other elements of the world system—entertainment, politics, sports, fads, and fashions—have invaded the visible body of Christ, filling it with the glamor of fast-flowing action, machine-age methods, and Hollywood-style productions. The church has gone out to the world and allowed the world to come into her. As a result, her mood is more social than spiritual, her manner more accommodating than aggravating, her methods more business-like than Christ-like.

In spite of the countless belief systems available in Christianity, so many denominations offer nothing that distinguishes their members from a humanistic society at large. They represent cleverly-packaged programs for approaching God with the self still intact and still seated on its throne.

Having committed spiritual adultery with the world, the end-time church has reproduced a host of worldly offspring. In fact, organized religion turns out some of the finest specimens the world has to offer. Covered with layers of sanctimonious jargon and pounds of praises and platitudes, they resemble Christians, but their lives express nothing of Christ. They claim the risen Savior, but they don't know Him. They talk of Christ, but their hearts are far from Him. They boast of walking as "strangers and pilgrims" through this world, but they never set foot outside the camp. Why? For one thing, they love camp life too much. (See Hebrews 13:13.)

New Age Christians keep one foot in the church and the other in every function, fashion, and festival the world has to offer. They are earthly-minded, in love with the world, not God. Yet, they would place Him in a box, asking Him to spring out whenever there is a need: *"... in the time of their trouble they will say, Arise, and save us"* (Jeremiah 2:27). They have no fear of God, so they are immune to the voice of a true prophet. They are above reproof, above correction, above sound doctrine and much of organized religion must bear the brunt of the blame.

Backslidden across the denominational spectrum, organized religion handily dismisses the doctrines of Christ as inappropriate for our generation. A worldly church views with disdain the difficulties of the first century apostolic fathers, explaining away their trials as undue hardness befitting none but the hapless martyrs of that inglorious era. Worldly Christians boast of their freedom from hardship, reducing spiritual giants like Paul, Peter, and James to moral midgets who needlessly labored under a cross until it finally killed them. So-called believers are allowed, even encouraged, to pass off as outmoded our great Christian heritage and to demean the testimonies of those who suffered and died that the legacy might live on.

Sadly, most of this encouragement comes from the clergy; most of the nonsense proceeding from modern pulpits sounds more like Christianized humanism than world-hating holiness. With Christ's return about to spring on the world as a trap, the church is less prepared, less eager to see Him than ever before. Cradled in the arms of the world, she carries on business as usual but without the convicting and transforming presence of Almighty God. She continues her religious functions but without distinctiveness and vitality. She goes through the routines but without any life. She maintains a pretty form but without any power.

FORM OF GODLINESS

End-time Christianity has been seduced into thinking that the sinful elements of the world are permissible as long as they are covered by a thin veneer of godliness. Latter-day man, playing church while he practices sin, must therefore, of necessity, erect religious structures that appear godly on the outside but are void of the power of true godliness on the inside: *"This know also, that in the last days perilous times shall come. For men shall be lovers of their own selves ... Having a form of godliness, but denying the power thereof: from such turn away"* (2 Timothy 3:1-2, 5).

To deny the power of godliness is to reject the Holy Ghost, for He is the medium through which God's energy is transmitted to man: *"But ye shall receive power, after that the Holy Ghost is come upon you"* (Acts 1:8). To reject the Holy Ghost as God's agent for enduing man with power is to deny man's need of the Spirit and to disclaim the Spirit's ability to "come upon" man demonstratively and impact his life: *"And my speech and my preaching was not with enticing words of man's wisdom, but in demonstration of the Spirit and of power"* (1 Corinthians 2:4).

The rejection is not only of the Holy Ghost's obvious manifested power, but it extends to His inner transforming power as well. His function as the "Spirit of Truth" sanctifies us, sets us free from the bondage of sin and enables us to live holy: *"According as his divine power hath given unto us all things that pertain unto life and godliness ... "* (2 Peter 1:3). God made the demand for holiness so high that none of us could live it without the power of the Holy Ghost living it through us. God's power is therefore indistinguishable from His holiness; the two must mutually coexist because power produces holiness while, ironically, purity is perfected by the indwelling Holy Ghost. There can be no real power without purity and there can be no true holiness without the power of the Holy Ghost.

Therefore, those with a form of godliness repudiate not only the power of God by which they are made over into the image of Christ but they renounce by their actions the overall concept of holiness as well. In short, they continue in sin and will die in their sins because they reject the One who can endue them with the power to live above the sinful, beggarly elements of this world. They will always have a formalistic, dead, dry form of worship because they refuse the holiness-producing power of the Holy Ghost. And, because power deniers are an integral part of the world's religious structure, those who would live holy by the power of God's indwelling Spirit must *"from such turn away."*

FORM OF POWER

Other end-time believers accept the indwelling presence of the Holy Ghost, but they will not renounce their sins to get it. Like Simon the sorcerer, they clamor for God's power but want nothing to do with His purity: *"... Give me also this power, that on whomsoever I lay hands, he may receive the Holy Ghost"* (Acts 8:19). Peter rebuked the man: *"... thou art in the gall of bitterness, and in the bond of iniquity"* (v. 23). Like Simon, modern power seekers often walk in sin, wed to the world, but they still want the power operating in their lives. Dazed by the good life and their penchant for sin, they would sever (if it were possible) the indispensable link between an untarnished temple and a holy inhabitant, between morality and manifestations. They would have a form of power but deny the godliness thereof. There can be no God-sent blessings for those with sin in their lives, only releases of pent-up pressures or self-induced exhibitions of the flesh, only outward demonstrations as the old man has his turn at religious showmanship in a lukewarm mixture of pretentious praise, worldly worship, and super-spirituality.

Without holiness, worship becomes perfunctory, not free; pretentious, not sincere; forced, not spontaneous; smoke with no fire. Without holiness, the Spirit of God will not abide, and the smoke that some call "fire" is not from God. Instead, as influenced by humanism, their power hails from the dynamic force of the universe into which they unwittingly tap through the manipulative abilities of their own minds. However, there really are no latent powers in the human psyche and, since there are only two spiritual power sources in the universe, workers of iniquity (religious or otherwise) obviously receive theirs from Satan. Any power that the impure possess comes from Hell and represents nothing less than an intrusion from the demonic realm. Any time unholy ones circumvent the power of God and, through their own supposed mental prowess, tap into the unseen forces of the universe, they are calling upon the *"prince of the power of the air"* (Ephesians 2:2) to alter the visible world for them. And he can do it, for it is his world to change (Luke 4:6).

Soon, Satan will intrude into the physical plane with greater intensity when, during the Great Tribulation, he is *"cast out into the earth"* (Revelation 12:9). His supernatural onslaught slays (spiritually) the wicked, for he empowers the man of sin *"Even him, whose coming is after the working of Satan with all power and signs and lying wonders"* (2 Thessalonians 2:9) and the False Prophet so that he *"... deceiveth them that dwell on the earth by the means of those miracles which he had power to do ..."* (Revelation 13:14). Additionally, Satan will send forth legions of religious demons during this fateful three and one-half year period who, with wondrous works, deceive all but the elect, and they just barely escape: *"For there shall arise false Christs, and false prophets, and shall show great signs and wonders; insomuch that, if it were possible, they shall deceive the very elect"* (Matthew 24:24).

Preparatory to Tribulation signs and wonders, unholy miracle workers will prophesy and cast out demons while they offer but token resistance to sin. They have power, but theirs is concocted. They have tongues, but theirs are taught. They have dances, but theirs are choreographed. They sing and shout and praise the Lord, but, in their sin, they do so without the sanction and anointing of the Holy Ghost. With their deceptive mixture of sins and signs, they pave the way for the great deceiver, conditioning the world into accepting the New Age messiah (Antichrist) by proving that the unholy can call fire from Heaven the same as holy men of God.

Of course, such a fraudulent end-time mixture of power and impurity has been condemned by our Lord:

> "Many will say to me in that day, Lord, Lord, have we not prophesied in thy name? And in thy name have cast out devils? And in thy name done many wonderful works? And then will I profess unto them, I never knew you: depart from me, ye that work iniquity." (Matthew 7:22-23)

Clearly, power is not necessarily indicative of godliness, nor is power reserved for the godly. Particularly in these last days, sinners will perform miracles without the sanction of God Almighty and by that deceive many who, as babes in Christ, are swayed by every balmy breeze of false doctrine that drifts in from Hell. Is it any wonder that the great falling away occurs simultaneously with the latter rain outpouring of the Holy Ghost?

10
Apostate Leaders

"... this is a rebellious people, lying children, children that will not hear the law of the Lord: which say to the seers, See not; and to the prophets, Prophesy not unto us right things, speak unto us smooth things, prophesy deceits:" (Isaiah 30:9-10)

O ur generation wallows in the filth of its own sin, and then declares itself clean: *"There is a generation that are pure in their own eyes, and yet is not washed from their filthiness"* (Proverbs 30:12). Behind this declaration of self-proclaimed purity lurks a host of spiritual hirelings who fuel our lust and leave our sin untouched. Paul prophesied of our end-time love affair with ear-tickling teachers: *"For the time will come when they will not endure sound doctrine; but after their own lusts shall they heap to themselves teachers, having itching ears"* (2 Timothy 4:3). That is exactly what we have, and plenty of them!

Apostate Laodicea is laden with leaders who often appear outwardly clean but, without holiness, are ministers of darkness transformed by Satan into deceptive angels of light: *"… Satan himself is transformed into an angel of light. Therefore it is no great thing if his ministers also be transformed as the ministers of righteousness …"* (2 Corinthians 11:14-15). Laodicea is loaded with false prophets pouring out lies from their own hearts, every one a coward, afraid to sound a warning of coming judgments, afraid to lead the sinner from his judgment-bound way: *"… if they had stood in my counsel, and had caused my people to hear my words, then they should have turned them from their evil way ..."* (Jeremiah 23:22). Laodicea is burdened with mercenaries who care nothing for the flock—the sheep are theirs for the fleecing. Laodicea is bloated with priests whose high tolerance for sin forces them to *"... put no difference between the holy and profane, neither have they shewed difference between the unclean and the clean ..."* (Ezekiel 22:26).

[For the sake of simplicity and convenience, the term "false prophet" will, in this chapter, encompass all levels of leadership and instruction in the Laodicean church. It will include preachers, pastors, teachers, evangelists, writers, etc.]

False prophets, regardless of their positions in the church, lure the unsuspecting with their many winds of strange doctrine while avoiding the essential issue of holiness. This army of deceivers defiles the temple of God (His people) with their false teachings, leading organized religion into the throes of crippling apostasy.

False prophets play no small part in provoking God to cast a spirit of slumber over those who refuse the truth: *"... God hath given them the spirit of slumber, eyes that they should not see, and ears that they should not hear ..."* (Romans 11:8). As angels of light, they enslave souls to their sins, ensuring their blind allegiance to the rising world leader and their unquestioned acceptance of the Antichrist spirit that already hovers over the church.

To most people in our carefree, "feel good—do it" society, nothing is sin. Attribute this to humanism and to an army of soft-on-sin false prophets who dare not point the finger at any man's iniquity. To keep the numbers high, the dollars plenty, and the buildings big, false prophets preach a compromised gospel, offering only lip-service to holiness. They deny moral absolutes and scoff at moral accountability. They embrace and excuse sin; they console and appease sinners. They prophesy smooth things, deceitful things, and easy things.

False prophets twist the Scriptures to soften God's hatred of sin and His inevitable judgment of sinners. They offer no definition of sin, no call to repentance, no Holy Ghost conviction, no thunder, no fire and brimstone. Instead, they promise life to the sinner, binding him to his sin, forever damning his soul: *"... ye have ... strengthened the hands of the wicked, that he should not return from his wicked way, by promising him life"* (Ezekiel 13:22).

The bulk of our modern-day prophets have become highly respected, highly successful businessmen, converting their calling into a profession, used to their financial and social advantage. With a drive that would put many capitalists to shame, the new professionals push for the best ministerial positions, jockeying and politicking until they get their way. They fret over the best benefit packages, fighting for churches with the greatest potential for advancement. They busily protect their own interests as they strengthen the authority of their beloved denomination.

The new professionals are well trained, and their training along with their pleasing personalities usually lands them lush pastoral jobs, saved or not. Yet, with all their education and all their degrees, in the eyes of God, they are stupid: *"For the pastors are become brutish, and have not sought the LORD ..."* (Jeremiah 10:21).

Typifying their spiritual dullness, the new professionals minister by worldly methods, struggling for worldly recognition, respectability, and acceptance. They preach the headlines and the latest bestsellers. They counsel from Freud, Jung, and Rogers. They politick; they promote. They scheme; they dream. They spend; they steal the Lord's glory.

To conceal their spiritual denseness, the new professionals become intellectual, witty, and winsome. To hide their ignorance of God, they develop soothing personalities, synthetic smiles, and shrewd understandings of human nature. Full of phony sentiments and apparent love for all, they care no more for their neighbor than for the baby sparrow that has fallen from its nest. The prophet Micah said, *"The best of them is as a brier: the most upright is sharper than a thorn hedge ..."* (Micah 7:4).

With cartloads of charisma, the new professionals shine in the pulpit but not as students of the Holy Ghost. They preach without the anointing; they parade without the unction. They operate on their own, for they have not sought the Lord's counsel; they have heard no voice from above. They have no history, no depth with God. They have no revelation of His greatness, no awesomeness of His holy presence, no trembling at His Word.

Without that flesh-rending respect for God and His Word, the new professionals unashamedly misconstrue His holy oracles and minimize His divine intent for man. They undo our Lord's plain instructions for separation and sobriety by giving liberal interpretations and intricate explanations. They pass off as commandments of God a host of meaningless activities. They bury the saints in a mountain of chaff; they flood the saints with a torrent of trivialities. The new professionals deal with doctrine, not experience; with mental assent, not spiritual transformation; with the consequences, not the cause; with the symptoms, not the disease.

PROSPERITY PROPHETS

Spilling from the world of commerce into an increasingly business-minded church, the false notion of God as a divine Santa Claus praises the believer for his selfishness and his total disdain for the ways of our Heavenly Father. No other lie from Hell so debases the cross of Christ. No other lie so desecrates His precious atonement. No other lie so defiles His holy command to *"... seek ye first the kingdom of God, and His righteousness ..."* (Matthew 6:33).

Yet, this lie is propagated by a virtual army of prosperity prophets who scoff at poverty and sneer at those who take joyfully the spoiling of their goods. Sedated by the good life, they press relentlessly for their own materialistic gain: *"... they are greedy dogs which can never have enough ... they all look to their own way, every one for his gain, from his quarter"* (Isaiah 56:11). Accordingly, they prophesy for money: *"... the priests thereof teach for hire, and the prophets thereof divine for money"* (Micah 3:11). To line their own wallets, they merchandise saints of God by selling guaranteed formulas for success and wealth.

To seduce their faceless sponsors, prosperity prophets devise a convenient gospel compatible with the lifestyles of those who can contribute the most money. They sanctify covetousness by offering blessings in exchange for financial support. For the sinner, they extend the prospect of material gain as a viable motive for accepting Christ. For the saint, they interpret God's promises in a materialistic way, with faith and prayer as tools to make life easier, healthier and richer. For all, they belie the austere pattern set by the gospel's lowly author.

The church that has for hundreds of years only smiled upon prosperity as a sign of God's approval upon the believer's life is now openly encouraging the aggressive pursuit of wealth and fame among the children of God. No other lie hatched in the basement of Hell so praises the Christian for his selfishness, while it locks him in the clutches of capitalism. Spilling from the world of commerce into an increasingly business-minded church, the prosperity gospel is the Harlot's chief means of Christian entrapment.

She works especially through false prophets by first seducing them into following after gain:

> "His watchmen are blind: they are all ignorant, they are all dumb dogs, they cannot bark; sleeping, lying down, loving to slumber. Yea, they are greedy dogs which can never have enough, and they are shepherds that cannot understand: they all look to their own way, every one for his gain, from his quarter." (Isaiah 56:10-11)

Then, with little more than 3 John 1:2, *"Beloved, I wish above all things that thou mayest prosper and be in health ..."* (which, incidentally, is nothing more than a wish that all is well) and a handful of Old Testament verses, these greedy shepherds pull millions of Christians into the Harlot's lap with them. They easily convince their covetous flocks that gain is proof of their godliness, that God, in fact, wants all His kids to be rich. They applaud blind ambition, self-indulgence, and personal fulfillment. They promise life more abundantly while they sow seeds of eternal damnation. They sanctify covetousness by offering blessings in exchange for financial support. They prophesy for "filthy lucre" and merchandise saints of God by selling guaranteed formulas for getting rich and living forever—*"... through covetousness shall they with feigned words make merchandise of you ..."* (2 Peter 2:3).

Since health and wealth must rightfully belong to the child of God, prosperity prophets encourage saints to demand their rights from God. Nothing new; stubborn Jews did the same thing in the wilderness. God gave them their heart's desire, and then slew them:

> "And they tempted God in their heart by asking meat for their lust ... So they did eat, and were well filled: for he gave them their own desire; They were not estranged from their lust. But while their meat was yet in their mouths, The wrath of God came upon them, and slew the fattest of them, and smote down the chosen men of Israel." (Psalms 78:18, 29-31)

Like rebellious Israel, any people who claim all their rights have no time to lean on Jehovah. The strong have no need of the great I AM. On the other hand, the weak could not survive without God and His Son. They look to Christ and the cross, not to self and the world. They say with Paul, *"But God forbid that I should glory, save in the cross of our Lord Jesus Christ, by whom the world is crucified unto me, and I unto the world"* (Galatians 6:14). They delight in their infirmities, for they know that in their weakness, Christ's power manifests itself—*"... Most gladly therefore will I rather glory in my infirmities, that the power of Christ may rest upon me ... for when*

I am weak, then am I strong" (2 Corinthians 12:9-10).

Old Testament saints thought little of their rights, but they knew a great deal about suffering and deprivation. How unlike today's effeminate confessors of health and wealth were those old saints, tried and tested but forever true:

> "They were stoned, they were sawn asunder, were tempted, were slain with the sword: they wandered about in sheepskins and goatskins; being destitute, afflicted, tormented; (Of whom the world was not worthy:) they wandered in deserts, and in mountains, and in dens and caves of the earth." (Hebrews 11:37-38)

Strewn behind their tortured and slain bodies is a trail of tears and blood and a testimony that screams in holy anger against this blasphemous filth from Hell of asserting oneself in the sight of God.

Assertiveness and the active pursuit of riches and recognition have never been God's way, not even under the Law. The prophets could not have been clearer in their declarations of God's love for the poor and His hatred of a proud, independent spirit. Likewise, the overriding tone of the New Testament is one of submission and sacrifice. Because Christ made the ultimate sacrifice of Himself for our sins, God, in return, requires that we lovingly offer ourselves back to Him as a *"living sacrifice"* (Romans 12:1-3). He expects us to say with Paul, *"... what things were gain to me, those I counted loss for Christ"* (Philippians 3:7).

Hardly anyone today is much interested in crosses and losses, pain and perplexity, suffering and shame. Of more importance is prosperity and worldly position, building monuments of self-achievement. Hardly any live such self-denial that they cry out in agony, *"If in this life only we have hope in Christ, we are of all men most miserable"* (1 Corinthians 15:19). Yet, the soul that is determined to break out of Babylon at any cost will gladly give up all if necessary.

PEACE PROPHETS

Prosperity prophets are usually advocates of peace as well. Like the humanists, they seek *"a world in which peace, prosperity, freedom, and happiness are widely shared."*[34] Through their positive confessions, they allege that peace will prevail in our nation and eventually envelop the world. All is well, they say. You are prosperous. You are full. You are at peace.

With their empty promises, peace prophets soothe the frayed edges while they seduce the body of Christ: *"The prophets prophesy falsely ... They have healed also the hurt of the daughter of my people slightly, saying, Peace, peace; when there is no peace"* (Jeremiah 5:31; 6:14). They console with positive statements of continued peace and prosperity. They preach a smooth gospel in the face of impending doom.

As long as Lucifer rules this world and sin reigns in the heart of man, there can be no peace: *"There is no peace, saith the Lord, unto the wicked"* (Isaiah 48:22). Because Satan came to steal, kill, and destroy, his servants will forever lift their weapons in battle against one another. This is particularly true in the last days as our Lord forewarned: *"And ye shall hear of wars and rumors of wars ... For nation shall rise against nation, and kingdom against kingdom ..."* (Matthew 24:6-7). Promises of peace may sedate the host of lost and deceived humanity, but the actual evidence of violence and war but alert the children of light that their redemption draweth nigh. Jesus is soon coming back, but until He does, there will be no true peace.

Yet, peace prophets persist, and, by their ploy, many will be taken unaware when the Prince of Peace breaks forth as a thief, having already been deceived into accepting the man of sin as earth's long-awaited savior. By rocking their sin-prone followers to sleep, peace prophets pave the way for the son of perdition, himself an advocate of apparent peace. Daniel said of Antichrist, " *... he shall magnify himself in his heart, and by peace shall destroy many ...*" (Daniel 8:25).

UNITY PROPHETS

Prophets of peace and prosperity have become so earthbound, so in love with this life, that they have invented doctrines designed to give them the world. They refuse to make Christ Lord over their lives, yet they push for dominion over the earth. They reject biblical standards of holiness, yet they politick for morality. They loathe the unifying message of sanctification, yet they press for the integration of all religious doctrines and disciplines. They would consolidate the entire religious world, reconciling all its differences by compromise, conformity, and confusion of the truth.

Despite its pleasant sound, the unity movement, as well as all of dominion theology, is fraudulent and should be shunned. Christ needs no help from man to establish His earthly kingdom. He will, Himself, subdue the mighty world system and take dominion over it during the Millennium when *"... he shall have put down all rule and all authority and power. For He must reign, till He hath put all enemies under His feet"* (1 Corinthians 15:24-25). This occurs after Armageddon, at which time He will *"... smite the nations: and He shall rule them with a rod of iron ..."* (Revelation 19:15). Then, after Antichrist and his armies are defeated, the saints possess the kingdom with Christ: *"I beheld, and the same horn [Antichrist] made war with the saints, and prevailed against them; Until the Ancient of days came, and judgment was given to the saints of the most High; and the time came that the saints possessed the kingdom"* (Daniel 7:21-22 brackets added). Then, and only then, do holy ones take dominion over the earth.

Christ, Himself, wanted nothing to do with establishing a physical kingdom by natural means: *"... if my kingdom were of this world, then would my servants fight ..."* (John 18:36). Like Christ, Paul insisted that Christians not fight the world system: *"... we do not war after the flesh: (For the weapons of our warfare are not carnal) ..."* (2 Corinthians 10:3-4). *"For we wrestle not against flesh and blood, but against ... spiritual wickedness in high places"* (Ephesians 6:12).

Christians do not wrestle with the world system; they reprove it of sin. So, as long as iniquity abounds, there will be discord between the righteous and the unrighteous. Darkness hates light. The world of sinners hates reproof and will always resist those who testify against their sin. Therefore, it is impossible for sin-hating saints to establish a physical Christian kingdom without lowering their standards and taking on the ways of the world. And when they do, they become a band of religious activists waving a sin-stained banner at a world they would only convert to their own brand of mediocrity.

Furthermore, the idea that self can prematurely usher in the Kingdom Age hails from a humanist handbook. It implies that God is unable to establish the kingdom Himself, and man must take matters into his own hands. This heresy, cleverly disguised in soothing theological terms, discredits the omnipotence of God, discounts the coming Tribulation, and disavows all knowledge of the great apostasy that is even now gutting the visible church.

11
WORSHIP IN THE FLESH

*S*adly, most Christians in this Laodicean Age know nothing of personal communion with God. Wed to the world in a defiling mixture of sacred and secular, they keep up the routines of worship but know nothing of the spontaneity and intimacy of spiritual worship. Lacking a burning desire to know Christ, their church-going is ritualistic and dead; their service, mechanical and meaningless. So driven are they with activity that Christ is left out; so in love with precedent and process that spirituality is squeezed out.

In Christendom, much of what is called worship is really activity-oriented routines of the flesh, much of it designed to comfort those enveloped in their own spiritual shallowness. These shallow ones simply feel emotionally relieved by going to church. They assemble in their "synagogues" at the appointed time, sing a few songs, pay their tithes (sometimes), nod through another sermon, then go their way—business (or pleasure) as usual. Having made the Sunday show, their conscience is cleared for another week. Having followed the ritual, they are happy. They have offered God a little time and a little money, but commune with Him, they haven't. Yet, they are comfortable with their Sunday brush with God, convinced that, under the New Covenant, God only requires the visible expression of holiness, that somehow the Son's sacrifice sanctified the superficial and sold it to the world as grace.

And, if a little sacred effort is pleasing to the beleaguered soul, then much eager-beaver religious work satisfies even more. So, more and more lukewarm Christians are becoming extremely busy "for God." Through much noise and bluster, they would please and endear themselves to Him. Even sincere saints are caught up in the hustle and bustle of meaningless movement, misinterpreted as Christian service, all to their soul's dismay.

The gospel of works may well ease the conscience, but it does precious little to appease a jealous God. He is not nearly as interested in our external observance of rites and customs as He is in what we are. Religious activity can have spiritual relevance but only after a genuine transformation of the inner man and only as a harmonious complement to our secret history with God.

ENLIGHTENMENT

In this information age, we all seem to be driven by a mad quest for knowledge, a craving for details, facts, and figures. Christians are caught up in the whirlwind, too. These information-crazed believers devour books and tapes, lectures and lessons, yet never really learn God. They don't get to know Him for, from their form of worship, He is gone.

God is gone because He has been educated out of His own temple, chased away by man's endless quest for natural knowledge, irrelevant historical data and tantalizing current events. Daniel accurately prophesied that in the last days *"knowledge shall be increased"* (Daniel 12:4). Then Paul concluded that this knowledge, if of a religious nature, would be wasted; apostate Christendom would be intellectually wise but void of sanctifying truth: *"Ever learning, and never able to come to the knowledge of the truth"* (2 Timothy 3:7). Without God's presence and without His truth, the intellectual saint may delight to worship at the shrine of scholastic achievement, but his soul lays parched within him, his hungry heart famished from lack of *"the wisdom that is from above"* (James 3:17).

EXCITEMENT

In certain circles, some Christians go to church for excitement. To them, commotion replaces communion, parade overshadows performance, hype outsells holiness, and action passes for unction. Even in God's sacred temple, excitement-prone professors clap irreverently when the entertainer pleases them. They trample on the hallowed with their lightness and frivolity. They carelessly and flippantly approach God's holy throne, claiming as King's kids their covetous hearts' desires. Is it any wonder that church attendance in pleasure-mad America has little impact on a person's ethical views and behavior?

Stemming from worship services that are filled with excitement and in keeping with a humanist objective that "religion must work increasingly for joy in living,"[35] churches have become entertainment centers with built-in bowling alleys, massive sports programs, convenience-packed fellowship halls, etc.

But where is Christ in all the festivities? Where is the exhortation to righteous living, the encouragement in trials, the comfort in distress? Where is the gathering of "family," the binding together of "kin" against a common enemy? Where is the sound doctrine and godly examples so needed to instruct and inspire a malnourished body onward to maturity? Indeed, where are the "patriarchs" of the latter-day church? Look around—they are playing games like the rest of Laodicea, sleeping while Antichrist slips a net of empty promises over a pleasure-riddled, peace-seeking world.

WORSHIP IN THE FLESH
(Law vs. Grace)

Those whose encounter with God has degenerated into worthless acts of appeasement, enlightenment, or excitement are, in effect, back under the mechanical rites of Old Testament Law. Their failure to yield directly to God causes them to turn, as did the Jew, to rituals of the flesh for their worship. Devoid of a real heart for God, they erect idols of religiosity to satisfy their *"... zeal of God, but not according to knowledge ... going about to establish their own righteousness, have not submitted themselves unto the righteousness of God"* (Romans 10:2-3). Quite often fashioned after authentic works of godliness—e.g., soul winning, eschatological studies, church attendance, praise and worship—even these divine duties quickly deteriorate into formality because they are not accompanied by the full expression of God's reaction to a sin-cursed world.

When that happens, worshipers in the flesh *"fall from grace"* (Galatians 5:4) back into the sin-prone *"ordinances of divine service"* (Hebrews 9:1). This they do even though Christ abolished *"the law of commandments contained in ordinances"* (Ephesians 2:15) and condemned the Jewish establishment for heaping tradition and man-made rules onto the holy Law of God:

> "... Thus have ye made the commandment of God of none effect by your tradition. ... This people draweth nigh unto me with their mouth, and honoureth me with their lips; but their heart is far from me. But in vain they do worship me, teaching for doctrines the commandments of men." (Matthew 15:6, 8-9)

God had given the system of sacrifices and ordinances to the Jews as a means to approach and appease Him; they were not an end within themselves. So, when His chosen people continued their divine services, even after mixing with the world, they did so without life, vision, and purity. Their worship became mechanical and formal with no real purpose.

The same is true today, not just in Judaism, but in much of what is called Christianity. Because it is, and in spite of their Sunday-morning ceremony, Christians who worship in the flesh remain detached from God and attached to self, handcuffed by the weakness of their own flesh to achieve that which their spirit often aspires to do. The spirit longs to live righteously, but the flesh, unmoved by Old Testament-like rituals and ordinances, dominates the life, and sin remains.

This ageless conflict within the heart of man is vividly portrayed in Romans 7 where Paul outlined his Old Covenant struggles with sin and flesh. Looking back to his Pharisaic past, he said of himself: *"... for what I would, that do I not; but what I hate, that do I ... For the good that I would I do not: but the evil which I would not, that I do"* (Romans 7:15, 19). Trying to live above sin by the Law was, and still is, impossible because, as Paul said, *"we were in the flesh"* (Romans 7:5), i.e., the flesh was not crucified. Although he knew the right way and offered sacrifices to atone for the wrong (which he hated), his heart remained uncircumcised and unaltered by the physical acts of appeasement: *"... by the deeds of the law there shall no flesh be justified"* (Romans 3:20). The will to live above sin was there, but was negated by "the sinful impulses" of the flesh *"which were by the law"* (Romans 7:5). As Paul confessed, and as all who worship in the flesh can attest, the will to do better *"is present with me, but how to perform that which is good I find not"* (Romans 7:18).

They may hate the evil in their hearts, but with no godly remorse or resolve to turn from it, worshipers in the flesh turn instead to works and rituals. They turn to the Law (in its ceremonial form) as their mediator because they are afraid to go directly to God; they fear His holiness and His intolerance of sin. Since they have no control over sin, they choose to plead for leniency according to dutiful principles established under the Law, then conveniently and carelessly call it grace.

Ironically, grace no longer accepts offerings of the flesh as atonement for sin. God has made one final offering for sin, thereby relieving the Law of its authority to redeem. As a result, the law is no longer a mediator between man and God; Christ is! And all who mechanically worship God with deeds of the flesh, while chained to their sins, are just as far from Him as the unbelieving Jew.

Like the Jew, Christians who submit to routine, fleshly worship for absolution of their sins are bound by Old Covenant-style legalism. As then, legalism is still outward expressions of righteousness through works, which have no tangible effect on the soul. The performance of these deeds register no merit in the eyes of God, but tend, rather, toward His disfavor, as they are commandments and doctrines of men. And those who worship God in the flesh are just as works-oriented, just as legalistic as the ritual-prone Jew.

Old Testament legalism failed, climaxing in the Pharisee fiasco. They were the strictest Jewish sect, yet Christ condemned their sin-blackened hearts: *"Woe unto you, scribes and Pharisees, hypocrites! for ye are like unto whited sepulchres, which indeed appear beautiful outward, but are within full of dead men's bones, and of all uncleanness. Even so ye also outwardly appear righteous unto men, but within ye are full of hypocrisy and iniquity"* (Matthew 23:27-28). Fasting, praying, alms-giving, church-going—all these made the Pharisees look good, but inwardly they were more corrupt and contemptible than the vilest sinner. They maintained a high level of external morality, but Christ, in no uncertain terms, demanded more righteousness of those who would follow Him (Matthew 5:20).

Like the Pharisee, New Covenant legalists often observe the visible and obvious commandments of God, yet their motives clash violently with the spirit of the Law. For their fleshly worship, the world often considers them holy, but with lust and pride burning out of control in their hearts, God does not. Nor does He condone the appearance of righteousness when jealousy and hatred ravage their unsanctified spirits. And hate they do.

They especially resent those who reject outward shows of piety for inner transformation into the glorious realm of light, apart from dead works.

As in Christ's day, Laodicean legalists are particularly antagonistic toward holiness. They scream foul when some hungry soul breaks out of the world's mold and then look feverishly for ways to condemn and crucify his Christ-centered life. As a smokescreen for their own divided hearts, the new breed of legalists ironically label as "legalism" all sacrifices of the one who rejects the lusts of this world, who casts off the entanglements of flesh, who gives himself wholly to the things of God, who wants holiness more than life itself. In this sense, legalism becomes a buzzword for the host of ritualistic worshipers who feel condemned by the separatist and who wish to discredit his sanctity and dispel his kind altogether from their company of conformists.

Lacking sound doctrinal footing, much of modern Christendom will fall away from God in the last days, victimized by the overwhelming spirit of this age—the seductive spirit of deception. This spirit is even now at work; the great apostasy is already upon us, pillaging the church, devouring all who refuse the walk of holiness, who refuse to separate from the darkness of this world. Having their understanding darkened (Ephesians 4:18), their lights grow dim and they limp through life as the blinded ones of which Isaiah spoke: *"… we wait for light, but behold obscurity; for brightness, but we walk in darkness. We grope for the wall like the blind, and we grope as if we had no eyes: we stumble at noonday as in the night …"* (Isaiah 59:9-10). As then, deluded believers still grope for a word from God, and there is no word. They wait for truth, then stumble over it at high noon. They look for brighter days, but glide callously into the darkest days of human history.

Section IV

The End of Time

12

THE COMING TRIBULATION

The darkest days of human history will come at the end of human history, at the end of time during the great Tribulation. Sprinkled throughout Scripture are references to matters of the end time: the Day of the Lord, the Day of God's Wrath (Psalm 98:9); the resurrection (Isaiah 26:19-20); the restoration of Israel, the fall of Lucifer from Heaven, the Last Trumpet (Isaiah 27:13).

It is Daniel who introduces and outlines the seventy weeks of years which are *"… to make an end of sins … and to bring in everlasting righteousness …"* (Daniel 9:24). It is his seventieth week, actually a period of seven years, that has come to be known as the Tribulation (see Christ's reference to the second half of the week as a period of "great tribulation," Matthew 24:21).

According to Daniel, the period begins when the Antichrist confirms the covenant with many [probably Jews]. It disintegrates in the middle when he causes the sacrifice and the oblation to cease [the abomination of desolation] (Daniel 9:27). It is marked by an increase in knowledge that had been shut up (Daniel 12:4). Many are tested and purified, while the wicked do wickedly (Daniel 12:10). It ends with the resurrection of the dead (Daniel 12:2) and the deliverance of Israel (Daniel 12:1).

Then in Matthew 24, Christ Himself adds more details about the seven year period. He tells us what to expect with the beginning of sorrows in the first half, confirms Daniel's mid-week abomination of desolation as the beginning of "great tribulation," and concludes the period with the promise of His return and the gathering together [Rapture] of His elect *"... from one end of Heaven to the other"* (Matthew 24:31).

Paul, too, has something to say about the Tribulation, but in response to concerns of the early church, his focus is on the Rapture of the saints. In 1 Thessalonians 4, Paul exposes the chronological order of the catching away, but in 2 Thessalonians 2, he addresses the preconditions to the final gathering—that the church must fall away first and the Hinderer (Holy Ghost) be removed from earth allowing the man of sin (Antichrist) to be revealed. At his revealing, he desecrates the temple of God *"... and exalteth himself above all that is called God, or that is worshipped; so that he as God sitteth in the temple of God, showing himself that he is God"* (2 Thessalonians 2:4).

The Apostle John brings it all together in the Book of Revelation. He describes the fate of Israel and Christians, the fall of Satan to earth, the rise of Antichrist, the return of Christ, the defeat of Antichrist at Armageddon. The Revelation not only reveals the Christ in His Second Coming with power but was given by God to Christ *"... to show unto his servants things which must shortly come to pass ..."* (Revelation 1:1). So, here, we have a clearer, more complete picture of the end of time and, most specifically, the Tribulation period, void of contradictions to prior references, yet full of complementary and cumulative information.

Throughout the Bible, there are references to all or portions of the Tribulation, especially the last day, which is the Day of the Lord, or the Day of God's Wrath. These references do not necessarily associate that day with a preceding period of great Tribulation. The Resurrection and Rapture likewise have references (Old and New Testaments) independent of their connection to the Tribulation period. But, in context and with careful superimposition, the sometimes random references to the Rapture, God's wrath, and the worldwide dominion of the Antichrist do make sense and do give us plenty of insight as to what the last generation can expect and when they might expect it.

We summarize our cursory look at the Tribulation like this. It is a seven-year period at the end of time. It begins with the confirmation by Antichrist of the covenant with many people (probably the Jews). This writer believes the covenant is not a peace treaty, as many suppose, but a reference to God's covenant with Israel to *"... make of thee a great nation ..."* and *"... bless them that bless thee, and curse him that curseth thee ..."* (Genesis 12:2-3). I also believe it is Antichrist's affirmation of Israel's right to exist—a deceptive ploy to take advantage of Israel's desperate situation on the world stage. The confirmation breaks down mid-Tribulation when the Antichrist exalts himself as God and commits the abomination of desolation. He turns on Israel, makes war with Christians, destroys Babylon, and rules the entire world. His end, and that of the Tribulation, come at Armageddon when Christ returns in power with His then-raptured saints [see Appendix A] and destroys the Antichrist and his armies that have gathered against Israel from every nation, including America.

So controversial, so mysterious and misunderstood, yet so infinitely significant in the lives of Christians, the Tribulation warrants a close look, not only for the curious, but especially for those of us who are troubled by our perilous times and feel, but aren't sure, that we are headed for even worse times as the end of this age approaches.

For our closer look at these worst of times, we will break the discussion into four parts: the two halves of Tribulation, the events that mark the sudden shift to Satan's on-site influences in mid-Tribulation, and the end of it all on the Day of God's Wrath. First, we will present an outline of the four parts followed by some questions that have challenged us through the years. Then we will dig deeper into significant events of each part and attempt to answer some of these questions and, hopefully, shed some light on the whole end-time subject as we address the perplexities of this mysterious period.

First Half

- Antichrist alive but, as yet, not revealed
- Antichrist confirms the covenant with Israel
- Steady worsening of conditions
- The beginning of sorrows
- Christians refined
- Christians hated by all nations → some probably killed
- Compared to second three and one-half years, relatively uneventful
- Love grows colder as man becomes more sinful
- Capitalism continues to bow to liberal socialists' demands

Mid-Tribulation

- The Holy Ghost removed from Earth

- The Antichrist is revealed
- Satan and his angels are cast to earth
- Satan empowers the Antichrist; he rules for three and a half years
- The Antichrist commits the Abomination of Desolation
- The Mark of the Beast becomes mandatory universally
- The two witnesses begin to preach
- Satan makes war on Israel
- Satan singles out Christians and the mass killing begins
- Beginning of the Great Tribulation

Last Half – Satan's Wrath

- Antichrist reigns with totalitarian control for three and a half years
- With the mark, he isolates and exterminates all opposition
- He kills most of Israel and chases a remnant into hiding
- Christians deprived but refined, then most, if not all, are killed
- The False Prophet deceives by miracles—gives life to the image of the Beast—kills those who do not worship the image
- The ten kings are given power for "one hour"; they destroy Babylon in that "one hour" and then give their power to the Antichrist
- There is peace by default, for none can resist the Antichrist
- Freedom, private property, free market, true Christians: all gone

Last Half – God's Wrath

- The seven seals are opened by Christ
- The trumpets, woes, etc., are expressions of God's wrath
- God's punishment of the wicked occurs → most are killed
- God makes a full end of sin and brings in everlasting righteousness (Daniel 9:24)

Last Half – God's Promise

- Elijah is promised
- 144,000 Jews sealed and protected
- Two witnesses (of God) preach for three and one-half years and are killed
- The gospel preached to the whole world by an angel (Revelation 14:6, Matthew 24:14)

The End – The Day of God's Wrath

- Sun darkened; Moon sheds no light; Stars fall (Matthew 24:29; Isaiah 13:10); Moon like blood (Revelation 6:12); Heaven departed as a scroll
- The last trumpet sounds (Isaiah 27:13)
- Christ comes in power
- Angels gather the elect from the four winds (Rapture)
- All nations (including America) gather in Israel (Zephaniah 3:8, Zechariah 14:2, 4-5)
- Armageddon is fought—We win! Antichrist and his armies defeated
- Destruction of man and few men left (Isaiah 28:22, 26:21, 24:6,19, 13:9-13). They hide in caves (Isaiah 2:19, 21; 42:13, 14)
- When they say peace and safety, sudden destruction comes
- Antichrist and False Prophet cast into Lake of Fire
- Satan cast into bottomless pit for a thousand years
- All Israel saved when they look upon Him whom they pierced
- Thousand Year Millennium begins (Zechariah 14:16-21)

Note: At the end of the Millennium, Satan is released from the bottomless pit, organizes a final rebellion against God, is defeated, and this time is thrown into the Lake of Fire where he joins his old buddies—Antichrist and False Prophet.

So, what of this Tribulation? What do apostate, deluded Christians have to look forward to during the Tribulation? To the broader point, what can we all expect as we, saint and sinner, slide into the darkest period in human history? How will we know when we have slid in? Once in, what do we do, and is there a way out? Will it end? How?

As we attempt to answer these questions, we would first like to pose other questions that have challenged us through the years. As we broaden our knowledge of the Tribulation, perhaps others, too, will be motivated to seek and receive an even better understanding of what is to be.

Questions that have troubled us include:

- Why is there a Tribulation in God's plan for man?
- Why is there an Antichrist? Is there a reason to bring in a man more wicked than any before him?
- Why is there a Mark of the Beast?

- Is it possible that Christians would even welcome the Tribulation in spite of the inevitable consequences for the elect? If so, why?
- Why is there a Millennium?
- What happens to Israel?
- What happens to Christians, and where are they during the Tribulation?
- Is all mankind either raptured or killed?
- Does God allow or even initiate the horrendous events upon His own creation? If so, why?
- What is Satan's role and purpose in this calamitous culmination of time as we know it?
- What is the difference between God's wrath and Satan's wrath?
- Is the Day of the Lord the same as the Day of God's Wrath? Is it just one day?
- Which seals, bowls, trumpets, etc., in Revelation describe the Day of God's Wrath, and which describe pre-wrath but God-allowed perils?
- Is there a chronological order to the seals, bowls, trumpets, etc., in Revelation? When is the first seal opened? Who is impacted—saint, sinner, or both?
- Which events actually announce the return of Christ? Which trumpets?

FIRST HALF OF TRIBULATION

As Christ pointed out (Matthew 24:15, 21), the great Tribulation occurs in the last half of the seven years. This is after the Hinderer is removed and Antichrist is revealed. So it is likely that the first half of the Tribulation is relatively uneventful as compared to the second half.

Still, it will see *"the beginning of sorrows"* (Matthew 24:8), which include: wars and rumors of wars, false Christs, nation against nation, famines, pestilence, earthquakes—many of the same things our generation already experiences. The beginning of the beginning is probably not very far off as Tribulation-like events unfold and intensify and the condition of man worsens.

Unrestrained and unfearful sinners pollute the earth with their meanness and hatred and total disregard of and disrespect for the God of this universe. They fear Him not, for, to them, He does not exist, or He is just a forgiving old "Daddy" who overlooks all their sinful ways.

The wise will see this dramatic turn toward evil and the paving of the way for, even the necessity of, a world leader. He apparently will come in as leaders do, with hope and promise. He even takes the unimaginable step (which inaugurates the Tribulation) of confirming the covenant with Israel, thereby decreeing her right to exist. The Antichrist world leader is obviously alive in the first half, but he is not yet revealed as the wicked one. He likely will perpetuate the already stylish hatred for Christians, even promoting more widespread killing of true believers.

Between the confirmation of the covenant and the abomination of desolation, the elect of God will be persecuted increasingly. By design, this testing of their faith and their resolve to please God is for their purification. The pure will then lead many others to righteousness and, as Daniel explained, perform exploits which we might surmise would include miracles of a divine nature.

Their lives will stand in stark contrast to the unrepentant wicked who will continue to do wickedly and will not understand the nature of the times, where it is all heading, and who they are worshiping.

Because the wicked have pleasure in their sins and refuse the truth of God in His Word, God will send them strong delusions so that they will fall for the Antichrist, the world's secular savior. So deluded are they that in the second half of Tribulation, they will fight and die for the losing team none the wiser, go to Hell, and remain throughout eternity with the ones to whom they cast their lot. Then they will know they were wrong—too late.

Contrast that with the elect who know right from wrong, who love not their lives, and who will yield their heads to the executioner as their way of overcoming the Beast and entering their Heavenly refuge while the world of sinners is punished. Those who might miraculously escape being killed will suffer from deprivation and starvation, but they will certainly be refined and shine as the light of sun in a sin-darkened world. See Daniel 11:35 and 12:10.

Man is a spiritual being, so he will always allow his spirit to worship someone or something—the state, the emperor, the king, a god, Jehovah God, the self, the earth, a cow. Those who now refuse to worship anything but self will worship the image of the Beast then. The one to whom they have paid silent homage (via humanism) they will overtly worship then. The author of their "non-religious" religion will emerge as the idol they must worship then.

MID-TRIBULATION

Here is where everything comes apart. In short order, God reverses the supernatural power structure here on earth. He kicks Satan out of the Heavens down to earth, and, we believe, lifts His Holy Spirit out of the way as what has been a force holding Satan in check. When this God-authored twist is made midway through the Tribulation, the beginning of sorrows abruptly becomes exceedingly sorrowful—dreadful times *"such as was not since the beginning of the world"* (Matthew 24:21).

The history of Satan has been a sordid one from the time pride was found in him and he was ejected from Heaven to become "prince and power of the air." Full of hatred and wrath and forever deceitful, he has done a good job of leading man astray, tempting him to sin, and sending millions to Hell. In the Garden of Eden and ever since, he has lured mankind to sin against his Creator, even so bold as to stand before God accusing His own people.

But there were limits to his power and influence—the Spirit of God working through His people always stood in the way. The dawning of the end of time is about to change all this as Satan's literal presence on earth fully unleashes and increases dramatically his damnable influence over man. With the Holy Spirit out of the way and knowing his time is short, Satan races to set up an unchallenged kingdom here on earth. Life to him holds no value as he runs roughshod over humanity. Man, after all, is God's creation and just an object in his quest to make subjects of them all—or kill them if they don't submit. And he does.

Satan has always met with opposition, but, to date, he has never been bound up, rendering him ineffectual to tempt man to sin. But the Holy Spirit has operated over the millennia to keep evil somewhat at bay by acting as a restraint to Satan's unquenchable desire to steal, kill, and destroy. The Holy Spirit has also placed a manageable restraint on the Devil's power to deceive us with his web of lies so cleverly disguised as to appear to be the truth. As the "Spirit of Truth," the Holy Spirit has held Satan's ability to deceive somewhat in check. Until mid-Tribulation.

Mid-Tribulation, we believe, God's Spirit is taken out of Satan's way (2 Thessalonians 2:7) giving him free reign to deceive and otherwise do with man as he pleases. To make matters worse, his powers over man are heightened exponentially when, in mid-Tribulation, he and all his angels are *"cast out into the earth"* (Revelation 12:9) by Michael the archangel. With the Holy Spirit set aside and Satan and his demons literally here on earth with no restraints placed on their power to kill and deceive, they take full control, and unimaginable sorrows set in—for their opposition.

Working with Satan to wipe out all opposition is the very antithesis to Christ, the Antichrist. Empowered by Satan, he becomes the first world leader, albeit the worst leader the planet has ever had. Apparent friend to Israel in the beginning, after three and one-half years, the Antichrist Beast is revealed for his true self, what he really is, when the Holy Spirit no longer stands in the way of his full exposure. The veneer that glossed over his true intentions disappears as Satan empowers him, and he commits the abomination of desolation.

Another indicator that the Great Tribulation has begun, this act of defiance as predicted by Daniel (Daniel 9:27) and confirmed by Christ (Matthew 24) witnesses the Antichrist in full self-loving fashion. Inspired by his leader, he turns on Israel after his "revelation" and desecrates the temple of God, exalts himself *"... above all that is called God, or that is worshipped; so that he as God sitteth in the temple of God, showing himself that he is God"* (2 Thessalonians 2:4). With this declaration, Satan, acting vicariously through the Antichrist, officially and boldly proclaims his true intentions—universal worship.

Universal worship, Satan's goal from the beginning, now rises as an attainable obsession. Heretofore, he pursed his dream through the likes of Hitler and Stalin, but it was not to be, not just yet. Until now, Satan has no worldwide kingdom with subjects from every nation to adore and worship him. In the second half of the Tribulation, everything changes.

With our second half discussion, we will look further into Satan's methods for attaining his goal. Suffice it to say here that he is not responsible for all the troubles then, but as it relates to killing those who oppose him, he is. There can be no opposition to his plans now that he is god—or so he thinks. Secular man feels the Devil's wrath, but it is the Christian and the Jew who are specifically marked for extinction.

Ironically, Satan marks his foes by their refusal to be marked. Coincident with his fall to earth and Antichrist's rise to power, the second beast (the False Prophet) appears, performs miracles that deceive man into making an image to the first beast (Antichrist), gives life to the image, then mandates that every human being worship that image or receive his mark of ownership (commonly called "the mark of the Beast") in the right hand or forehead in order to buy and sell any product.

It is quite a sure way to quickly and unmistakably identify supporters and, more importantly, dissenters. Once identified, dissenters are doomed. Refusal to worship the Beast's image results in death. Refusal to take the mark eventually results in starvation. Again, it is Satan's way of ridding the earth of all who would oppose him, of singling them out for slaughter or for starvation. After all, that is his moniker—kill, steal, and destroy—and the nature of his wrath as he seeks worldwide dominion. Killing is a tactic he has employed throughout history and which his disciples (liberals and the like) now wish they could do. Yet a little while and they, too, will get their wish. In short, Satan devises a marking mechanism whereby all commerce and consumer activity is strictly regulated, with rules enforced and violators removed from the process by death.

All men are specifically forbidden by God to receive Satan's mark of ownership under penalty of being *"… tormented with fire and brimstone … forever and ever"* (Revelation 14:10-11). Once taken, they are forever doomed to the Lake of Fire, not a matter to be taken lightly or frivolously dismissed as just another modern method of avoiding ID theft, credit card fraud, or to speed up all money-related processes. Christians, and any biblically-informed person for that matter, know they must say no and suffer the consequences, whether it be the firing squad or sure starvation. Either is infinitely better than the Lake of Fire, forever and forever.

It is, therefore, mid-Tribulation when Satan drops in and takes over. After mocking their God and their worship, he breaks his promise with Israel, kills two-thirds of them, chases the rest into their wilderness place of refuge, fails to make a complete extermination, and then in anger makes war with the *"… remnant of her seed, which keep the commandments of God, and have the testimony of Jesus Christ"* (Revelation 12:17). In other words, Christians. Through the mark, he singles them out, and the second half, mass killing begins.

SECOND HALF – SATAN'S WRATH

Christ, when referring to the second half of the Tribulation, said that after the abomination of desolation (mid-Tribulation) *"… then shall be great tribulation ... "* (Matthew 24:21). He foresaw the wrath that Satan would pour out on His people (Jew and Christian). He knew it would be a time of refinement, then slaying of His elect. He knew, too, that it would be a time for choosing whom we would serve, of separating from the Satan-led world system, of being different from the world, of making life and death choices for our Lord, of choosing to be overcome in death so that we might overcome the one who killed us (Revelation 12:11), of looking up for our redemption would finally be here.

Never forget this: the second half of Tribulation appears to be Satan's time and Antichrist's time. Together, through war and peace, deception and delusion, marks and images, they subdue all foes, saint and sinner alike. Through Satan, Antichrist has power *"... over all kindreds, and tongues, and nations. And all that dwell upon the earth shall worship him, whose names are not written in the book of life ... "* (Revelation 13:7-8). And they worship Satan, too, for giving his power to the Antichrist (Revelation 13:4). Power likewise comes to him from the ten kings (the ten horns of the Beast) who themselves receive power for "one hour," then yield that power to the Antichrist. (During their time of empowerment, the ten kings destroy the Babylon whore, another move to secure all power for the Antichrist).

Two and one-half chapters in Revelation are dedicated to the great Harlot, so we have devoted one chapter ourselves to her identity—Chapter Six, especially since Christians are commanded to come out of her. Because God put it in their hearts to do so, Babylon is destroyed by the ten kings who are given power one hour with the Antichrist. Isn't it strange, though, that such an evil as Babylon would in the end be destroyed by evil entities, the ten kings who are partnered with the Beast? Why doesn't God Himself destroy Babylon? Could it be because it is an institution so woven into the fabric of the economics of the world system that it would be best if those comprising the world system actually destroyed her from within?

Babylon and the Beast coexist, work hand-in-hand to corrupt mankind, so it is fitting that the Beast should end it all for the Harlot. If, as we suppose, they are cooperative antagonists, the time will have come when the cooperation is no longer needed, and the Beast chooses to tyrannically own and operate all means of productive distribution and selection of who partakes in the buying and selling of those goods. With full control of that power, he easily picks winners and losers in the games of life.

With Babylon out of the way, with the remnant of Israel in hiding, and with all other nations conquered, incredibly weakened, or voluntarily acquiesced to Antichrist, there will be peace toward the end of Tribulation. Granted, it is a peace by default, for none *"... is able to make war with him"* (Revelation 13:4), but it is peace nonetheless.

However, it is not a pleasant peace by any means, for the totalitarian reign of Antichrist will be characterized by the total absence of freedom, a free market, Biblical Christianity, and freedom of worship. It will be the culmination of political and economic forces already entrenched in the American process and poised for a complete takeover when conditions are right. It is more of the same, just a deluge of it, even a suffocating blanket of tyranny, deceit, and bondage smothering all evidences of freedom from our planet.

For those of us at ease in Zion, it is highly likely that we cannot even imagine how horrible life will become after mid-Tribulation. With the Spirit of Truth lifted, the spirit of lies and deception will rule. Deceit has always been Satan's skillful tactic used to win converts. He has to, for evil must be viewed as good for most men to accept it. In the Tribulation, he goes all out, *"... he shall cause craft [trickery, or deceit] to prosper ... "* (Daniel 8:25 *brackets added*). Given all the deception flooding us today (especially from our leaders) it is hard to imagine it could get worse, but it will, exponentially. Add to that, Satan's literal presence on earth casting his ominous cloud of oppression, darkness, and fear. No peace, no joy, no Spirit's drawing power for the unregenerate; for them, there is only despair, depression, and hopelessness.

Can they be saved post mid-Tribulation? Who knows? But to this writer, it does not look good, especially for willful procrastinators. From Satan's point of view, most of the second half is a great time. He savors his worldwide following and relishes the pure power he exercises over man and the absolute freedom with which he is able to kill Christians. His hand is loosed to completely remove any vestiges of Biblical Christianity. The mark is his ultimate and outward device for isolating God's people from his own flock. It is his cleverly designed segregating process that will assuredly single out Biblical Christians for death. Humanist liberals finally succeed in weeding out their opponents and killing them. Their apparent goal for many years is finally realized in the Tribulation.

Indications are that Satan does successfully make a full end of true Christians during the second half for *" ... it was given unto him [Antichrist] to make war with the saints, and to overcome them ... "* (Revelation 13:7 brackets added). "Overcome" is Revelation code for kill (Revelation 11:7). Daniel confirms the destiny of the righteous under Antichrist for he *" ... shall wear out the saints of the most High ... "* (Daniel 7:25) and *" ... shall destroy the mighty and the holy people"* (Daniel 8:24). See also Daniel 12:7.

Given that, how could the saint escape? Sure, we can store up supplies, lay up some gold, or purchase mountain hideaways, but supplies run out, and everyone, no matter where they live, has to worship the image of the Beast, or else. There is no getting around it, what with all the technology and GPS tracking systems available to modern man. It might take a short while, but Antichrist will eventually "wear out the saints."

The well informed notwithstanding, it is our opinion that only the holy will refuse to bow the knee to Satan's image or allow his soul-damning mark on their body, for they alone possess the indwelling Spirit (that role is not gone) and His power of discernment that keeps them from being taken in by the arch deceiver. Only they will have the resolve to obey their convictions, even though execution or starvation awaits. How do they do this? By means of a mindset most of us don't have today—*" ... they loved not their lives unto the death"* (Revelation 12:11). Even if it means death, they will not take his mark or worship his image.

What makes the change in believers from the lukewarm, feel good, Pharisees who name the name of Christ today? In a word—refinement. The fiery trials of hatred and demonization—even murder—directed at Christians leading up to and during the first half of Tribulation will have a purifying effect on those who will accept it. No doubt many will turn back to the world, but the elect will be *" ... purified, and made white, and tried ..."* (Daniel 12:10). The purifying process will intensify in the second half as saints lose all attachments to this life and can say with Paul, *"For to me to live is Christ, and to die is gain"* (Philippians 1:21).

After all, what do these few years have to compare with an eternity in Heaven? Especially when this life narrows down to little more than deceit, deprivation, starvation, and hatred? Loosened are the attachments to this world that once we held so dear. As Paul said again and we then will attest, trivialities down here become as refuse when we finally cast our sights on the supernal joys of the eternal. I believe that the release of Satan's fury on Christians will do much to flush the stains of this world's charms from our lives, and with the love and lusts of this world finally gone, we can focus our eyes on Jesus, and gladly so. Maybe then we can say (and finally mean it) with John the Revelator, *"... Even so, come, Lord Jesus"* (Revelation 22:20).

SECOND HALF – GOD'S WRATH

As devastating as Satan's wrath is during the second half of The Tribulation (especially for Jews and Christians), the unleashing of God's wrath (culminating in the Day of God's wrath) pales that of the wicked one. After all, it is the Revelation of Jesus Christ—Satan just happens to be one of the appointed players in the unfolding of events leading up to the return of Christ at the end of Tribulation. It would appear that Satan, who masquerades as God, has actually assumed god-like powers but, never forget, God is still God during the Tribulation. The powers permitted Satan are just that, permitted by God (Isaiah 45:7) as part of His overall divine plan for mankind. We hope to examine some of these paradoxical purposes later in Chapter Thirteen after a look at the cause, chronology, and climax of God's wrath.

Part of understanding Revelation is properly delineating between Satan's wrath and God's wrath, realizing that God, who is the only God, has initiated or allowed all that befalls man and earth in this time of great trouble. Revelation witnesses two supernatural titans, both in anger, acting simultaneously in time and space here on planet earth—same platform but opposite goals: one is to punish, the other is to prevail. They run on separate tracks for three and one-half years only to meet at the end in a colossal and conclusive clash called "Armageddon." Satan's wrath, as we have seen, is focused on killing all his opposition (especially Jews and Christians) en route to an unopposed worldwide kingdom. God's wrath comes as punishment of the wicked, as the eradication or subjugation of the impure, as preparation for His Millennial reign. While Satan and Antichrist wreak havoc on the way to a worldwide following, God punishes those deluded followers who, despite it all, remain obstinately unrepentant.

While Satan singles out and kills God's people, God is tormenting Satan's followers in an enhanced version of Old Testament style destruction.

It is a struggle of epic proportions, all with divine purposes.

- Saints suffer at Satan's hand, are refined, do exploits, and then willingly die for their Savior, missing the Day of His wrath while they wait in their chamber of refuge "until the indignation is past."
- Sinners, on the other hand, suffer at God's hand but remain unrepentant, die from the seventh seal plagues and pestilences, go to Hell where they await Judgment Day and their slot in the Lake of Fire with their masters—Satan and Antichrist.

Satan, here on earth. The Holy Spirit, set aside. Christ, yet to appear in power. For the saint, it might seem that all hope is gone. But remember, God in Heaven still rules the affairs of man, even in the Tribulation. He authors it all, directly or permissively indirectly, to accomplish His purposes. He evicts Satan from the Heavens and allows him to establish his temporary kingdom devoid of any participation from Jews or Christians (as if we would want to). His methods of identification for elimination are sure and swift but serve a definite purpose in God's plan, as we shall see later in Chapter Thirteen.

A synopsis of Satan's wrath and the full details of God's wrath are disclosed with the opening of the seven seals in the book of Revelation. Unless the seals were opened, we would not know what is soon to come upon those who deny our Lord and denigrate all the good that flows continuously from His throne. John even wept when he thought no one worthy to reveal the depths of Satan's depravity and to open the floodgates of God's wrath on the depraved. He, too, wanted to know and, perhaps, welcomed the fall of those who had killed all his disciple brethren and would continue to mercilessly kill God's people throughout the ages.

Weep no more, John, for Christ, the slain Lamb, opens the seals of God's wrath containing a series of real torture on the wicked, visions of the sainted dead and the end of sin and of Satan (for a time). The seven seals show in detail the progressive punishment and eventual destruction to come on sinful man, the certain death of the elect at the hands of Satan, and the wrathful return of Christ in power.

The first four seals offer us an overview of Satan's short but treacherous Tribulation tenure as depicted by the "four horsemen of the Apocalypse." As is Satan's way, the four horsemen, led by Antichrist, trample mankind, taking peace from the earth, making war, conquering and killing one fourth of the world's population, the results of which are shortages of precious produce resulting in worldwide famine. These are trademarks of the cunning and cavalier Satan—killing and destroying at will with no concern for the side effects on the living (sound familiar, abortionists?). After all, people are only a means to an end for the wicked one. If you contribute to his goals, you may live. If not, you will die.

The fifth seal looks under the altar in Heaven at the souls of them that "just said no" to Satan and were summarily slain. Some have suggested that the fifth seal souls represent the one fourth of mankind killed by the pale horse rider in seal four. It is possible, but to this writer the number seems too high unless there is a good bit of refinement going on between now and the early part of the second half of Tribulation. Hopefully there will be a widescale reformation real soon.

At any rate, Revelation gives us several glimpses of martyred saints—their pleas for judgment, their great number, their means of overcoming Antichrist, and their ultimate reward for faithfulness to their Lord. The fifth seal martyrs pleaded with God saying *"... How long, O Lord, holy and true, dost thou not judge and avenge our blood on them that dwell on the earth?"* They were told to be patient *"... for a little season ... "* until others *"... that should be killed as they were, should be fulfilled"* (Revelation 6:10-11). Obviously, the "mark" would take "a little season" to fulfill its purpose, but it will, and when all those that "should be killed" were killed, then God would begin avenging their blood on the killers. That would be God's wrath, and it will not affect His people.

Our position is that most if not all saints will be killed by Antichrist after his mark is mandated. Their souls will await the resurrection and glorification of their bodies from their "chambers" in Heaven. They are not touched by God's wrath. When the seventh seal is opened, God's chosen ones are hidden away in the wilderness (Jews) or safe on the "sea of glass" (Revelation 15:2) in Heaven (Christians). Otherwise, they would be tormented by scorpions, intense heat, hailstones, and the like by God Himself. Not going to happen. The wrath of God is directed at heathens, not saints.

Those who disagree with our hypothesis generally subscribe to a pre-Tribulation theory (See our detailed response to this in Appendix A) as a means of removing saints from the seventh seal scenario. They would rightly argue that God would not impose Tribulation-style punishment on His own people—hence the Rapture must of necessity occur before the Tribulation begins or no later than mid-Tribulation. The missing link in this argument is that death also removes one from the earth, a truth especially needful during the Tribulation—*"The righteous perisheth ... none considering that the righteous is taken away from the evil to come"* (Isaiah 57:1).

Murder of the saints delivers them from God's wrath, but in yielding to the executioner's axe, they achieve an even greater purpose—that of overcoming the Antichrist Beast. It is a divine paradox—that, in dying, one defeats his enemy—that began with the crucifixion of Christ and will culminate in the death of innumerable masses at the hands of Antichrist— *"And they overcame him by the blood of the Lamb, and by the word of their testimony; and they loved not their lives unto the death"* (Revelation 12:11).

In death, Tribulation saints gain victory over the Antichrist (Revelation 15:2). They, and only they, defeat him (prior to Armageddon) by willingly dying for Christ. How would they so easily do this? The answer—they were already dead—dead to self and love for their own lives. Tribulation's fiery trials will burn the love for this world out of their hearts. Its appeal no longer embedded in their lives, they might well yearn to depart.

We might keep that in mind today as we, too, confront the Antichrist spirit of self love. Alive in John's day (1 John 2:18), that spirit is rampant today. Paul confirmed that the Antichrist spirit would pervade society in the last days, and it does as never before and will only grow worse as the Beast, full of pride and self-love, proclaims himself to be god.

We cannot so casually die for our Lord, defeating his foe, while living by the same proud and lustful spirit that drives him, the Antichrist. We cannot defeat him in the flesh, but as we slay the flesh and yield to the sanctifying power of the Spirit, we will not succumb to his soul-damning power. Death and only death defeats Antichrist and his humanistic spirit—death to self in this dispensation and literal death at his hands during Tribulation. As already discussed, holiness then becomes our only hope of overcoming him and his spirit that even now envelops the globe and, with each passing day, tightens its grip on the masses. (Section Five offers our vision of the pathway to holiness.)

THE SEVENTH SEAL

The first four seals signal Satan's unfettered rule over man, the results of which are death, famine, and martyrdom of many. The fifth seal pictures those he martyrs, *"... a great multitude, which no man could number ... which came out of great tribulation ... "* (Revelation 7:9, 14).

The sixth seal introduces the Day of God's wrath (Revelation 6:17), with natural and atmospheric upheavals: a great earthquake, the sun turns black, the moon turns to blood, stars fall, the Heavens depart, every mountain and island moves out of their place. So frightening are God's disturbances and dislocations of His own creation that men hide in caves and plead for cover from the mountains and rocks.

The seventh and final seal steps back from the sixth to cover an unspecified period of time in the second half of Tribulation up to and including more details on the Day of Wrath. When opened, it releases God's long and patiently pent-up wrath and retributions on the world of non-believers and the unholy of all persuasions.

For most of the second half of Tribulation, the contents of the seventh seal parallel, to a degree, those of the first six seals. Within the seventh seal of God's wrath are series of Heaven-sent miseries and death of His foes up to and including the final battle. This seal houses seven trumpets, seven thunders (which John is forbidden to write about), three woes, and seven bowls of the wrath of God. Each issuance from the seventh seal is a form of punishment upon those who have refused His gracious offer to believe, repent, and pursue a path of self-denying holiness. Each is an expression of the vengeful side of God. It is under the seventh seal that Satan, alas, receives his just reward, when the slain Lamb returns in glory to vindicate Himself.

Trumpets one through six sound off in Revelation chapters eight and nine. Clearly, they represent God-sent plagues inflicting distresses, destruction, and a great deal of death. The first four trumpets bring: (1) hail and fire mixed with blood burning up one third of trees and grass; (2) a great mountain burning with fire cast into the sea, turning one third of it into blood, killing one third of sea creatures, and destroying one third of the ships therein; (3) a great star (wormwood) falls from Heaven into one third of rivers, killing many men; (4) one third of the sun, moon, and stars are darkened so that one third of day and night are likewise in darkness.

The fifth, sixth, and seventh trumpets are so bad that, before they sound, an angel cries with a loud voice *"... Woe, woe, woe, to the inhibiters of the earth by reason of the other voices of the trumpet of the three angels, which are yet to sound!"* (Revelation 8:13). The three woes, as they are called, synchronize with the final three trumpets.

Trumpet five and woe number one release locusts from the bottomless pit that for five months torment all except the sealed 144,000 Jews. Trumpet six and woe number two release 200 million horsemen spewing out fire, smoke, and brimstone by which one-third of mankind is killed. Before the seventh trumpet sounds, seven thunders are uttered, but John is forbidden to expose their contents. God's two witnesses are introduced; they prophesy unharmed for three and one-half years, are slain by Antichrist, and then are resurrected while their enemies look on.

THE DAY OF GOD'S WRATH

Then comes the seventh trumpet. This, the last trumpet and the third woe, ushers in one truly remarkable, literally earth-shattering day—the Day of God's Wrath. There is God's Wrath as expressed at various times throughout history on limited scales, and manifest with a vengeance in the second half of Tribulation, and then there is the Day of God's Wrath—date specific, universally felt, and highlighted by the return of Christ.

References abound in Scripture about the Day of God's Wrath, also known as the Day of the Lord. Many could have been selected, but we refer you to:

- Zephaniah 1:14-16, "The great day of the Lord is near ... That day is a day of wrath, a day of trouble and distress, a day of wasteness and desolation, a day of darkness and gloominess, a day of clouds and thick darkness, A day of the trumpet ..."

- Romans 2:5, "But after thy hardness and impenitent heart treasurest up unto thyself wrath against the day of wrath and revelation of the righteous judgment of God ..."

- Take a close look also at Isaiah 13:4-13.

Some say the Day of God's Wrath is a period of time as we might say "in our day and time" or "in his day." But we feel it is of duration just one day, a day of extreme vexation and destruction upon the wicked, a day of ominous age-ending calamities that cap off the several prior months of God's agony-producing anger.

When the seventh trumpet sounds, voices in Heaven announce the end of the Gentile Age and the beginning of the Kingdom of God: *"... The kingdoms of this world are become the kingdoms of our Lord, and of his Christ; and he shall reign forever and ever ... thy wrath is come, and the time of the dead, that they should be judged, and that thou shouldest give reward unto thy servants ..."* (Revelation 11:15, 18).

Transitioning from Satan's worldly kingdom to God's eternal kingdom involves some fast-moving and sometimes simultaneous events for which saints have long awaited—Christ returns to *"reign forever and ever."* As He does, there is the resurrection—*"the time of the dead"*—of martyred saints, and the Day of God's Wrath—*"thy wrath is come."* Then comes the Millennial Kingdom when Tribulation saints are rewarded, in one way, by ruling with Christ over the surviving remnant of heathens.

We see the deadly extent of this as John tells us more and the seventh trumpet unleashes a firestorm of devastation. Coincident with Christ's return, God is still sending afflictions from above by way of the contents of the seven golden bowls containing the seven last plagues that *"... in them is filled up the wrath of God"* (Revelation 15:1). The bowls contain painful sores, seas and rivers turned to blood, scorching heat, the beast's kingdom full of darkness, Jerusalem divided into three parts, cities fall, islands and mountains disappear, the Euphrates dried up preparing the way for the kings of the east, the greatest earthquake ever, and huge hail beating down on man.

Further evidence that the seven plagues signal Christ's return are two things that occur between the sixth and seventh bowls: Demons sent out by Satan; the Antichrist and the False Prophet gather the world's leaders and their armies to do battle at a place called Armageddon on *"... that great day of God Almighty"* (Revelation 16:14). That day, the Day of His Wrath, is also the day of the Lord's return, for Christ announced, *"Behold, I come as a thief. Blessed is he that watcheth, and keepeth his garments ..."* (Revelation 16:15). Furthermore, after the world comes together in Israel, the seventh bowl is poured out with the proclamation, *"It is done."*

While Satan rages here on earth, God punishes from His throne in Heaven, that is, until His Son returns on the Day of God's Wrath. His torments are issued from above and below but not from a divine presence on the planet. That presence will come in the form of Christ when He returns to wage war with Antichrist and his multi-national armies. His soon return will not be in humility as before, but this time taking vengeance on those who have rejected His gracious offer, mocked His Word, denied His Father's existence, and killed His followers. God's wrath is manifest throughout the second half of Tribulation, but it is from a distance until the last day when, in the form of His Son, He, too, makes a visit to earth and confronts His enemies face to face at a place called Armageddon.

At Armageddon, the returning Son of God defeats Satan and his entire crew. At this, His Second Coming, Christ smites the Antichrist and the world's armies, after which He casts the Beast and False Prophet into the Lake of Fire and Satan into the bottomless pit where he stays bound for a thousand years. Then Christ and His resurrected Tribulation saints rule what's left of the nations with "a rod of iron." And the rod will guarantee a thousand years of peace and order with governance the way it should be—truly theocratic.

13

WHY HAVE A TRIBULATION?

Christ, John the Revelator, Paul, the prophets, and others have all contributed insights into what is, to most of us, the mystery that is the end of time, the Book of Revelation, the Rapture, and the Day of God's Wrath. We have attempted to look into this mystery and make some sense of it so that we all might know what is soon coming to this rapidly changing world of ours. That done, now we will look a little deeper into this mystery of God, even the presumed purposes of all the tragic faces and forces about to be released on the world—saint and sinner alike.

The thoughtful might well ask, "Why is there a Tribulation? Why would God end this age with seven dreadful years and a monstrous leader who makes everyone take his mark or worship his image just to survive? Couldn't God just as easily end time abruptly, judge the wicked and reward the righteous without sending the world through a time of great trouble such as the world has never seen?"

Surely, the answer must be yes, but remember, everything in God's scheme of things has meaning. So, why would God cause (or allow) such a horrible time to befall America, Israel, and His sainted elect? Why not skip the Tribulation, forget about the Millennium, just stop time, judge everyone, and then send them either to Heaven or Hell? There must be benefits to be gained, necessary adjustments to be made, wrongs to be righted, doors to be opened, perfecting to be pursued, retributions to be rendered in time and space, justice at last. Could God have a purpose in all the punishments?

We believe so because, when all is said and done, everyone still standing will know at last that our God is the only true God, that Christ is His Son, that the Bible was right after all. The world will see Christ in glory in contrast to His role as the meek and lonely Nazarene. The rejected One will, this time, be revealed in majesty and power, exercising extreme vengeance and inescapable punishment on the wicked, including any who have rejected Him, some of the punishments commensurate with the heinous acts committed against Christians down through the years.

Granted, the wicked receive their just reward in Hell, but the Tribulation serves as a worldwide stage in the here and now to reveal the righteous judgment side of God in contrast to His mercy and grace that this world has mostly ignored or taken for granted. They will not ignore Him then. For so long, God has held His peace and watched while the world's morals have spiraled downward, reaching to the very brim of the bottomless pit itself. Now, justice demands that retributions be made for the overt disregard for the laws of God. The Tribulation is the time that God's patience finally runs its course. Mine would have run out long ago if I were God. But for all our sakes, thank God, I am not God.

There is one exception—God extends His hand of mercy one final time in the Tribulation when He sends an angel to make a worldwide presentation of the Gospel (Revelation 14:6-7). Those who have never heard the Gospel will finally hear it. Some will likely repent. All will be given one last chance to repent, but with the Holy Spirit withdrawn, it is unlikely that the gospel hardened or humanist minded will repent, no matter what. But, none are without excuse then.

Could God also have a purpose in permitting the Antichrist to rule all of mankind and send them to their knees or to their grave if they refuse to bow? We believe there is good reason God would subject His elect to the sure death of denying the Mark of the Beast. We believe Antichrist fulfills a purpose in God's scheme of things. God does work in mysterious ways His wonders to perform. It is not up to us to question Him.

We believe God allows the Antichrist, with his defining Mark, as a way to reveal those who truly love Him instead of their own lives and to get them out of harm's way before His plagues and pestilences are released on the world. Christians will then have a clear choice with life and death implications. There will be no middle ground then. The demarcation lines will be drawn (with a Mark) for all to see and ably differentiate between the godly and the ungodly. No more guessing then. During the Tribulation the world will clearly see that, for some, their belief in God is worth dying for. Furthermore, saints must be taken out of the way, so the mark is used to definitively divide the elect from all the rest. God would not allow His elect to go through the outpouring of His wrath—their death at the hands of Satan's wrath accomplishes that.

Antichrist and his abominable programs further serve to enslave all mankind so that he can amass armies from all nations for the battle of Armageddon. Only a powerful, global leader like Antichrist could bring the world together and, in so doing, bring Christ back as the triumphant warrior to defeat him.

Antichrist is also used for the final punishment and salvation of Israel. Upon his ascension to power, he will chase Israel into their last exodus where they will hide for three and one-half years. Then, alas, they will accept Jesus as the Christ when He returns and they look upon Him whom they have pierced (Zechariah 12:10), realizing sorrowfully what their ancestors had done. At this point, as Paul said in Romans 11:26, *"... all Israel shall be saved ..."* To recap: with no Antichrist, there will be no Armageddon, no returning warrior King, no looking at the nail-pierced hands, no salvation for Israel.

The Tribulation does, however, bring about the salvation and restoration of Israel. This then enables God to reward His chosen ones, for during the Millennium, Jerusalem becomes the capital of the world. The Gentile Age is over. Finally, Israel will know peace—no more Hamas and Hezbollah. No more threats from Iran and others to wipe her off the face of the earth. Instead, she will see all nations once again gathered on her soil but, this time, to worship her God (Zechariah 8:23; 14:16). The tiny nation around which the world of hatred revolves today will then be exalted and made the center of the universe.

Perhaps the greatest and most obvious reason for the Tribulation is to prepare the way and set the stage for the Millennium. It takes the trauma of the Tribulation to unlock the door from the enclosed corridors of time into the unending vastness of eternity. These cataclysmic events provide the key and furnish the trumpet that beckons the Messiah back from His Heavenly home.

Life in the Millennium will be vastly different from today, so a host of changes are needed to get us there. First of all, the world must change. And it does. Because of the Tribulation, Satan is finally done in, tucked away in the bottomless pit for a thousand years. The ungodly, humanistic spirit of Antichrist, which has ruled the world for so long, is cast into the Lake of Fire. Gone, too, is the greed-mongering, empire-building harlotry of Babylonian capitalism. And most of the sinners will have been severely punished for their wicked ways or killed; most are probably killed and few men left, as the Bible says.

Secondly, we must change. And we will. God's refining fire and the Antichrist's hatred will serve to purge and purify the elect, with a purpose—to identify and select those who will rule with Christ in His theocracy, an honor not lightly bestowed or casually earned. The selection process is painful, as we will see in Chapter Twenty, but the rewards are almost incomprehensible, as we will see in Chapter Twenty-One.

Section V

THE END OF SELF

14

THE NEED FOR HOLINESS

How can we know we have what it takes to recognize and lay down our lives for our beliefs? How do we as Christians avoid entrapment in the lukewarmness of the end-time apostate church? How can we know that we are not part of the fallen away crowd, that we are members of the "elect," that we actually qualify for the Rapture? The answer: *"… seek righteousness, seek meekness; it may be ye shall be hid in the day of the LORD's anger"* (Zephaniah 2:3).

This little book is an effort to supply knowledge of the end of time—the Tribulation, the final battle, the timing and purposes of it all. Yes, it is good to have knowledge of the end times. We hope to have imparted some information on the eschatological places, players, and plagues. But, in the final analysis, we do feel that being ready, especially in these last days, by pursuing the pathway of holiness is all that will prepare us for the all-out wrath of Satan. And, if we are alive at the end, it is holiness that will hide us, by way of the Rapture, in the Day of God's Wrath.

Time races us toward Armageddon. The spirit of Antichrist smothers us with its charm and its promises of global peace and equally shared prosperity. And, yet, we slumber and stagger along under the weight of a host of humanist-inspired, flesh-driven sins.

America, it's time to wake up! It's time to shed the sin that so easily overwhelms us. It's time to subdue the flesh that will so easily be swayed by the deceitfulness of Antichrist. As never before, it's time to be holy.

Without a pursuit of holiness, no man shall rise to meet the Lord when He comes back for His own. In these last days, flirting with sin will leave us like the five foolish virgins, unprepared for Christ's Second Coming. The eternal consequences of impurity and the imminence of our Lord's return mandate a state of perpetual readiness, a constant pledge of purity, a relentless quest for personal holiness.

The Apostle Peter makes the connection between upcoming end-time events and the need for a holy walk before God:

> "But the day of the Lord will come as a thief in the night; in the which the heavens shall pass away with a great noise, and the elements shall melt with fervent heat, the earth also and the works that are therein shall be burned up. Seeing then that all these things shall be dissolved, what manner of persons ought ye to be in all holy conversation and godliness ... Wherefore, beloved, seeing that ye look for such things, be diligent that ye may be found of him in peace, without spot, and blameless." (2 Peter 3:10-11, 14)

Of His people, God has always demanded holiness. To the Old Testament Jew, He said, *"... ye shall be holy; for I am holy"* (Leviticus 11:44). To the New Testament Christian, He said, *"... as he which hath called you is holy, so be ye holy in all manner of conversation"* (1 Peter 1:15). As Paul saw it, *"... he hath chosen us in him before the foundation of the world, that we should be holy and without blame before him in love"* (Ephesians 1:4).

Granted, the atonement for sin differs under the two covenants, but the requirement for holiness, like God Himself, never changes. We live under grace now, but static unholy behavior, regardless of our confession, will still send us to Hell. Without a change of character in which we are *"... conformed to the image of His Son ..."* (Romans 8:29), God will not allow us in His celestial presence: *"Follow peace with all men, and holiness, without which no man shall see the Lord"* (Hebrews 12:14).

Paul asked in Romans, *"... Shall we continue in sin, that grace may abound?"* (6:1). He answered his own rhetorical question, *"God forbid ..."* (6:2). Yet, without holiness, even if we are saved by grace, we will continue a lifestyle of sin after our regeneration experience. And, if we do, we will backslide, die in our sins, and go to Hell. (See Ezekiel 18:24, 30-31; Ezekiel 33:12-13; 1 Thessalonians 3:5; Hebrews 3:14; Matthew 24:13; Psalm 69:28.)

So, how do we, the children of God who have accepted Christ as our Lord and Savior, avoid this fate, especially living in a country overwhelmed by Satan-inspired, Christian-hating humanism? As the bride of Christ, how do we make ourselves ready for the Bridegroom? How do we actually live a holy life? To live holy, it is fair to say that we would need to ask, "What exactly is holiness?" As have countless others, we have put our thoughts on paper and hope they serve as a useful guide to attaining our own personal, holy walk before God.

What distinguishes Peter and Paul and men like Stephen from the lifeless, listless breed of half-converted imposters who call themselves saints today? It might help explain what holiness is if we first look at what it is not. Holiness is not religious rituals, though holy ones do religiously look to Jesus. It is not self-inflicted pain, though holy ones do suffer for righteousness sake. It is not vows of silence, though holy ones do bridle their tongues. Holiness is not canvassing the country carrying a literal, wooden cross, though holy ones do take up a cross of perplexity and persecution. It is not outward appearance, though holy ones do shun the world's fads and fashions. Holiness is not wearing a painted-on frown, though holy ones do lament the wickedness of this present generation. It is not redistribution of the world's wealth, though holy ones do share what they have with the needy.

So, what is holiness? In a word, it is Christ. It is the preeminence of Christ, and no method for attaining it (including the one advanced in this book) that does not exalt the name of Christ or that does not promote the cross of Christ should be dismissed as works of the flesh. Furthermore, holiness is abiding in Christ, *"... ye in me, and I in you"* (John 14:20), with Him living His life again on earth through us. It is manifesting Christ, declaring Him in words of fire, radiating Him from our countenance, revealing and reflecting His own purity through our lives. Holiness is a perfecting and progressive process in which we are transformed into the image of Christ. It is a continuous process of growing up into Christ, of pressing toward the mark for the prize of the high calling of God in Christ. And, it is living above the dominion of sin, *"But now being made free from sin, and become servants to God, ye have your fruit unto holiness, and the end everlasting life"* (Romans 6:22).

Because holiness is freedom from sin's reign, it is also victory over the flesh and release from years of bondage to humanism. In fact, holiness is the very antithesis of humanism, for self has no place in the pure heart. By the same token, holiness is the only cure for the humanist cancer in individual hearts and lives. Not too many years ago, when holiness was still preached, a familiar slogan was heard in the church, "It's holiness or Hell!" For today's self-enthroned Christians, we might appropriately revise the old adage to read, "It's holiness or humanism!" This is the choice of the end-time church.

HOLINESS — NO WAY!

In a day when self is god, the cross a relic of the past, and sin the national pastime, most Christians (closet humanists) want nothing to do with holiness. When God calls for purging, they usually answer with a polite, "No, thank you!" They have listened to Satan and self for so long, they find it incomprehensible that man could walk holy before God. They argue, "Man cannot live above sin; that's perfection and nobody's perfect—we all sin. As long as we're clothed in these robes of flesh, we're going to sin!" If they have read their Bibles at all, they didn't listen when God told Ezekiel that *"... if thou warn the righteous man, that the righteous sin not, and he doth not sin, he shall surely live ..."* (Ezekiel 3:21). They didn't listen when Christ told the impotent man, *"... sin no more, lest a worse thing come unto thee"* (John 5:14); and when He told the woman taken in adultery, *"... Neither do I condemn thee: go, and sin no more"* (John 8:11); or when He proclaimed, *"... Whosoever committeth sin is the servant of sin"* (John 8:34). They didn't listen to Paul, *"Awake to righteousness, and sin not ..."* (1 Corinthians 15:34); or to Peter, *"... he that hath suffered in the flesh hath ceased from sin"* (1 Peter 4:1); or to John, *"Whosoever abideth in Him sinneth not ..."* (1 John. 3:6).

Instead, like Israel at Mount Sinai, these Laodiceans rebel and worship another god because Jehovah God is too hard, too high, too holy, and they are too weak. They bow instead to a more understanding, less demanding god, one who will bless them without charge, asking nothing in return. They serve a god "... who winks at sin, who expects nothing more than their best efforts, and who overlooks certain sins and lets bygones be bygones."[36]

Christians in this category are generally good people, though not godly people. They are generally upright people, though not righteous people. They love education, entertainment, and appeasement, but they hate to be confronted with their sin. Mention holiness, and the very wrath of Hell is stirred. Mention holiness, and they lash out, "Preach anything, but leave my sin alone. A merciful God will not hold me accountable for my 'weaknesses,' so don't you. Times have changed; we live under grace now, so quit judging me! I'm no different from anybody else." With that, their heart is hardened; in their sin they remain. The Bridegroom makes His final preparations, and they are not ready for the Wedding because, to the call for holiness, they have answered, "No way!"

HOLINESS — MY WAY

Another much smaller group of Christians answers the call by vowing that they will live holy if it kills them. By sheer willpower and bulldogged determination, they try to suppress their sin. By outward displays and self-righteous thrusts of the flesh, they try to crush the evil that eats at their soul. Some join communes and monasteries. Others torture themselves. A few must dress and look a certain pious way. Many more do battle by giving up things (some perfectly harmless) until there is nothing left to surrender except themselves. Tozer said of these misguided zealots, "... their world of permitted acts becomes narrower year by year till at last they fear to engage in the common pursuits of life. They believe this self-torture to be a proof of godliness, but how wrong they are." [37]

This stubborn group chooses to deal with works rather than sound doctrine. They stress outward appearance rather than inner purity. They subdue the natural man but not the old man. They neglect the body but nurture the flesh (lust and pride). They "disfigure their faces," presuming as did the Pharisee, that a "sad countenance" reflects on their inner righteousness. They *"... make clean the outside of the cup and of the platter, but within they are full of extortion and excess"* (Matthew 23:25). They are *"... like unto whited sepulchres, which indeed appear beautiful outward, but are within full of dead men's bones, and of all uncleanness"* (Matthew 23:27). As with the Pharisee, their service to God is bondage; their religion, grim, hard, and loveless. Yet, they glory in their spiritual superiority: *"... Stand by thyself, come not near to me; for I am holier than thou ..."* (Isaiah 65:5). They presume piety, but, in the sight of God, they are not holy at all. God, who is a Spirit, has fashioned spiritual values so that a man's holiness may not be discerned altogether by his outward appearance or his strict attention to detail but by his full expression of the Lord Jesus Christ.

As our real enemy is within, we do not defeat him (the old man) by external deeds of the flesh. We do not stamp him out by punishing ourselves. We do not shut him out by isolating ourselves. We do not starve him out by arbitrarily denying ourselves the basic necessities of life. Abstaining from acceptable food, drink, and daily activities does not conquer but, rather, satisfies the flesh, for it is *"... commandments and doctrines of men ... a show of wisdom in will worship, and humility, and neglecting of the body: not in any honour to the satisfying of the flesh"* (Colossians 2:22-23). Self-denial and voluntary humility are not holiness, just sanctimonious surges of the flesh once again seeking recognition, but, this time, as we respond to God's call for purity, our way.

HOLINESS — GOD'S WAY

Yet another group of Christians responds to the call for holiness the New Covenant way by submitting to the righteousness of God in Christ Jesus. God no longer accepts man's futile efforts to live holy by his works; that was the Old Covenant way. God now makes man holy by what He does in him and by what man does for God after his sin nature is killed.

Since even our motives and attitudes can be sinful in God's eyes, we cannot be holy without first getting rid of our sin nature, *"... the old man, which is corrupt according to the deceitful lusts,"* and then putting on the divine nature, *"... the new man, which after God is created in righteousness and true holiness"* (Ephesians 4:22, 24). Yet, within ourselves, it is impossible to slay the old man and clothe ourselves with the new. If we could, then Christ died in vain, and the Old Testament system of sacrifices and ordinances of fleshly service would never have been banned. But, just as God has a way of saving us by faith, He also has a process whereby He crucifies our old man by faith, kills the power of sin over us, and puts us on the road to holiness—God's way. That process is sanctification; without it, no man shall travel the highway of God's holiness.

THE CRISIS

However, before any of us will submit to sanctification's cruel slaying of the very thing we have cherished all our lives (the self), we must reach a point of desperation, our personal deadline with God. We must first come to a life and death crisis in our relationship with God, a crisis where nothing short of a miracle will pull us through. We must feel sin's painful sting and hate ourselves for always giving in to the old man's lusts:

> "Then shall ye remember your own evil ways, and your doings that were not good, and shall loathe yourselves in your own sight for your iniquities and for your abominations." (Ezekiel 36:31)

We must want our old man dead, realizing that because of his pride, his lustful passions, his foolishness, his contempt for Christ, we are frustrated and miserable, empty and alone, heartbroken and restless, ready to crumble under the weight of God's unbearable demands. Because of him, all our self-imposed rules and resolutions we have broken; all our dreams of purity we have shattered. Because of him, we may not find the way to eternal life *"Because strait is the gate, and narrow is the way, which leadeth unto life, and few there be that find it"* (Matthew 7:14). Because of him, we face the consuming fire of God's wrath.

In our crisis, we sense the severity of God; yet, we feel completely helpless in our efforts to please Him. We know we should stop sinning and we want to, but we don't. We want to become a new man, a spiritual man, a holy man, but we cannot. That is exactly where God wants us—hungry for His righteousness but at the end of ourselves as how to attain it. If we are really serious about holiness God's way, we will turn to Him, surrender all of ourselves to Him, put all our faith in the finished work of Calvary, confess our sins, and determine that, with God's help, we can be free from the dominion of sin. Our struggle with sin then becomes His struggle with sin; His righteousness becomes our righteousness. Then, through God, we can have power over sin, power that begins with the death of our "old man" in the miraculous act of faith called "sanctification."

15

DEAD TO SELF
(THE OLD MAN)

*T*raditionally, sanctification has been defined in terms of what it does for the believer. For example, it is said to set him apart from secular use to a life of consecrated service unto God. The theologically minded will love the definition given by Louis Berkhof: "Sanctification is that gracious and continuous operation of the Holy Spirit by which He delivers the justified sinner from the pollution of sin, renews his whole nature in the image of God, and enables him to perform good works."[38]

Sanctification is indeed a continuous and progressive operation but only to the point that it renews, strengthens, and builds upon an initial, climactic act—a death-rending second work of grace in which the old man of the flesh is suddenly slain and the new man implanted in his stead.

In the flesh, believers will never establish a kingdom suitable for the reigning Christ; in the flesh, believers will never walk in the unity of the faith. Until the self is crucified and the mind of Christ indwells and humbles believers, there can be no melding of kindred spirits, no blending of godly goals, no joining together to wage spiritual warfare against the darkness of this midnight hour. Without sanctification, there can be no spiritual bond between God's people: *"And for their sakes I sanctify myself, that they also might be sanctified through the truth … That they all may be one …"* (John 17:19, 21). With sanctification, holy ones are bound together by their mutual love and high regard for one another: *"Fulfill ye my joy, that ye be likeminded, having the same love, being of one accord, of one mind. Let nothing be done through strife or vainglory; but in lowliness of mind let each esteem other better than themselves"* (Philippians 2:2-3). This is unity—the only kind God recognizes, the only kind that furthers the spiritual growth of His kingdom. Any other conglomeration of sinners, no matter how sweet sounding its goals, is of Satan and must be avoided.

IN CHRIST

The potential for sanctification begins when we get saved. When we genuinely repent and accept Jesus Christ as Lord of our lives, we unite with Him: *"... ye in me, and I in you"* (John 14:20). Upon acceptance of His atoning death and resurrection, we affix ourselves to the Vine (Christ); He enters us and we Him. We are "in Christ."

In Christ, we draw our spiritual life from Him as branches do from a vine. In Christ, we are new creatures, delivered from old sins. In Christ, we are saints in position, whether in practice we are or not. In Christ, we don't have to sin.

But, we will sin if we stop at salvation, because without a further sanctifying step and that which follows, we may be in Christ, but Christ is not yet formed in us. And He will never be fully shaped in us until we rid ourselves of the old man, until we dethrone self from its deified position in our hearts, until sanctification renders sin's necessity null and void. Granted, we never reach a point where we cannot sin, but, through sanctification, we can reach a point where sin no longer reigns over our lives.

Regeneration atones for *"... sins that are past ..."* (Romans 3:25); sanctification makes provision for sins present and future. Regeneration imputes Christ's righteousness to us; sanctification imparts it to us. Regeneration places us in Christ; sanctification makes possible an abiding relationship in Him.

In Paul's letter to the Colossians, we get a glimpse of sanctification as it relates to our positions in Christ: *"And ye are complete in Him ... In whom also ye are circumcised with the circumcision made without hands, in putting off the body of the sins of the flesh by the circumcision of Christ"* (Colossians 2:10-11).

Here, we are looking at sanctification in principle, the circumcision and removal from our hearts of the fleshly layer of self-will, the seat of all our lusts, unholy desires, and affections.

CRUCIFIXION

Principle must be put into practice. Paul, therefore, in his penetrating letter to the Christians in Rome, unveiled the believer's role in sanctification. When he rhetorically asked, *"... Shall we continue in sin, that grace may abound?"* (Romans 6:1), he answered with an emphatic, *"God forbid ..."* (v. 2). He then detailed the sin-delivering, holiness-producing process of practical sanctification.

First of all, to take advantage of our positions in Christ, we must acknowledge that, because we are in Him, we have been baptized into His death. In theory, our old man was, at the time of that baptism, crucified and buried with Christ, his sinful impulses destroyed by the mortal blow. Paul explained it like this:

> "Know ye not, that so many of us as were baptized into Jesus Christ were baptized into His death? Therefore, we are buried with Him by baptism into death ... Knowing this, that our old man is crucified with Him, that the body of sin might be destroyed, that henceforth we should not serve sin." (Romans 6:3-4, 6)

Theory becomes reality then as we, by faith, climb onto the cross with Christ and identify ourselves with His death. Again, Paul emphasized our responsibility in the cleansing process when he said, *"... reckon ye also yourselves to be dead indeed unto sin ..."* (Romans 6:11).

Through an honest association of ourselves with Him on the cross, our old self-life dies, our old ways become history. On the cross, there is no more human wisdom, no more human will, no more affairs with the world. Tozer said that "... the cross will cut into our lives where it hurts worst ... It will defeat us and bring our selfish lives to an end ... In coming to Christ we do not bring our old life up onto a higher plane; we leave it at the cross. The corn of wheat must fall into the ground and die."[39]

On the cross of sanctification, our flesh does die. T. Austin-Sparks knew of that death, for he well wrote of its consequences on the old sin nature:

> "In that death, you are regarded as having passed out of the realm of what you are, even at your best, and as having passed into the realm of what He is ... [The cross is] death to what we are in ourselves, a death of our own life, a death to a life apart from Him. We must go down with Him into death, and there, under the act of the

> Spirit of God in union with Christ buried, there is a transmission of His life to us ... [This death] breaks up our own natural life. It scatters it, pulls it to pieces, takes all its beauty away. We begin to discover that, after all, there is nothing in us but corruption ... we are losing all that beauty that was there from the natural point of view."[40]

Furthermore, by choosing the cross, we willingly give up that for which our Lord sacrificed His life. We show God that the very least we can do for Him is to lay down that thing for which His only Son died. Of our moral obligation to join Christ on the cross, J. B. Stoney wrote:

> "Christ, the Son of God, has borne the judgment, not that you should keep the man who was under judgment, but that you should be completely severed from him in Christ's death ... I do not see the cross truly if I only see it as opening a way of escape for me, and yet allowing that in me to escape which has incurred the judgment ... if Christ died for me, I am bound by every good and right feeling to lay aside that for which He died, and which needed His death."[41]

That thing in us is the old man. He must be left behind, nailed to the cross, for he was the cause of the offense that drove Christ to Calvary. If we do not reckon him dead, then Christ died in vain—we continue in sin.

RESURRECTION

After we acknowledge and accept the death of our old man, we must likewise recognize *"... that like as Christ was raised up from the dead by the glory of the Father, even so we also should walk in newness of life. For if we have been planted together in the likeness of his death, we shall be also in the likeness of his resurrection"* (Romans 6:4-5). Then, as with our crucifixion, we must reckon ourselves to be resurrected with Christ to newness of life, a life completely apart from ourselves and separated unto God: *"... reckon ye also yourselves to be dead indeed unto sin, but alive unto God through Jesus Christ our Lord"* (Romans 6:11).

The death of our carnal man and subsequent resurrection of the new—these are the two indivisible parts of sanctification.

FAITH

According to Romans 6, knowledge and faith are both required for our sanctification, but unquestionably, faith is the key ingredient—so much so that the Bible tells us we are *"sanctified by faith"* (Acts 26:18). All the high-sounding theology on sanctification and all the eloquent talk of death and resurrection mean nothing without faith.

Our hearts are purified when we, by faith, reckon that God's mandated union with Christ in His death and resurrection applies to us, and when we, by faith, accept our death with Christ and our resurrection with Him to walk in newness of life. We are cleansed when, by faith, our self-centered Adamic man is considered dead and our new God-oriented man is considered raised to a life dedicated unto God. When we truly accept this great miracle of God and apply it to our lives by faith, we are sanctified.

DIVINE PARTICIPATION

Then, because we are in Christ, attached to the Vine, and because we are sanctified, dead to self and alive unto God, we can draw spiritual strength from the Christ within us. Paul did: *"I am crucified with Christ: nevertheless I live, yet not I, but Christ liveth in me: and the life which I now live in the flesh I live by the faith of the Son of God, who loved me, and gave himself for me"* (Galatians 2:20).

Christ knew no sin, so, if He abides in us and we in Him, His righteousness and His faith enables us to live holy, the New Covenant way. Paul's recognition of his ineffectiveness against sin under the Old Covenant (Romans 7 gives his classic confession) and the power of God *"... to them which are in Christ Jesus ..."* (Romans 8:1) prompted him to pray that he *"... be found in Him, not having mine own righteousness, which is of the law, but that which is through the faith of Christ, the righteousness which is of God by faith"* (Philippians 3:9).

As evidenced by Paul's disclosures earlier in Philippians 3, this promise of God's righteousness working through us is conditioned upon our utter rejection of all that we once held dear and the total surrender of our lives to Him. When the world no longer casts us in its mold and God no longer has half our heart but the whole of it, His strength enables us to walk in holiness. Without Him, we would fail miserably; the hill of holiness is too high for anyone to climb alone.

But in Christ and through Christ, the sanctified have power over besetting sins, victory over runaway lusts and pride, freedom from slavery to their house-devil (self), for self is dead—dead to blame or praise, dead to fashion and human opinion, dead to ambition and earthly attachments.

Through Christ, the sanctified are delivered from the curse of humanism and introduced to the blessedness of holiness. Spurts of pride and spells with hurt feelings give way to humility and long-suffering. Hypocrisy and artificiality give way to sincerity and genuineness. Religion and ritual give way to spirituality and intimacy. Superficial concern for others gives way to honest, compassionate treatment of their fellow man.

NO SANCTIFICATION

If such a simple act of faith is so potent, why aren't all Christians sanctified? Why is the church not pure, powerful, and effective in bringing down Satanic strongholds? Why is holiness not a housetop cry, the buzzword of society?

Probably the greatest deterrent to sanctification in our day is end-time man's increasing disdain for the sacred, his building hatred for God's Holy Word. The majority of Christians in Laodicea content themselves with a sin-laden form of godliness but cringe at the thought of personal, substantive holiness. They excuse their own sins by exploiting Paul's confession in Romans 7—*"For the good that I would I do not: but the evil which I would not, that I do"* (v. 19)—as if he were practicing sin at the time against his will (those who believe that know nothing of Paul's life, nor do they understand the context of Romans 6, 7, and 8).

Lukewarm Christians rather enjoy their sins and their fleshly flirtations with this world's filth. They despise any reference to self-crucifixion or separation from the world, tabbing those efforts as outmoded and legalistic. David Wilkerson said this of these sin-loving, legalist-labeling Laodiceans:

> "If the Spirit moves on a pastor and he brings forth God's call to holiness, separation, self-denial—and the parishioners don't like it, they pack up their billfold, their membership card, and go shopping for a pastor who will accentuate the positive. That is why the terrible plague of Apathy is sweeping over religion today. We have been so afraid of works—so riled up about legalism that we have given obedience a bad name. The church has reached the zenith of apostasy when it calls obedience legalism."[42]

Ironically, most so-called "holiness" churches do not even stress purity anymore. Now, it is nearly impossible to distinguish them from the rest of organized religion (or the world, for that matter). Now, it is not uncommon for members of "holiness" churches to tell convenient lies, dirty jokes, and juicy gossip. Now, it is not uncommon for them to mistreat their fellow man and chase after materialism and success with an aggressiveness that would put some Wall Streeters to shame. But it is uncommon to hear the battle cry of saints of old; "be ye holy" is simply no longer in vogue.

REBIRTH SANCTIFICATION

Among those who teach or at least acknowledge the existence of this seemingly mystical experience, false teachings abound. Prevalent among the more liberal (and more famous) Pentecostals is the misconception that salvation and sanctification occur simultaneously. When we get saved, we are automatically sanctified by God. We don't have to seek for it, believe for it, or die (to self) for it. It is ours as part of the Redeemer's blessing pact with the redeemed.

Granted, the same royal blood that redeems us also purifies us (Titus 2:14), but regeneration and sanctification are different works of grace. They must be sought for different reasons, using different methods, with different results. To be saved, the sinner recognizes that he is lost, repents, and believes in the Lord Jesus Christ. To be sanctified, the believer recognizes that he is still bound by sin, reaches a point of desperation, then alas acknowledges and accepts, by faith, his death and resurrection with the Lord Jesus Christ.

By teaching the two acts of grace as one, sanctification is stripped of its sin-delivering power, leaving the believer with no foundation upon which to build a life of holiness. And, to confuse justification with sanctification is to imply that Christians are neither more nor less holy from the time they are born again to the time they die, which would be true if sanctification is lumped in with salvation, but is certainly not true of those who take faith's second sanctifying step.

ALTAR SANCTIFICATION

Most of those who teach a second, distinct work of grace nullify their commendable efforts with the notion that sanctification is nothing more than an "altar experience" in which God reacts to the seeker's vigil by sanctifying him and removing forever his desire to sin. This, they say, occurs when God plucks up and destroys the individual's root of sin, at which time he can expect to receive emotional confirmation that he has, in fact, been sanctified.

Followers of this teaching are led to believe that holiness and sanctification are one and the same, that the move to holiness stops at the altar. Therefore, if they have been sanctified, they are holy. They have sought God, He responded, and they live holy ever after. All they have to do now is go to church, pay their tithes, and Heaven is theirs.

The most damaging aspect of this fallacy is that its disciples, having failed to reckon their old man dead, remain bound by sin. So, when the lusts of the flesh flare up again, they become confused. They thought the desire to sin had been removed, that the old man had been rooted out and slain. Yet, now they're tempted to sin. And, without true sanctification, they will yield to the temptation, and commit sin. When they do, they begin to doubt their altar experience. If they don't backslide altogether, they are trapped in a sin/repent syndrome all their lives just trying to hang on to their salvation. Deep down they hope that a God of love will have mercy on Judgment Day.

Another error evolving from the doctrine of "altar" sanctification is that it inadvertently places responsibility, which rightfully belongs to us, back on God. It implies that God must react to our persistence, not our faith, and that if we seek Him long enough, He will answer.

However, God doesn't respond to vigilance, He responds to faith. We are saved by faith; we are healed by faith; we are filled with the Holy Ghost by faith; and we are sanctified by faith. He will not sanctify us until we receive the knowledge of our union with Christ in His death and resurrection and then reach out by faith and accept it. Whether this outreach of faith takes place at the altar or in our prayer closet is irrelevant, but it must take place.

Then, and only then, do our emotions (if there are any) signal a truly life-transforming change in our character. Then, and only then, are we delivered from the impulsive lusts and passions of the flesh, severed from everything that breaks our communion with Christ and dims our vision of Him. Then, and only then, are we outfitted for our continued pilgrimage along the highway of holiness.

16
KEEPING THE OLD MAN DEAD

*I*n Christ, we find sanctification. Our position in Him enables us, by faith, to assume our old man dead. But that is by no means the end of our quest for holiness; it must be perfected. That is by no means the end of our old man; he must be put off in practice.

Even sanctification is not complete without a purifying walk before God. Especially as we approach the return of Christ and the end of time, are we implored to pursue a lifestyle of Christian purity.

> "... when he shall appear, we shall be like him; for we shall see him as he is. And every man that hath this hope in him purifieth himself, even as he is pure." (1 John 3:2-3)

Granted, sanctification faith activates the power of God within to rid us of the old man's practices, but even this marvelous work of grace is not within itself a finished work. There must be growth in sanctification; progressing, perfecting that which has been planted in our hearts by faith. After we have received the second work, we cannot sit back, rest on our faith and expect to never yield to temptation again. Until the flesh is actually brought under subjection, we very likely will give in to ever-present temptation.

To bring our bodies under subjection, faith in the theoretical death of the old man must be followed by works which crucify him in the real world of practical experience. Faith places us in Christ; works keep us there, abiding in Him. Faith sanctifies; works purify. Faith assumes lust and pride to be gone from our hearts; works do away with their actual performance or consummation. Just as knowledge without faith leaves the heart cunning but cold, faith without works leaves the heart circumcised but susceptible. Theological discussions on faith and doctrine (including that of sanctification) mean nothing outside the classroom (or sanctuary) unless followed by cleansing action. If we claim our death with Christ, then we must, as Paul taught, literally and physically shed our earthly members of the flesh: (Colossians 2:20; 3:5, 8-9; Galatians 5:19-21; Ephesians 4:28; 5:4).

In addition to the old man's obvious infractions (spoken and unspoken), there are fistfuls of everyday practices which, on the surface, appear innocent enough but, underneath, are fueling the flesh and bolstering the carnal, Adamic nature. They too are offensive to God; if persistently partaken of, they will eventually result in sin. Because they are spawning ground for the world's sinful smut, they too must be purged: *"... let us cleanse ourselves from all filthiness of the flesh and spirit, perfecting holiness in the fear of God"* (2 Corinthians 7:1).

Satan has an arsenal of activities and adornments that are not within themselves sinful but, rather, are indicative of or promotion for a heart condition that is bent on lust and pride. For instance, fashionable adornments and artificial alterations to appearance can be mirror images of an inner propensity to violate God's holy laws; they usually indicate a heart laden with pride. On the other hand, such innocent looking pastimes as entertainment and recreation can lead to sin because they promote the lusts of the flesh and the pride of life. In time, if we continue to participate in the world's games and fill our minds with its filth, they will deteriorate our spiritual condition until the old man rears his ugly head and we sin. We sin because the flesh has been fed, while the new man starved to death.

Even so, I have reservations about naming externalities that are reflective of or conducive to sin because, for one thing, it is impossible to know them all; I do not and neither does anyone else. As we work out our own salvation, God Himself has to personally reveal some things that He knows will harm us: *"... if in anything ye be otherwise minded, God shall reveal even this unto you"* (Philippians 3:15). Too, naming outward hindrances and manifestations of sin tends to condone the inner and uglier dispositional sins of pride, jealousy, deceit, temper, faultfinding, covetousness, sensitiveness, resentfulness, etc., sins that are more difficult to detect and infinitely harder to put off. Plus, when you start identifying sin-breeding conditions and activities, you tend toward Phariseeism, spiritual pride, and outward holiness; inner sins go unnoticed and unshed. And, to the sanctified, pleasing God should not even be a matter of good or bad, right or wrong, but of truly expressing Jesus Christ to the world with every word and every deed; anything that does not manifest the Lord is rejected, if for no other reason than this: Christ would not do it.

In some circles not many years ago, naming "sins" was popular. Preachers thundered against smoking; chewing; dipping; drinking; swimming; movies; ballgames; make-up; jewelry; long hair; short dresses; sleeveless blouses; working, buying, or cooking on Sunday; etc., etc. "It is holiness or Hellfire and brimstone," they bellowed. The messages were so awesome that some sat in their pews in fear. Others apparently feared the wrath of God as well because, to a great degree, Christians in those days lived much cleaner lives. It was reflected in their worship services; the Spirit of God was much more evident.

Undoubtedly, excesses developed. Like our Puritan fathers, a few became overzealous in their efforts to stamp out all personal sin, naming in the process many things that were not wrong, things that were not indicative of a corrupt heart and in no way would ever lead to sin. The list of sins grew until it included such things as women crossing their legs, drinking soft drinks, or having indoor plumbing and electricity.

To their credit, however, they had good intentions, for they rightly recognized that sin must be eliminated from their lives if Heaven were to be their eternal home. So they tried to wipe out every sin, every appearance of sin, and everything that might engender sin. When they were wrong, at least they were wrong in the right direction.

Today, just the opposite is true. Our laxity toward sin and our repugnance of those "old-fashioned holiness doctrines" make us wrong in the wrong direction; hardly anything is considered a sin anymore; hardly anything breeds sin anymore; and society suffers the more for it.

So, for those who are serious about holiness and are determined that no sin shall have dominion over their lives, I will attempt to identify some of the popular American perversions that pose more as respectable pastimes and fads than as portraits and promoters of inner impurities, which they are. In so doing, it is not my intention to condemn those who are involved but, rather, to inform, warn, and urge us to purge the offensive members.

PLEASURE

Society does indeed suffer under the constant pounding of sin's hammer. Most of the pounding comes from America's vast and insidious entertainment mediums, all of which exist for the sole purpose of pushing fun on a fun-loving population. Paul prophesied that in the last days *"... men shall be ... lovers of pleasures more than lovers of God"* (2 Timothy 3:2, 4). How true that is of America. Ours is a nation possessed with its pleasure.

If they are to put off (and keep off) the old man of the flesh, the sanctified cannot join the world in its all out devotion to entertainment. They cannot pollute themselves with filthy movies, dubious social events, questionable clubs and wild parties: *"Thou shalt not also go into the house of feasting, to sin with them to eat and to drink"* (Jeremiah 16:8).

The sanctified cannot listen to music, secular or sacred, that demeans the deity of God, that glorifies man, or that appeals to or arouses the lusts of the flesh. The sanctified cannot read the world's literature where Christian ideals and their verbal expression have been replaced with more relevant humanistic terms and thoughts. The sanctified cannot become addicted to sports, either as spectators or participators. Our religious devotion to recreation, athletics, and athletes is an outright stench in the nostrils of God.

ENTERTAINMENT

The entertainment industry is probably the most obvious and most visible expression of the humanist-run world system. This primary medium of worldly swill and humanistic slime has penetrated and corroded every aspect of our lives, tantalizing the flesh to fornicate with the world and break our communion with God.

In the name of entertainment, the world is electronically piped into our living rooms, its dirt no longer having to be sought clandestinely in bars and peep joints.

> "Americans live no longer in homes, but in theaters. The members of many families hardly know each other, and the face of some popular TV star is to many wives as familiar as that of their husbands."[43]

There are consequences. Most Americans now believe that put-downs are funny, that life is entertainment, that things will make them happy, that sex, violence, wealth, and fame are the desirable norm.

> This is the day of arrogant iniquity. It struts and strides; it screams from the billboards; it flashes from the television tubes. In a day when crime and cruelty saturate the press and television news, the public thirsts for more. It devours television mayhem, murder, and sadomasochism. This is the day when all that is vile, vulgar, vicious, vain, and virtueless gets the headlines."[44]

Furthermore, our conversations have become open, obscene and non-discriminate regarding topic or audience. Even Christians no longer feel guilty when discussing vulgar or otherwise private matters in public and with anyone.

Thanks to the entertainment industry (movies, television, music, etc.) the dispersion of humanism in the American public has been greatly enhanced: "Television has been by far its [secular humanism's] chief disseminator. It would be almost impossible to overestimate its influence."[45]

Television networks knowingly push the humanist value system on millions of ignorant viewers. New Ager George Christie boasts that "the father's house is wired, and we can infuse that network with a living, vital positive energy that will transform the planet ... we are midwives of a birthing process to the New Age."[46]

In the name of entertainment, Americans readily accept the values of humanist ideologues shoved down their throats. But, "TV is more than just a little fun and entertainment. It's a whole environment, and what it does, bears an unpleasant resemblance to behavior modification on a mass scale."[47]

Thanks to Hollywood, throngs of Americans have a distorted picture of Christians. If they have any place in the script at all, believers are portrayed as narrow-minded, self-righteous, judgmental, incompetent, witless, irrelevant, etc. "In fact, when Christians are depicted in programs with modern-day settings, they nearly always are stereotyped as being hypocrites, liars, cheats, frauds, unfaithful in their marriage vows."[48]

Furthermore, "... religiously motivated characters are likely to be neurotics for whom religion is a form of sickness. Rarely are sympathetic characters presented whose lives are strengthened by prayer or the guidance of clergy."[49]

Thanks to Hollywood, Biblical Christianity is now considered by many to be the religion of freaks, fanatics, and futurists, of doomsayers, dullards, and defeatists. Thanks to Hollywood, millions never bat an eye as they trample traditional Christian values, principles, and prophecies. Hollywood glamorizes self-gratification while it degrades God's demand for self-denial and cross-carrying. Hollywood shuns the Christian's hope of eternal salvation and ridicules his fear of everlasting damnation. It avoids his warnings of God's judgments that are even now falling on America.

Yet, in spite of its distortion of Christian views, its promotion of humanist values, its destruction of family ties, and its electronic infusion of worldly filth into the home, the act of watching a movie or listening to music may not be a sin. The sin of worldly entertainment is its emphasis on the present and the tangible, its silence toward Heaven and the soul, its spurning of the spiritual, its fascination with the physical. It is not so much that entertainment is an idol before which we pay worshipful homage, but that it is a promoter of one of our greatest enemies—the flesh. Entertainment pampers the old man, reassures him of his preeminence and encourages him to practice his corrupt ways. Its message is the lust of the flesh, the lust of the eyes, and the pride of life. And when lust is conceived, sin always follows. So, we may not sin when we partake of this world's entertainment, but if we persist, we will.

Our minds are a battleground, and the battle is lost when the only food our soul receives is served up by the world. The next time we sit before a television filling our minds with sex and violence, we should ask ourselves if what we are doing is helping us to grow spiritually. We should ask ourselves if there is even the slightest difference between our applause of corruption and the ancient Roman's voracious appetite for the same, which the Apostle Paul condemned: *"Who knowing the judgment of God, that they which commit such things are worthy of death, not only do the same, but have pleasure in them that do them"* (Romans 1:32).

Paul also said to *"... have no fellowship with the unfruitful works of darkness, but rather reprove them. For it is a shame even to speak of those things which are done of them in secret"* (Ephesians 5:11-12). How much more of a shame is it to sit for hours applauding the darkest, most damnable filth Hell has to offer and one of Satan's most seductive means of secularizing society and polluting the soul. If we are to preserve our sanctification, we must be very selective of what we watch and listen to and be aware when the directors of humanism try to slip their religious messages overtly and subliminally into our minds through the medium of entertainment.

WEIGHTS

The world arena is also host to a multitude of problems and projects that heap heavy burdens on Christians and hinder their progress in the Kingdom of God. Like entertainment, the cares and affairs of life are not necessarily sinful acts, but, because they are not movements toward God or His holiness, they must be put off. Because they retard the Christian's spiritual growth and prevent him from bearing fruit, they must be set aside: *"… lay aside every weight, and the sin which doth so easily beset us, and let us run with patience the race that is set before us"* (Hebrews 12:1).

These cares of life (along with the pursuit of pleasure and riches) shove aside the Word of God, removing our cleansing agent and leaving a void that is easily filled by the world. In the parable of the sower, Christ categorized these pitfalls as seed that fell among thorns: *"He also that received seed among the thorns is he that heareth the word; and the care of this world, and the deceitfulness of riches, choke the word …"* (Matthew 13:22). As our growth is directly proportional to our intake and application of the Word, any problem or project (outside our means of making a living) that keeps our minds occupied and our hands busy needs to be reviewed and forsaken if it drives a wedge between us and our conformity to the image of Christ.

We Christians are in a war for our souls. With our eternal destiny at stake, we cannot afford to encumber ourselves with the temporal cares of this present life: *"No man that warreth entangleth himself with the affairs of this life …"* (2 Timothy 2:4). So let's shed the weights. Let's fight a good fight. Let's run until our earthly course is finished and life's race is won.

FASHION

Unlike entertainment, which leads to sin, and unlike weights, which lead to barrenness, the Christian's obsession with fashionable attire and adornment is usually indicative of existing impurities hidden deep in the heart. Lust and pride always manifest themselves in our dress, in the way we adorn and present ourselves to the world around us. The old man always tries to appeal to the senses or put himself above others by relieving plainness with pomp and showiness, by adding to the original with color and design, by setting off the simple with the superfluous, and by improving the intrinsic with the extraneous. The old man always strives for excellence, for attractiveness, for the striking appearance, for the unusual and the flamboyant because he ministers to ego-stroking man, not to a fear-invoking God.

The sanctified cannot follow the world's fads and fashions; conversely, every sad sack and plain Jane you pass on the street is not pure of heart either. Purity will express itself in the visible realm because the holy have no need for vainglorious displays of the flesh; but purity cannot be had by merely defacing one's outward appearance. Those self-righteous souls who pride themselves in their plainness, who gloat over their homeliness, who sit in arrogant scorn of all who don't look and dress as they, who have no love for the lost, who would send a man to Hell for his cigarettes and a woman for her earrings, yet see nothing wrong with backbiting, jealousy, or gossip, they are headed for Hell, too.

Spiritual arrogance is just as sinful as the pride that slaps on the jewelry, the make-up, or the silk suit, and then heads downtown to impress the world. C.S. Lewis said, "The devil ... is perfectly content to see you becoming chaste and brave and self-controlled provided, all the time, he is setting up in you the Dictatorship of Pride."[50] Granted, the holy will not decorate and adorn themselves like the world, but neither will they sit in Pilate's judgment seat and condemn to death those who do.

EVERYTHING A SIN?

Questions inevitably arise when someone starts naming sins (and weights): "What's wrong with going to movies? It's not a sin if I don't lust. What's wrong with watching off-color programs on television if I only do it for relaxation? What's wrong with worldly music; I never listen to the words, just the beat. What's wrong with taking a social drink so long as I don't get drunk? What's wrong with beautifying the body God gave me; I'm not trying to temp anyone to lust after me? What's wrong with having fun, as long as I don't hurt anybody? What's wrong with having a balanced life; I go to church and pay my tithes; can't I have a little fun, too?"

Some liberal soul has, by now, thrown up his hands, proclaiming that to this writer, everything must be a sin. No, but if it is not of or for God, then it either is sin, bespeaks of hidden sin, or eventually will lead to sin. If it is not of the spirit, then it is of the flesh. You say that is too close. Well, it is close. It is straight and narrow, the way leading to eternal life, and only a few will find it (Matthew 7:14). Until the refiner turns up the heat, perhaps only a faithful few will cleanse themselves of all impurities (hidden or otherwise), all hindrances, and all sin-breeding perversions, and prepare for His soon return. Only a faithful few will have such intense hope in His return that it alone ignites a fire hot enough to burn out all the chaff from their lives. Only a faithful few will purify themselves as He is pure.

It is high time and past time for a holy remnant to once again set the standard for holiness. It is time to lay down our sins, to cleanse ourselves of this world's filth, to purify the vessel of even its sin-producing seeds. We may scrub too hard in some spots, but at least the vessel will be clean. Praise God!

17
SEPARATING FROM THE WORLD SYSTEM

"For the LORD spake thus to me with a strong hand, and instructed me that I should not walk in the way of this people ..." (Isaiah 8:11)

Another mandatory move toward holiness that walks hand-in-hand with purification is separation from the world system. Like purification, separation logically and scripturally accompanies sanctification as a means of keeping the old man nailed to the cross, severed from his corrupt playmates that reside in the world:

> "Wherefore Jesus also, that He might sanctify the people with His own blood, suffered without the gate. Let us go forth therefore unto Him without the camp, bearing His reproach." (Hebrews 13:12-13)

The camp to which Paul refers is the complex system built and inhabited by corrupt men, administered by Satan, and more generally known as "the world." John, in his first epistle, defined the world in terms of its ungodly behavior. This behavior is not only characteristic of the individual old man, but typifies as well the collective body of all "old men," each one in hot pursuit of his own carnal lusts, each one brimming with Satanic pride:

> "For all that is in the world, the lust of the flesh, and the lust of the eyes, and the pride of life, is not of the Father, but is of the world. And the world passeth away, and the lust thereof: but he that doeth the will of God abideth for ever." (1 John 2:16-17)

When John speaks of lust and pride as being "things that are in the world," they are, but only because the world is comprised of scores of unsanctified "selves," each one asserting his own godhood and each one following the dictates of his own evil heart. There is a collective body of worldlings bent on lust and pride, but only because those same tendencies manifest themselves in the individual lives of those who give their old man free reign.

For purposes of definition, I will treat the "things that are in the world" as characteristics of the unregenerate or unsanctified individual, though it well describes the spiritual composition of our entire humanistic society.

- ***The lust of the flesh*** is the old man's illicit craving for a good time or a good feeling. It is his longing to reach beyond God's legal limits and indulge himself for the sake of a physical or emotional high. It is his desire for the consumption of things, or the physical interaction with people, all for the sole purpose of bringing pleasure to himself. It is his insatiable appetite for food (especially delicacies). It is his yearning for drugs, alcohol, or tobacco. It is his raging passion for illicit sexual relations.

- ***The lust of the eyes*** is the old man's covetous craving to possess things of the world that are not basic necessities. This unholy desire of the eye goes beyond fleshly appeal and reaches out for anything thought to bring pleasure merely by its possession. It is serving the god of "things"—houses, cars, clothes, furniture, etc. It is preoccupation with and the pursuit of material possessions. It is always grasping for more, driven by a nagging discontentment with the status quo. It is accumulating and gathering beyond actual need, squandering everything on self. It is a craving, not for just one particular thing, but a reaching Achan spirit (Joshua 7) that is not satisfied until it has one of everything. With so many things to offer, the world system tempts the old man to let his wants race out of control, then tantalizes him by promising that happiness is his if only he could own them all.

- ***The pride of life*** is the old man's inordinate desire to always excel, to get ahead and go places in the world system. It is his hunger for the applause and acclaim of others within the world order. It is his desire to always have the biggest and the best. It is his preoccupation with self-improvement, always trying to look, talk, and think better than the other fellow. It is his unquenchable quest for the "number one" spot in career, in sport, in personal relations. For the proud, the world system is structured so that the ambitious might stroke their egos by climbing the ladder of success (on their job and in their games), but neither the top rung nor any between ever affords them the rest they seek—they must always find another mountain to climb.

In the physical realm, the world is a multi-faceted system boasting of political, military, and economic might and teeming with man-centered educational, religious, and entertainment structures. In each process, the lust of the flesh/eyes and the pride of life dominate its every precept and principle. They are standard procedure, its normal modes of operation. Through them, the world works us, pampers, programs, and entertains us. It cultivates, educates, and recreates us. It demands all of our attention, all of our time, talents, and thoughts until there is nothing left for God.

That driving force—that preoccupation with self and alienation from God—is purposefully instilled within the world system by its leader, Lucifer, "... *the prince of the power of the air* ... " (Ephesians 2:2). Because Satan is king, the world crucifies the Son of God, desecrates His cross, persecutes His children, and secularizes all His sacred traditions. With Satan at its helm, the world system is covered by darkness, blinded by the humanist lie, destined to worship the Beast, and on its way to a lake of fire.

That being the case, can we as Christians be united to Christ and intimately joined in an adulterous relationship with the world system at the same time? No, because spiritual adultery breaks our marriage vows to the Lord. No, because spiritual adultery forms a psychosomatic union with the world, binding us in a profound and mysterious way, making us one with the world, robbing us of our sacred relationship with God. No, because spiritual adultery enslaves us to the world, making us mass-produced clones stamped out in the world's mold, its adulterous ways having become our ways. No, because spiritual adultery weaves us into the "invisible tapestry," the tangled web of New Age networks, which bind the world together as one ominous force marching dutifully toward Armageddon.

Furthermore, we are the light of the world, and light does not mix with darkness: *"... for what fellowship hath righteousness with unrighteousness? and what communion hath light with darkness?"* (2 Corinthians 6:14). When we fellowship with sons of darkness, our own lights grow dim, and our Christian witness is silenced. Because the children of this world would introduce darkness back into our lives, we have but one choice if we are to continue manifesting Christ to them: *"... have no fellowship with the unfruitful works of darkness ..."* (Ephesians 5:11). *"Wherefore come out from among them, and by ye separate, saith the Lord ..."* (2 Corinthians 6:17). Tozer, accordingly, warned against spiritually incongruent relationships: "The wheat grows in the same field with the tares, but shall they seek to interbreed? The unjust and the just enjoy the same rain and sunshine, but shall they forget their deep moral differences and intermarry?"[51]

Absolutely not! In fact, end-time saints must "turn away" from those with unholy, covetous lifestyles and unChristlike, selfish tendencies; from those with the world's pleasure-loving stamp printed indelibly on their every move and motive; from those who claim Christ but deny His purifying power in their lives. Christ, Himself, was *"... holy, harmless, undefiled, separate from sinners ..."* (Hebrews 7:26); can we who abide in Him do any less than withdraw from the pleasure-crazed, pride-filled, possession-minded, power-denying sons of Satan? Must we fall in with the crowd of worldly clones? Must we keep in step with the Romans just because we live in Rome? No, no, never!

By the same token, shouldn't we demonstrate our love for God by separating from His enemies: *"... whosoever therefore will be a friend of the world is the enemy of God"* (James 4:4) ... *"Love not the world, neither the things that are in the world. If any man love the world, the love of the Father is not in him"* (1 John 2:15). Shouldn't we, as sons of God, hate the world's ways so much that we ache inside until we set our faces against the icy winds of conformity? Shouldn't we be so repulsed by its godless manner that we dare to swim against the raging currents of conventionality? Shouldn't we be compelled by the Spirit within to keep ourselves unspotted from the world's iniquities, *"Choosing rather to suffer affliction with the people of God, than to enjoy the pleasures of sin for a season"* (Hebrews 11:25)? Yes, yes, forever!

Yes, for our Lord commands it. Yes, for our sanctification demands it.

Sanctification potentially crucifies the old sin nature, but even this powerful act of faith will not keep the sinful impulses under subjection if we allow the old man to run with his former playmates and if we provide him with outlets for the perpetuation of his uncontrolled lusts and pride. By exposing ourselves to the world's impurities, seeds of flesh are re-sown in our hearts, the old man and his passions take root again and, inevitably, burst forth as sin. If we do not separate from the world, the old nature will not remain dead; it will not be put off for long. Our sanctification will be lost as lust and pride creep back in and take dominion over our lives once again.

So, in everything we do, we must ask ourselves if it be of God or of the world; does it cater to our flesh or feed our spiritual new man; does it fuel our lusts and pride, or is it bearing the fruits of holiness. In every relationship, in every involvement and every association within the world system (be it secular or religious), if toward God and His purity it is not leading, from it we must separate.

In a world full of an unimaginable array of allurements, the list of this world's offensive activities is obviously enormous. Each of us must examine ourselves for the culprits that would hinder our own quest for holiness. Even so, we would implore us all to separate or come out of three particular damaging institutions: The apostate church, Socialism, Capitalism.

THE APOSTATE CHURCH

The Word and the Spirit compel us to withdraw from every religious order that does not teach holiness. Without holiness, none of us will see God, but more than that, all of our religious exercises turn out as nothing more than form with no power, knowledge with no truth, power with no godliness. That kind of religion makes no substantive change in our lives and no valid contribution to the kingdom of God at large. That kind of hypocrisy makes organized religion as it was in the days of our Lord, one of the greatest deterrents to spiritual growth in the entire world system.

False prophets pervade the hierarchy of organized religion. Consequently, God's true sheep hardly find pasture for their hungry souls anymore: *"My people hath been lost sheep: their shepherds have caused them to go astray, they have turned them away on the mountains: they have gone from mountain to hill, they have forgotten their restingplace"* (Jeremiah 50:6). George Warnock explains it this way: "God's sheep are longing for true guidance and true leadership, but their hearts grow weary and their souls become dry and thirsty as they go from one pasture to another looking for true rest ... Eventually many of them simply give up in despair and either settle down in some ecclesiastical structure or withdraw completely from anything that bears any semblance to a meaningful fellowship of the Body of Christ."[52]

Two thousand years ago, God's people were likewise starving for the meat of His Word. So, God raised up a true prophet from outside the tainted religious establishment. His name was John. Speaking of the "wilderness" man and his unorthodox ordination, David Wilkerson said, "The Holy Spirit bypassed the entire religious system, the rabbinical schools, the educated Pharisees and scribes, and even the highest officials of the church and sent the true word to a man of God shut up in the wilderness. The word came to John, to a man outside every religious body of that day, to a man educated by the Holy Spirit alone. The religious big shots, those pious church officials, had not a single word from the Lord. They could drone on for hours exhorting dead Scriptures, but they had nothing fresh and life-giving from the throne of God. But John! He was non-materialistic, separated, God-consumed, and possessed by a single vision—the coming Christ."[53]

In these last days, God is once again going outside the established religious structure to find prophets for His people. The call to repentance and righteousness will be heard once more, but not from within the denominational network. As David Wilkerson so succinctly puts it, "It is not going to be a denomination that delivers the Word of the Lord to this cursed generation ... While the angels of the apocalypse go forth to smite the earth, denominations and religious leaders will be hard at work protecting their interests and strengthening their authority, drawing up bylaws and resolutions."[54]

God will once again have leaders who have no Lord but Him, no role models but His Son, no teachers but His Holy Spirit. God will once again have genuine prophets with enough courage to sound the trumpet of impending judgment, enough concern *"... to warn the wicked from his way ... "* (Ezekiel 33:8), enough conviction to thunder Hell, fire, and brimstone. God will once again have submissive shepherds who love and feed His sheep: *"And I will give you pastors according to mine heart, which shall feed you with knowledge and understanding"* (Jeremiah 3:15). God will once again have talented teachers who shun success, who make of themselves no reputation, who walk in meekness, who have not learned Him in a seminary but, like the lowly Nazarene, know Him on an intimate, one-to-one basis. God will once again have a royal priesthood, a godly lineage through whom He can define the way of holiness: *"And they shall teach my people the difference between the holy and profane, and cause them to discern between the unclean and the clean"* (Ezekiel 44:23).

God will once again have an independent voice to which hungry souls can turn for a pure word from Heaven. Even now, He is raising up prophets who have been shut in with Him, broken, and transformed by a vision of His holiness. Saints do have a choice again! Let every one with a hunger for God flee from the harlotry of organized religion. Let every one with a heart for holiness depart from the host of false prophets.

SOCIALISM

What is wrong with socialism, some say. What is wrong with everyone sharing, more or less equally, this world's goods, instead of some few having most of the wealth while masses barely get by or simply die of starvation? Sounds good on paper, but, in reality, socialism is a gateway drug to irresponsibility and to the draining of man's incentives to invent, sacrifice, and out-produce in the marketplace. It silently enslaves its followers as they become addicted to the handouts and the parental type cradle-to-grave care promised by the state. Never mind that in exchange for the ballot-bought security, the victim has lost his soul and guaranteed his allegiance to socialism's soon coming, clench-fisted cousin, communism—the battering ram of Antichrist.

Christians should especially be wary of the seductive promises of socialism to care for this world's less fortunate. As Christians, such should be our goal as well, but we do so out of love and not as part of some state-coerced taxation and redistribution packages.

Sadly, the love of humanism's state-sponsored equalization programs has won the hearts of many who call themselves Christians. Christian liberals, especially, fall prey to the pervasive doctrines of socialism. Lacking a life-changing relationship with God, Christian socialists are readily seduced by promises of human liberation and emancipation from repressive institutions, especially economic ones. Devoid of any spiritual insight into God's Word, they accept the socialist lie that the evils of the world are not the result of man's sinful nature, but are products of institutions whose removal would bring happiness and allow the expression of man's true essence through creative freedom. Since the primary institution of evil is capitalism, they would eliminate it by ending all private business and replacing it with public (social) ownership (socialism does not restore private ownership, which capitalism strips away from the average citizen, but rather passes possession to the state to hold in common all land and all means of production).

Christian socialists feel that nothing less than the death of all wealth will correct the mammoth inequities in today's economic structures. Well do they mimic their humanist masters: "extreme disproportions in wealth, income, and economic growth should be reduced on a worldwide basis."[55] Well do they echo the sentiments of their former Russian role model, Mikhail Gorbachev: "In a future world community that will be different from the one we have today, we will have to work together again to find ways of distributing wealth among all the countries of the world."[56]

Christian socialists go so far as to teach that true Christianity is, in fact, Marxism and that Christ was a political activist bent on overthrowing any government or economic system that oppressed the poor. Consequently, they, like their secular brothers, attempt to aid the poor by imposing constraints on economic and political freedom. Ironically, Christian socialists endorse the use of force to fulfill the demands of Christian love and to create a better social order. To achieve their dreams of economic equality, they allow the state to assume full power and dictatorial control.

Socialism is obviously anti-Christian and must be forsaken by all who desire to walk in holiness before God. They must turn from it with all their heart, for socialism, no matter how cleverly disguised in religious vernacular, is still humanism expressed in economic terms, and as we have seen, humanism is clearly antithetical to all that God stands for. Consequently, God will accept no man's religious exercises until he acknowledges his personal accountability for sin, the absolute necessity of repentance, and the eternal consequences of rebellion against His propitiatory work at Calvary.

18
COMING OUT OF BABYLON

Christian socialists excluded, believers living in capitalist countries have been conditioned over the years to accept the lie that Christianity is quite compatible with capitalism. In fact, the profit-oriented capitalistic system has evolved over the centuries into such a well-conceived snare that it has won virtually unanimous Christian allegiance to a Babylon force that stands in stark contrast to values for which saints throughout the ages have given their lives.

As God foreknew that capitalism would, in the last days, enlarge Babylon's sphere of influence to include most of Christianity, He issued a solemn warning to end-time saints—*"... Come out of her, my people, that ye be not partakers of her sins, and that ye receive not of her plagues"* (Revelation 18:4). Because Christians who sleep with the Harlot soon behave like her, a holy God must insist that His people separate from the sin-drenched system. A decree directed to Jews captive in ancient Babylon applies equally well to latter-day saints enslaved in her modern counterpart—*"Depart ye, depart ye, go ye out from thence, touch no unclean thing; go ye out of the midst of her; be ye clean, that bear the vessels of the LORD"* (Isaiah 52:11).

While God's holiness demands separation, His love makes provision for the exodus. Through Isaiah, God promised to accompany His children out of the city of merchants, assuring them that their departure need not be with frenzied haste or restless frustration—*"For ye shall not go out with haste, nor go by flight: for the LORD will go before you; and the God of Israel will be your reward"* (Isaiah 52:12). Through Micah, God gave latter-day saints not only the assurance of divine escort away from worldly attachments (including Babylon) but a pledge of supernatural intervention in their quest for purity—*"The breaker is come up before them: they have broken up, and have passed through the gate, and are gone out by it: and their king shall pass before them, and the LORD on the head of them"* (Micah 2:13).

Two thousand years ago, God intervened in man's hopeless, Old Covenant struggles with impurity and mixture (Romans Chapter 7 describes Paul's conflict with sin under the Law) by sending the "breaker" forth—a Hebrew name for the Messiah—to remove sin's restraining walls and set the captive free (John 8:32-36). Christ, in dying, also shattered all barriers separating man from God so the two could become as one in a harmonious and holy New Covenant relationship based on love and obedience rather than laws and sacrifice. The potential for oneness occurred when Jesus, as the breaker, passed through the gate, suffering outside the camp for sanctification (a work of grace which embodies the power to separate believers from their sins and set them apart for their God)— *"Wherefore Jesus also, that He might sanctify the people with His own blood, suffered without the gate"* (Hebrews 13:12).

We would fail miserably, however, in our efforts to separate from the world and become one with the Father if we did not first appropriate Christ's sanctifying power in our own lives. Any serious confrontation with sin and worldliness must begin with Christ and an association of ourselves with Him in His death and resurrection. This mystical union of saved and Savior occurs as we, by faith, consider ourselves dead with Him, thereby crucifying (in theory) the old man of the flesh with his affections and lusts. The old man slain, in principle, he must then be subdued in practice. This constant battle could never be won without another act of faith, that of uniting with Christ in His resurrection unto newness of life. Matching faith with works, we nurture our resurrected new man and put off the crucified old man in reality by yielding to God, obeying His commandments (Romans 6) and choosing to *"... Walk in the Spirit, and ye shall not to fulfill the lust of the flesh"* (Galatians 5:16).

The old man is further subdued as we utilize sanctification's power— actually, Christ's power, since we are one with Him—to physically separate from the world. The breaker has crushed the walls surrounding all worldly establishments, particularly Babylon, but it is up to us to walk through the gate and join Him outside the camp of convenience, comfort, and security—*"Let us go forth therefore unto Him without the camp, bearing His reproach. For here have we no continuing city, but we seek one to come"* (Hebrews 13:13-14). It is up to us to choose, like Moses, *"... rather to suffer affliction with the people of God, than to enjoy the pleasures of sin for a season; esteeming the reproach of Christ greater riches than the treasures in Egypt ..."* (Hebrews 11:25-26). It is up to us to separate from all elements of society—economical, political, religious—that are compromised and mixed with the world—*"... come out from among them, and be ye separate, saith the Lord ..."* (2 Corinthians 6:17) and *"... have no fellowship with the unfruitful works of darkness ..."* (Ephesians 5:11). It is up to us to withdraw from those, saint or sinner, who are bound by their lust of the eye to capitalistic greed, who actually believe that gain is godliness—*"Perverse disputings of men of corrupt minds, and destitute of the truth, supposing that gain is godliness: from such withdraw thyself"* (1 Timothy 6:5).

It is also up to us to avoid the Beast when we break out of Babylon's camp. Many professing Christians who recognize the evils of chasing after gain have withdrawn from capitalism, only to fall prey to the perverse doctrines of "Christian Socialism." Because they left Babylon of their own volition, without the conviction of God, these so-called believers have unwittingly entered the camp of the next world leader—Antichrist. Because they leave in ever-increasing numbers, the most popular version of Marxism today, outside Russia and the like, is the humanistic interpretation—that adopted by Christian Socialists.

Coming out of Babylon and jumping onto the Beast (no matter how cleverly disguised with religious vernacular) is not God's solution to the inequities that exist in our world. The plight of the poor is not erased by forced economic redistribution and by overthrowing institutions alleged to cause poverty and oppression. Nor is there created a philanthropic desire to feed the poor simply by synthesizing Marxism and Christianity. This blend of Heaven and Hell is little more than a worthless mixture of satanic self-serving lies and a perversion of Scripture portraying Christ as a political activist determined to overthrow any government or economic system that oppressed the poor. Consequently, Christian Socialists, like their secular brothers, attempt to aid the poor by imposing constraints on economic and political freedom. Ironically, they endorse the use of force to fulfill the demands of Christian love and create a better social order.

Another incongruence in socialist philosophy is their use of the state to achieve economic equality, in effect, allowing the government to assume the role of the displaced and hated corporate entity. Which proves one thing—neither economic structure offers true freedom. Until the beast slays the Harlot, there will be either exorbitant consolidation of power by giant corporations or by the government. There will be either a dictatorship of the capitalists or a dictatorship of the state. There will be either parity in the market place favoring those with capital (money, property, resources), or there will be political allocations of resources biased in favor of the elite. There will be economic control of prices and commodities marked by freedom to choose within certain economic constraints, e.g., prices, employment opportunities, availability of jobs. Or, there will be statist manipulation of resources and people with a group of omniscient planners to forecast the future, set prices, and control production.

Faced with the options, believers have but one choice—to come out of both economic systems and to work (even if for less money) within the constraints of private enterprise free of the Babylon influence. God did not call us to convert the world's political and economic establishments through deeds of the flesh (Satan forever tempts man to solve his own problems without God and to strive for utopia by his own efforts). Nor does He wish that we support either as correct in opposition to the other. God wants to change the world through the heart of man. Rather than attack symptoms, He does war with the root cause, man's fallen nature. God's supreme interest has always been the man, not the institution. He has always advocated departure from rather than modification to the existing world structure. The kingdom of God is not of earthly compositions. We do not wrestle against flesh and blood but *"... against principalities, against powers, against the rulers of the darkness of this world, against spiritual wickedness in high places"* (Ephesians 6:12). We do not fight the established order—we leave it!

CONTENTMENT

A bonafide break with Babylon must include an effective treatment of covetousness, a major cause of our captivity. Departure is blocked until "things" no longer possess us and we no longer look on them as our possession—*"... and they that buy, as though they possessed not"* (1 Corinthians 7:30). Freedom forever alludes us until, like Achan, our covetousness is killed (not curbed), our love for "things" subdued, and our "grasping" brought under subjection.

The key to victory over this lustful craving of the eye rests in our willingness to accept the status quo—*"Let your conversation be without covetousness; and be content with such things as ye have ..."* (Hebrews 13:5). No matter how much we have, we want more until we learn Paul's secret: contentment—*"... for I have learned, in whatsoever state I am, therewith to be content. I know both how to be abased, and I know how to abound: every where and in all things I am instructed both to be full and to be hungry, both to abound and to suffer need"* (Philippians 4:11-12).

Without contentment, covetousness dominates our lives, and like so many Christians, we eagerly accept the false teaching that gain is godliness. Gain is not godliness, as Paul argued, *"But godliness with contentment is great gain. For we brought nothing into this world, and it is certain we can carry nothing out. And having food and raiment let us be therewith content"* (1 Timothy 6:6-8).

PASSION FOR CHRIST

Christ also recommended contentment as an antidote for covetousness, but with it He prescribed additional therapy for the dreaded disease of the eye: *"... Take no thought for your life, what ye shall eat; neither for the body, what ye shall put on ... And seek not ye what ye shall eat, or what ye shall drink, neither be ye of doubtful mind. For all these things do the nations of the world seek after ... But rather seek ye the kingdom of God; and all these things shall be added unto you"* (Luke 12:22, 29-31).

To overcome covetousness, contentment must be reinforced with a passion for Christ. Conquering the spirit of acquisition and breaking out of Babylon involves more than selling prized possessions, discarding stocks and investment portfolios, quitting a job. It is more than turning from the Harlot and her ways. It is also a complete turn to God and His ways. It is pursuing Him with the quality portion of our time, talents, and energy. It is a heartfelt desire to please God and to obey His Word at any cost. It is a yearning to emulate the life of Christ, to be a true expression of the Head, to conform to the image of the Son of God. It is living in the resurrection realm *"... dead indeed unto sin, but alive unto God through Jesus Christ our Lord"* (Romans 6:11). It is holiness.

Only those with a passion for Christ and His holiness will join Him outside the camp. They gladly give up all, if need be, for they know that "things" keep them from enjoying full fellowship with their Lord and from knowing Him and the power of His resurrection. Paul recognized this, for he admitted, *"... I have suffered the loss of all things, and do count them but dung, that I may win Christ, and be found in Him ... That I may know Him, and the power of His resurrection, and the fellowship of His sufferings ..."* (Philippians 3:8-10).

This desire to surrender everything for God comes only after we have glimpsed His glory and recognized the utter worthlessness of our selves. When we have stood in His presence, like Paul, stripped of all fleshly ambitions and aspirations, then self becomes nothing, and He becomes not just first in our lives but everything, not just the center but all in all. In His majestic presence, the things of this world lose their value. Earthly accomplishments shrink to a pitiful heap of dirty rags. Nothing else matters but Him.

One who has stood in His presence, still longing for an ever-expanding revelation of His greatness and purity, will desire no material gain. He is blind to everything not of God: *"Seeing many things, but thou observest not ..."* (Isaiah 42:20). "Things" are as refuse to him because he travels this life as a pilgrim looking for a city whose builder and maker is God. As he has nothing down here to lose and everything up there to gain, he naturally can join Paul in saying, *"For to me to live is Christ, and to die is gain"* (Philippians 1:21). Nothing moves him except a longing to be with Christ, for then and only then does he meet face to face the object of his affection.

TRUST

For more than 5900 years, man survived without the layers of security blankets that now cover the Western world. Yet, in the last century, a self-preservation craze has swept over affluent First-World countries. Saint and sinner alike seem possessed by a preparedness paranoia, convinced that economic calamity haunts and will destroy them unless shielded by an array of insurance, medical, and retirement packages.

Covetousness drives Christians to Babylon, but their craving for security guarantees a lifelong relationship with the Harlot. Welfare capitalism caters to their dreams of uninterrupted prosperity and provision, but in return, it asks believers to substitute servitude for freedom, paychecks and welfare checks for faith in God. The cost of necessities (food, health care, housing), which the state eagerly doles out to its poorer and older citizens, are driven inexcusably high; government costs, in turn, skyrocket and, along with them, taxes. Welfare recipients are bound to the state, and workers are tied to their jobs to pay for oppressive taxes and overpriced goods and services. Furthermore, to protect against all interruptions to their current lifestyles, working Americans have saved, insured, and invested in every security package known to man. Dependence on God, family, and church has been replaced by protection plans purchased from and with money earned in the capitalistic system. No longer can we as a people proclaim, "In God we trust." In our pride and self-sufficiency, we neither love nor obey, much less trust, the One who ultimately makes all our provision possible.

Yet, breaking out of Babylon is impossible until we learn to trust God and reject man-made security blankets as we would a bed that is too short or cover that is too narrow—*"For the bed is shorter than that a man can stretch himself on it: and the covering narrower than that he can wrap himself in it"* (Isaiah 28:20). Only then do we overcome self-reliance and dependence on the flesh-driven institutions of capitalism. Only then can we rest securely in God, confident in His desire and ability to care for us, confident that our supernatural supplier will meet every need. Only then can we say with David, *"I have been young, and now am old; yet have I not seen the righteous forsaken, nor his seed begging bread"* (Psalm 37:25).

This confidence is the very thing God expects of His people when confronted with a choice between Himself and a system whose principles are so self-centered that they mock even the most feeble references to trust in the Almighty—*"Blessed is the man that trusteth in the LORD ... "* (Jeremiah 17:7). God is waiting for a people who will wait for Him to provide and protect—*"And therefore will the LORD wait, that He may be gracious unto you, and therefore will he be exalted, that he may have mercy upon you: for the LORD is a God of judgment: blessed are all they that wait for him"* (Isaiah 30:18). God is longing to fill with peace those who focus their attention on spiritual matters rather than scheming to solve problems through their own abilities—*"Thou wilt keep him in perfect peace, whose mind is stayed on thee: because he trusteth in thee"* (Isaiah 26:3). God is yearning to bestow spiritual blessings on those who live moment to moment rather than securing their future through strategic planning, those who live each day grateful for God's provision and trustful that He will do likewise tomorrow. God is searching for others like Shadrach, Meshach, and Abednego who will trust Him for all in spite of all, who will "yield their bodies" to the fiery furnace of deprivation and despair to prove that trust.

Many, reasoning in their natural minds, will question whether anyone has enough faith to cast aside the Harlot's security and rest confidently in God. Who, they ask, is strong enough to stand when everyone else is bowing to the golden idols of materialism and self-sufficiency? Indeed, *"... who is sufficient for these things?"* (2 Corinthians 2:16).

None of us is sufficient within our own strength and by our own faith, but, through God, we have the resources to reject man's programs and promises of perpetuity—*"And such trust have we through Christ to God-ward; Not that we are sufficient of ourselves to think any thing as of ourselves; but our sufficiency is of God"* (2 Corinthians 3:4-5). Those abiding in Christ have the added luxury of Christ's indwelling faith enabling them to fight when others run, to conquer when others surrender—*"... the life which I now live in the flesh I live by the faith of the Son of God ... "* (Galatians 2:20). *"... not having mine own righteousness, which is of the law, but that which is through the faith of Christ, the righteousness which is of God by faith"* (Philippians 3:9). God will even help give us faith by putting us in positions (if we refuse to put ourselves there) that force us to trust Him—*"... we were pressed out of measure, above strength, insomuch that we despaired even of life: But we had the sentence of death in ourselves, that we should not trust in ourselves, but in God ... in whom we trust that he will yet deliver us"* (2 Corinthians 1:8-10).

Notwithstanding the sufficiency and longsuffering of God to woo and sometimes push us into a trusting relationship with Himself, there comes a time when He responds with judgment to our persistent refusal to rely on Him. God is good, but He is also severe (Romans 11:22) so, when unction does not sever our binding relationship with His enemies, force will. Christians who turn to man for protection (physical as well as financial) are cursed of God—*"... Cursed be the man that trusteth in man, and maketh flesh his arm ..."* (Jeremiah 17:5). Christians who refuse to break their alliance with capitalist-backed security programs will fall with the Harlot as did Israel when she aligned with Egypt thinking Egyptian horses, horsemen, and chariots would secure her from Assyrian attack. God condemned both parties to failure:

> "Woe to them that go down to Egypt for help; and stay on horses, and trust in chariots, because they are many; and in horsemen, because they are very strong; but they look not unto the Holy One of Israel, neither seek the LORD! ... Now the Egyptians are men, and not God; and their horses flesh, and not spirit. When the LORD shall stretch out his hand, both he that helpeth shall fall, and he that is helped shall fall down, and they all shall fail together" (Isaiah 31:1, 3).

THE CHRISTIAN SOLUTION

The Bible is not an economics book, but it does offer a course in financial priorities and pursuits. It does furnish instructions for man's financial interactions with man. It does provide economic absolutes without which man would forever flounder in the depths of doubt, indecision, and irreconcilable differences, e.g., capitalism versus socialism. It does supply solutions to extreme variances in the appropriation of this world's goods.

The Bible clearly teaches, and we have shown, that neither capitalism nor socialism represents the Christian ideal of "Do unto others as you would have them do unto you." The peaceful capitalistic exchange of goods and services errs in that it says, "If you do something good for me, I'll do something good for you." On the other hand, the violent socialistic transfer fails, for it says, "Unless you do something good for me, I'll do something bad to you."

Christianity offers the only suitable alternative to both worldly economic systems. It does not reserve its blessings for those who meet corporate behavior and productivity standards. It does not threaten with physical abuse those who fail to perform according to government expectations. Nor does it, through the state, forcefully take from producers and distribute to non-producers. Instead, it asks the possessor of capital to voluntarily share from his abundance with those less fortunate than he—
"Give to him that asketh thee, and from him that would borrow of thee turn not thou away" (Matthew 5:42). Granted, not all poverty results from capitalistic

exploitation, but assuredly, poverty remains because those with money are generally unwilling to share enough of it. By the same token, if sharing were carried out according to Biblical mandate, the state would be relieved of its coercive duties to wring funds from reluctant capitalists and redistribute them to the poor.

Christianity would accomplish what capitalism, in its greed, is unwilling to do and socialism, in its godless quest for power, is unable to do. It would offer relief to the poor, for it encourages giving as proof of God's abiding love—*"... whoso hath this world's good, and seeth his brother have need, and shutteth up his bowels of compassion from him, how dwelleth the love of God in him? My little children, let us not love in word, neither in tongue; but in deed and in truth"* (1 John 3:17-18). It would eliminate famine in the midst of plenty, for it directs its member to voluntarily give even to the point of economic equality—*"... I mean not that other men be eased, and ye burdened: But by an equality, that now at this time your abundance may be a supply for their want, that their abundance also may be a supply for your want: that there may be equality; As it is written, he that had gathered much had nothing over; and he that had gathered little had no lack"* (2 Corinthians 8:13-15). [This in no way implies that God condones laziness or that everyone should quit work and lie around waiting for Christ to return. Paul, when confronted with this slothful attitude, declared, *"... if any would not work, neither should he eat"* (2 Thessalonians 3:10)].

To attain equality, the first Christian church went so far as to adopt a lifestyle in which everyone *"... sold their possessions and goods, and parted them to all men, as every man had need"* (Acts 2:45). *"... neither said any of them that ought of the things which he possessed was his own; but they had all things common ... Neither was there any among them that lacked: for as many as were possessors of lands or houses sold them, and brought the prices of the things that were sold, And laid them down at the apostles' feet: and distribution was made unto every man according as he had need"* (Acts 4:32, 34-35).

Christians today do not necessarily need to pool their resources in collective societies, but they are still commanded to share with each other. If everyone who claimed Christ as their Savior would give, with parity as their goal, many of the wounds inflicted by capitalistic greed and socialistic force would be healed; profit-taking would dry up, the competitive drive to excel would disappear, forced redistribution would be stifled. And equally important, sharing would create financial interdependence among believers making mass exodus from Babylon a possibility that hardly exists when everyone pursues his own self-interest.

Regardless of the mode of separation, collectively or as individual efforts, God wants His people out of Babylon. Although Christ removed the walls surrounding the sinister city, none will leave until they sense the impact of her corruption on their lives, until their covetousness is killed by contentment and zeal for God, until their self-sufficiency is destroyed by trust, until their financial independence is eliminated by sharing. Satisfied with the little they have, seeking God with all their heart confident that He will supply every need, sharing from a heart of love—these are the ones who will break out of the Harlot system. *"Come out of her, my people."*

19
ALIVE UNTO GOD

*S*elf is theoretically brought under subjection in sanctification, the flesh cleansed in practice during purification, and the world with its many lusts forsaken with separation. Unfortunately, these works of grace are not within themselves enough to ensure a holy walk before God. Sanctification alone will not keep the self subdued. Purification in a vacuum will not keep sin out of the heart. Separation by itself will not keep the world at bay. Without consecration, other moves toward God would be left wanting; the self would resurrect itself, the flesh would rekindle its fiery lusts, the world would rush back in.

The void created by sanctification, purification and separation must be filled with a commitment to walk with God, a clinging unto Him as one that is *"… dead indeed unto sin, but alive unto God through Jesus Christ our Lord"* (Romans 6:11). Death to self and the world must be accompanied by a resurrection unto "newness of life," a literal putting on of the new man of the Spirit: *"If ye then be risen with Christ … put on the new man, which is renewed in knowledge after the image of him that created him"* (Colossians 3:1, 10). Indeed, the crisis of crucifixion must be answered by the renewal of resurrection, ascending with Christ into the heavenlies, there to consecrate all in His hallowed presence.

The consecrated new man is, of necessity, a spiritual man. In other words, he walks in the Spirit. In the Spirit, he nurtures his abiding relationship in Christ: *"There is therefore now no condemnation to them which are in*

Christ Jesus, who walk not after the flesh, but after the Spirit" (Romans 8:1). In the Spirit, he instinctively denies the flesh of its many lusts: *"... Walk in the Spirit, and ye shall not fulfill the lust of the flesh"* (Galatians 5:16). In the Spirit, sins of the flesh fade into the forgettable past; the new man doesn't have to continuously sin, then drag himself back to God hoping against hope that he will be forgiven just one more time.

Encompassing the whole of a Christian's walk before his Heavenly Father, consecration then becomes the bond that cements his union with God, the means by which he further perfects his holiness in the fear of God: *"Blessed are they that keep His testimonies, and that seek him with the whole heart. They also do no iniquity ..."* (Psalm 119:2-3). As such, consecration is interwoven with purification and separation to form three distinct, yet indivisible and overlapping processes in the saint's approach to God's holiness. Together, they seal his sanctification as the experiential crucifixion of the old man and subsequent resurrection of the new.

Yet, in spite of its sin-delivering simplicity, many Christians miss the mark on this very issue of consecration. They conveniently cast it aside as an unnecessary elective for the few who choose to live that way. Any Scripture that speaks of total sacrifice and crucifixion of the flesh, they either ignore or spiritualize into anemia. Outwardly religious, their hearts have drifted far from God. They will believe in Him and testify of Him, but they will not waste themselves for Him; they will not give back to God that which was lost to sin—their very lives.

It seems that people haven't changed much since Isaiah complained, *"... there is none that calleth upon thy name, that stirreth up himself to take hold of thee ..."* (Isaiah 64:7), or since Paul levied his indictment against man's slackness toward God: *"For all seek their own, not the things which are Jesus Christ's"* (Philippians 2:21). Many in our day are so entangled with materialism, pleasure, and career that they will not empty themselves in a poured-out life of sacrificial service.

For a time, even the disciples sacrificed everything but themselves to follow Christ. Flesh and its carnal ambitions still ruled on the throne of their hearts. Until Christ's death, they expected Him to establish an earthly kingdom so they could rule with Him as princes over the house of Israel.

Then, somewhere between the cross and Pentecost, the disciples died to self and emptied out all their flesh-driven dreams. Then and only then did they become useful to God as witnesses of His sacrificial love and redeeming grace. Then, rather than pursuing earthly kingdoms, they would surrender all their worldly ambitions to follow Christ into the ascended life of the resurrection realm. Then, rather than deny their Lord, they would deny themselves, gladly giving their lives in exchange for the glorious calling of God in Christ Jesus.

LIVING SACRIFICE

Like the disciples, we, too, enter the resurrection realm by dying. So, for those who have been crucified with Christ (sanctified), the door to consecration is already open. The theoretical death of the old man has conditioned their hearts to accept the literal sacrifice of self in the realm of the transfigured.

Regrettably, most Christians associate death with the Old Covenant, extending it into the New only as far as the Cross. There they stop. Christ did all the suffering and, by His grace, they are saved and secured from all harm to body, mind, soul, and selfish intent.

However, that's not God's way for this dispensation of gracious giving, sacrificial living and submissive death.

For us, God has prepared a new way, a way which begins at the Cross and extends into the holy confines of intimacy with Himself. Under the Law, this intimacy with God was precluded by religious works of the flesh. The Old Covenant *"... ordinances of divine service ... stood only in meats and drinks, and divers washings, and carnal ordinances, imposed on them until the time of reformation"* (Hebrews 9:1, 10). But the way into the "holiest of all" was barred: *"The Holy Ghost this signifying, that the way into the holiest of all was not yet made manifest, while as the first tabernacle was yet standing"* (Hebrews 9:8). Then Christ, by His own blood, dissolved dead ordinances and prepared a passage into the holiest place. In the holiest place, we find this new way of conquering (not covering) sin. There, we find the living way, the consecrated way: *"Having therefore, brethren, boldness to enter into the holiest by the blood of Jesus, by a new and living way, which he hath consecrated for us ..."* (Hebrews 10:19-20).

Few, if any, would argue that entry into the divine way is infinitely easier under the New Covenant than was the case under the Old. Who could deny that salvation and forgiveness of sins is simpler by God's grace and

His redemptive work at Calvary? Who could deny that the new way is a better way with one sacrifice for sin, one faith in that atoning sacrifice, one reckoning of ourselves dead with Christ and alive unto God? Who could deny that the new way is an intimate way with Christ in us and we in Him, wedding us to the sacrificial Lamb, affixing us to the body of Christ right here on earth?

And who could deny that the new way is a spontaneous way with loving submission rather than forced servitude?

But, for those who now enter the fold through faith, repentance and confession, the way within is intensely more difficult: *"Because strait is the gate, and narrow is the way, which leadeth unto life, and few there be that find it"* (Matthew 7:14). Looking and lusting are now as sinful as the adulterous act itself. The will to sin is just as damning as the deed. Unholy motives condemn as quickly as the actual affair. And now, rather than offering animals to atone for sin, we must allow ourselves to be slain upon the sacrificial altar of personal surrender: *"I beseech you therefore, brethren, by the mercies of God, that ye present your bodies a living sacrifice, holy, acceptable unto God, which is your reasonable service"* (Romans 12:1).

We have been liberated from the ceremonial aspects of the Mosaic Law. The system of ordinances and sacrifices has been discarded, no longer needed for entry into the family of God, no longer indicative of godly behavior. As a result, the only sacrifice the Father now accepts is that of ourselves. As Christ died, so too must we, not to be forgiven of our sins but to grow in grace, to abide in Christ, to overcome the flesh, to find holiness.

Our salvation cost Christ His life; it will cost us ours, too. As Paul told the Corinthian believers, *"... know ye not that ... ye are not your own? For ye are bought with a price: therefore glorify God in your body, and in your spirit, which are God's"* (1 Corinthians 6:19-20). We are "bought" with a price; no costlier offering could have been made than the Son of God Himself. Christ's death, His shed blood, entitles Him to claim us as His own, even His "purchased possession." And it entitles Him, as we are no longer our own, to ask that we give our lives back to Him in consecrated service. Because He died for us and purchased us out of sin's slave market, we present back to Him the only acceptable gift we have—ourselves.

God, therefore, desires the whole man—body, mind, and soul—to be surrendered and subjected unto Him. As A.W. Tozer explains, He must be our all: "The true believer owns Christ as his All in All without reservation. He also includes all of himself, leaving no part of his being unaffected by the revolutionary transaction."[57] And, God must have our all: "Before the judgment seat of Christ my service will be judged not by how much I have done but by how much I could have done. In God's sight my giving is measured not by how much I have given but by how much I could have given and how much I had left after I made my gift ... No man gives at all until he has given all."[58]

God seeks consecrated service with man at His disposal rather than, as many suppose, religion that would have God at man's disposal. I like Paul's description of Christ's dedication: *"For in that he died, he died unto sin once: but in that he liveth, he liveth unto God"* (Romans 6:10). Because Christ died in our stead, we should, in turn, commit all of ourselves unto Him: *"And that he died for all, that they which live should not henceforth live unto themselves, but unto Him which died for them ..."* (2 Corinthians 5:15).

As alive unto God, we recognize His sovereignty and our subservience and that we are love slaves to the Almighty, the omnipotent and jealous God. We acknowledge our true worth and that we have value only because God values us, that only by His grace were we purchased out of sin's bondage and allowed into the family of God as heirs and joint-heirs with Jesus Christ.

As heirs of a celestial inheritance, anything that even smells of flesh is discarded. Like Paul, we gladly give up and consider as dung all fleshly accomplishments and acquisitions and worldly acclaim, grasping instead for more of God's grace and goodness, pressing instead for the mark of total perfection in Christ. Like Paul, we dispel all notions of success and position down here, praying instead that we may be found in Him at His return. Like Paul, we surrender all things previously considered gain and forget about them. And when, like Paul, we have given all, endured all, and forsaken all to follow Christ, then we can truthfully say that we love Him with all our hearts.

To please Christ, to see Him, serve Him, love Him—nothing else matters but Him and what we know of Him. When we find this Pearl of great price, worldly possessions mean nothing; our old plans and dreams mean nothing. All are gladly cast aside so that Christ, the Pearl, becomes not just first in our lives but everything in our lives, not just the center but all in all.

LOVING SACRIFICE

An extension of the New Covenant relationship (Christ in us and we in Him) is the new law of Christ. This new commandment springs from God's everlasting love, love so powerful that He gave His only begotten Son that we, too, might be called the sons of God (1 John 3:1). In return, God requires that we *"... walk in love, as Christ also hath loved us, and hath given himself for us an offering ..."* (Ephesians 5:2).

Moses' law demanded love; the new law is love. Therefore, in the resurrection realm, less and less is it a question of dead rules and timid confessions, but more of an all-consuming love for God. That much love for the Heavenly Father makes all others secondary: *"He that loveth father or mother more than me is not worthy of me ..."* (Matthew 10:37). At the same time, such vigorous love for God makes Christianity not so much a religion of rules (although these abound) but of a mindset in harmony with God. Such love distinguishes true Christianity as a union of man's purpose and will with those of the Father, a oneness of his character and conduct with those of the Son, and a wedding of his thoughts and feelings with those of the Holy Ghost.

Therefore, we do not surrender all that once we held dear merely for the sake of punishment, or endurance, or rebellion against the world order. We do it because we love God. If we truly love God, nothing will suit us but Him. Freely we have received forgiveness and adoption; with the same spontaneity, we should lovingly yield ourselves back to God in consecrated service. Because we are "bought with a price," this giving of ourselves back to Him flows unforced from a thankful heart, a heart that gladly obeys the Master's commandment, *"... If any man will come after me, let him deny himself, and take up his cross, and follow me"* (Matthew 16:24).

Not only does sacrificial love bow joyfully to the demands of God, but it bends willingly for the rights and feelings of others. Those who would live in the resurrection realm extend their love to all men. They love because they know that man is loveable if for no other reason than that he is *"... made after the similitude of God"* (James 3:9). They love because the meek and lowly Christ within them suffered and died for the very ones who rejected and killed Him. They love because the same love that drove Christ to the cross *"... is shed abroad in our hearts by the Holy Ghost"* (Romans 5:5).

Those who would live in the resurrection realm must, like Paul, love even when they are not loved and give of themselves even when they receive nothing in return: *"And I will very gladly spend and be spent for you; though the more abundantly I love you, the less I be loved"* (2 Corinthians 12:15). Paul knew how difficult it would be, but he still encouraged the saints to follow his example of selfless devotion. He knew that in the loving sacrifice of themselves for others, the consecrated find true holiness: *"And the Lord make you to increase and abound in love one toward another, and toward all men, even as we do toward you: to the end he may stablish your hearts unblameable in holiness …"* (1 Thessalonians 3:12-13).

In spite of our attainments up the heights of holiness, true love demands that we regard ourselves as nothing, that we esteem others better than ourselves, that we seek another's welfare before our own: *"Charity [love] … vaunteth not itself … seeketh not her own …"* (1 Corinthians 13:4-5). Though we may be totally divorced from the world with no known sin in our lives, we may still err in our attitude, our haughtiness, and our lack of burden for those still chained to sin and worldliness. Flesh loves to be exalted, to be the greatest, and to be "holier than thou." But Christ said that he who would be the greatest must become the least. That is love.

LOVING SUBMISSION

According to humanist logic, all men are replaceable and, as such, have no particular part to play in life's cosmic drama. Christianity, on the other hand, teaches that each of us has a purpose in life and therefore becomes an integral part of its eventual outcome.

However, the will of God expresses itself not only in the purpose of our existence, but in the actual existence itself, even in our daily walk before God. God's intention for every believer goes beyond the call to teach, or preach or prophesy to the true manifestation of Christ to a deluded and dying world. To that end, we surrender ourselves to Him.

Those dead to self-will and alive unto God's will are raised up with a Heavenly vision and a purpose of heart that declares with Isaiah, *"… Here am I; send me"* (Isaiah 6:8). Like Paul, they press forward all their Christian lives in search of the fullness of God's divine intention for their lives: *"… if that I may apprehend that for which also I am apprehended of Christ Jesus"* (Philippians 3:12). They make Christ Lord of their lives, Lord of every interest, Lord of every intent, wholly committed, as was He, to doing the

Father's will.

Christ came to earth, single-minded in purpose: *"... I seek not mine own will, but the will of the Father which hath sent me"* (John 5:30). From that goal, He never departed, though popularity, power and prestige hounded Him throughout His ministry. Standing tall as our example, Christ was totally submitted, willing to suffer and die that God's will might be done through Him. Accordingly, He *"... made himself of no reputation ..."* (Philippians 2:7) though He easily could have. He established no earthly kingdom, though He easily could have. And, *"... he humbled himself, and became obedient unto death ..."* (Philippians 2:8), refusing to avoid it though He easily could have.

A similar obsession with God and His will may well gain us the reputation of being so Heavenly-minded that we are no earthly good. In a sense, that may be true, but doesn't our sanctification faith demand more than cursory glances in the Master's direction? Doesn't it compel us to see everything, as did Christ, from God's viewpoint, to make eternity judgments instead of time judgments? Don't those who are risen with Christ *"... seek those things which are above ..."* (Colossians 3:1)? Don't they naturally set their *"... affection on things above, not on things on the earth"* (Colossians 3:2)? And, aren't they unaffected by the lure of this world's charm, untainted by its many lusts, unmoved by its possessions—observing but not touching, using but not abusing, owning but not possessing (1 Corinthians 7:30, 31)? Yes. In every case, yes!

Section VI

THE END OF MEDIOCRITY

20

The Worst of Times

"... we must through much tribulation enter into the kingdom of God."
(Acts 14:22)

Because humanists actively "strive for the good life, here and now,"[59] they repudiate the idea of suffering. They violently oppose the principle of pain as "some kind of foolish mistake that could be avoided by a better understanding of human dynamics."[60] As most of man's misfortune and malady is head related (attitude, outlook, etc.), so too is the cure. With such a simplistic approach to eluding and relieving misery, there is, accordingly, no room and even less tolerance for suffering in a humanistic society. Pain, perplexity, and persecution are "negatives" that must be avoided and, should they slip into our lives, must be expulsed as swiftly and painlessly as possible.

Such thinking permeates the lukewarm religious establishment. New Age Christians, with all their refined manner and articulate form, simply dismiss tribulation from the oracles of God. Who could possibly enhance their self-image while carrying a cross with its humiliating exposure, its flesh-rending agony, and its disfiguring decay? Self-loving Christians refuse the ego-shattering work of the Cross, but the righteous accept and even welcome its harshness, not that they have a "martyr complex," as some suppose, but because of their genuine belief in the Word and their deliberate choice to participate in the sufferings of their Savior. And participate they will, for holiness is the very antithesis of life in the world system and sinners cannot stand to have their sins exposed by its light. Sinners don't bring reproach on their own kind. It is only when one rises out of the ranks of the unrighteous and determines by the help of God to live above the dominion of sin that the wrath of Hell is unleashed in his face.

Tribulation is to be expected; it is part of the purity package, for *"... all that will live godly in Christ Jesus shall suffer persecution"* (2 Timothy 3:12). If we truly are representatives of Christ's interests here on earth, we will suffer in His stead: *"For unto you it is given in the behalf of Christ, not only to believe on him, but also to suffer for his sake"* (Philippians 1:29). If we truly are heirs of God with Christ, we will, like Him, bear this world's reproach: *"And if children, then heirs; heirs of God, and joint-heirs with Christ; if so be that we suffer with Him ..."* (Romans 8:17). If we truly are enamored with Christ, determined that whether by life or by death, He will be magnified, we will rejoice when a portion of His anguish comes our way: *"... rejoice, inasmuch as ye are partakers of Christ's sufferings; that, when his glory shall be revealed, ye may be glad also with exceeding joy. If ye be reproached for the name of Christ, happy are ye ..."* (1 Peter 4:13-14).

In His suffering, Christ established a pattern for His children: *"... Christ also suffered for us, leaving us an example, that ye should follow his steps ... Who, when he was reviled, reviled not again; when he suffered, he threatened not ..."* (1 Peter 2:21, 23). Christ was hated, mocked, falsely accused, and crucified, yet He refused to retaliate. To that exemplary sacrifice we look for leadership (Hebrews 12:2). And, as members of His body, we continue the sacrificial tradition to *"... fill up that which is behind of the afflictions of Christ ... for his body's sake, which is the church"* (Colossians 1:24).

If the Bible is true, we can expect tribulation, but, at the same time, we don't have to wallow in it. In this chapter, we present the "negative" side of Christianity to show what we must expect when sold out to God, not to cast a shadow of gloom over the children of light. We can still dwell on those things which are true, honest, pure, lovely, and of a good report (Philippians 4:8) even while we hurt. We can still say, like Paul, *"... as dying, and, behold, we live; as chastened, and not killed; as sorrowful, yet always rejoicing ..."* (2 Corinthians 6:9-10), even as we join with Christ in the grief and privation of total surrender to God.

LONELINESS

Some of the hurt stems from our commitment to walk with God, a walk that often leads away from public clamor and private discourses into the solitude of the soul. From patriarch to prophet, from Savior to apostle, the walk of loneliness and sorrow has been a common thread and a necessary price all have paid to commune with their God. Leonard Ravenhill spoke of this oft-needed and spontaneous withdrawal from society:

> "The aspirant for spiritual wealth and for the ear of God will know much loneliness and will eat much of 'the bread of affliction.' He may not know too much about family or social opposition; on the other hand, he may. But this is sure, he will know much of soul conflict, and of silences (which may create misunderstandings), and of withdrawal from even the best of company. For lovers love to be alone, and the high peaks of the soul are reached in solitude."[61]

Then, at other times, loneliness creeps involuntarily upon the seeker of God. All of us long for human companionship, particularly with those of similar interests and ideologies. But the man (or woman) who walks close to God seldom has those who will walk with him: *"… all they which are in Asia be turned away from me … all men forsook me …"* (2 Timothy 1:15; 4:16). He seldom has those with whom he can share his innermost thoughts and feelings. He wants to open his heart, but few, if any, will listen. So, once again, he turns inward and upward, seeking solace from the One who truly understands. Said Tozer of that lonely soldier of the Cross:

> "His God-given instincts cry out for companionship with others of his kind, others who can understand his longings, his aspirations, his absorption in the love of Christ; and because within his circle of friends there are so few who share his inner experiences, he is forced to walk alone … He finds few who care to talk about that which is the supreme object of his interest, so he is often silent and preoccupied in the midst of noisy religious shoptalk. For this he earns the reputation of being dull and over-serious, so he is avoided and the gulf between him and society widens."[62]

REJECTION

Loneliness turns to isolation as holy ones are rejected outright—forsaken by family, forgotten by friends—for their opposition to this world's ways. End-time saints who are genuinely committed to holiness will assuredly encounter the same social banishment as their Savior and His imperiled followers down through the years. Paul told Timothy that, in the last days, *"... men shall be ... despisers of those that are good"* (2 Timothy 3:2-3). Therefore, as the Second Coming draws near, the godly will increasingly become victims of fallen man's hostility and hatred: *"Yea, truth faileth; and he that departeth from evil maketh himself a prey ..."* (Isaiah 59:15). As the world's quarry, saints will meet with resistance from its vast and hostile corps of Satanic henchmen *"That make a man an offender for a word, and lay a snare for him that reproveth in the gate, and turn aside the just for a thing of nought"* (Isaiah 29:21).

This is particularly true in a society like ours that has been reduced by humanism to "... a drab hive of look-alikes and talk-alikes droning the same stories, buzzing with self-concern ... an abrasive collection of selves, each one pressing his claim to the limit."[63] A world of ever-expanding, ever-competing selves makes for less room for any of us to live without confronting the bulging ego of another. Where can we go today that another is not staring defiantly as if to gain psychological superiority over our common turf? Where can we go that another is not scheming and plotting, in hopes of securing an advantageous position over us? Where can we go that the self is not on display as all men are being transformed into celebrities looking for a hero's welcome into our hearts? Indeed, where can we go that the spirit of Antichrist is not already at work, strutting brazenly down Main Street, defiantly challenging everyone who is honest, meek, and godly?

You make yourself Hell's target when you die to this world, purify your flesh, consecrate your all to God, and worship Him in spirit and truth. Because your "self" is crucified, demonic legions will be unleashed against you as they were against Christ, Paul, and all the others who presented their bodies a living sacrifice. On Satan's behalf, the humanistic world system will attack in force, for they see something in you that is different, something that clashes with and antagonizes their god—self. Your "self" is dethroned, Christ is now your Lord, and because the world hated Him, they will hate you as well. For no apparent reason, they will ridicule, falsely accuse, and *"... say all manner of evil against you ..."* (Matthew 5:11). Now that you are detached from their company, you have suddenly become weird and unbalanced, a religious fanatic in need of psychiatric help. Now that you no longer worship with them at the altar of success, you are wasting your life, your talents and your time.

As the visible church silently succumbs to humanism, it too will increasingly reject those who identify with Christ in His suffering and death. As the religious hierarchy rejected Paul for his doctrine of suffering, men-pleasers of the end times will likewise turn against those today who are prisoners for Jesus Christ. As the religious hierarchy openly stoned Stephen, men-pleasers of the end times will likewise lift the rocks of verbal abuse and bodily harm on the troubled outcasts of this last generation.

Separated saints will be badgered by compromisers whose greatest desire is to fit in, to be pleasant and popular, to be liked by everyone. Worshipers in the Spirit will be bruised by legalistic worshipers who insist that their zealous brethren have gone overboard in their search for God. Repentance preachers will be battered for resisting the religious order, for rebuking, reproving, and exhorting *"... with all long suffering and doctrine"* (2 Timothy 4:2). Watchmen will be banned for sounding the trumpet of impending judgment and persecution. Alas, the pure will be beaten; modern-day Pharisees will join their secular kinsmen in crucifying the spiritually minded, thinking as always that they do God a great service (John 16:2).

DEPRIVATION

As the world's enemy, part of our suffering may well include deprivation of many of its goods, even the loss of things once considered basic to survival. Paul, in his quest for perfecting knowledge and resurrection power, *"... suffered the loss of all things ..."* (Philippians 3:8). He ministered *"In weariness and painfulness, in watchings often, in hunger and thirst, in fastings often, in cold and nakedness"* (2 Corinthians 11:27). Clearly the man lacked the material possessions with which to make his life comfortable. And, if we, like him, forsake all to take up our cross and follow Christ, so too might we.

This is particularly true in today's inflated economy. Cross-carrying Christians have the added burden of just getting by when everything costs so much. Even now, many face the uncertainty of not knowing how long their jobs will hold out, how all the bills will be paid, where next week's grocery money will come from.

In tomorrow's regulated economy, things will get even worse. All of

God's holy remnant will experience the trauma of not being able to sell their goods and services at all, of not being able to buy any groceries at all. Without the mark of the Beast, Tribulation saints will be locked in a wilderness where things are, to the natural mind, narrowed down to God.

As with saints of old and as with saints under repressive regimes today, believers in the West will soon witness the "spoiling" of their goods, their houses bankrupt, their lives shipwrecked, fears within, and fightings without. Unable to buy or sell, life's basic necessities will soon be depleted and, like Paul, they will, for the first time, experience *"hunger and thirst ... cold and nakedness."* And like the heroes of faith (Hebrews 11), many may again wander about in deserts and mountains, hiding in dens and caves, destitute, afflicted, and tormented. But, as weary pilgrims exiled on this lonely planet, they do not despair. They gladly give up worldly possessions, for their citizenship is in Heaven, their desire is for a better country, their hope is in that eternal city whose builder and maker is God. Death would be a welcomed end to it all and a gateway to that eternal city.

DEATH

Saints of God have always suffered physical abuse. Of the Old Testament heroes of faith, James said, *"Take, my brethren, the prophets, who have spoken in the name of the Lord, for an example of suffering affliction, and of patience"* (James 5:10). Most were outcasts, the refuse of society. Some escaped the hangman's noose while *"... others were tortured, not accepting deliverance; that they might obtain a better resurrection: And others had trial of cruel mockings and scourgings, yea, moreover of bonds and imprisonment; they were stoned, they were sawn asunder, were tempted, were slain with the sword ..."* (Hebrews 11:35-37).

New Testament warriors of God likewise suffered and died on the battlefield of faith. In the first century, the hills of Palestine were dotted with crosses of Christians who chose to die rather than deny their Savior. Christ had told His disciples to take up their cross, never fearing, for *"... he that loseth his life for my sake shall find it"* (Matthew 10:39). Many did just that; following Christ's example, they gladly bore the cross upon which their lives would later be taken.

Paul, as an apostle *"born out of due time,"* would particularly bear his cross *"... in afflictions, in necessities, in distresses, in stripes, in imprisonments, in tumults, in labors ... in deaths oft ... Thrice was I beaten with rods, once was I stoned, thrice I suffered shipwreck ..."* (2 Corinthians 6:4-5; 11:23, 25). His divine visitation on the road to Damascus had filled him with an overwhelming passion for Christ and left him with a hunger not only to know the risen Lord but the power of His resurrection as well, even the fellowship of His sufferings—to which, God obliged. Paul knew Christ as few have known Him, but for that knowledge, he paid pain's debt as few have paid it. He too would give his life in pursuit of the prize of the high calling of God in Christ Jesus.

Through the years, this same willingness to yield their bodies *"... that they might not serve nor worship any god, except their own God"* (Daniel 3:28) has led throngs of Christians to an early grave. Millions have been burned at the stake, hunted down like animals, beheaded, drowned, thrown to the lions, buried alive, and shot.

And the killing goes on, even now, in totalitarian regimes hostile to the gospel of Jesus Christ.

What's worse, the barbaric stripping of human life will spread and become universally practiced and accepted during the upcoming Tribulation. The whole world will then witness the climax of man's inhumanity to his fellow man, particularly if that fellow man happens to be a Christian. Even as we approach this time of great trouble, believers are being murdered for their testimony, but most of the unprovoked treachery will occur during the final seven years of this present dispensation: *"Then shall they deliver you up to be afflicted, and shall kill you: and ye shall be hated of all nations for my name's sake ... then shall be great tribulation, such as was not since the beginning of the world ..."* (Matthew 24:9, 21).

John the Revelator saw the departed spirits of those destined to be slain by the wicked one, *"... a great multitude, which no man could number ... These are they which came out of great tribulation ... "* (Revelation 7:9, 14). A countless number of saints will come out of the Tribulation, but to get out, they leave their heads behind, reckoning life a fair exchange for their glorious inheritance and a small price to pay to worship their God and Him only: *"... I saw the souls of them that were beheaded for the witness of Jesus, and for the word of God, and which had not worshipped the beast ..."* (Revelation 20:4).

Biblical Christianity is the only remaining obstacle to a complete socialist/humanist takeover, so when Antichrist is revealed and filled with Satan's power, he will set out to crush the Gospel of Christ and slaughter all who confess His name and keep His commandments (Revelation 12:17). The forces of evil are working, albeit somewhat subtly, against Christianity now, but once socialism (communism) is firmly entrenched, worldwide open and forceful persecutions will erupt. The man of sin will be enraged at the rebels who refuse to take his mark or to worship his image, and will commence to annihilate them until it is complete: *"And it was given unto him [Antichrist] to make war with the saints, and to overcome them"* (Revelation 13:7 brackets added). *"And he shall speak great words against the most High, and shall wear out the saints of the most High … and when he shall have accomplished to scatter the power of the holy people, all these things shall be finished"* (Daniel 7:25; 12:7).

I firmly believe that most, it not all, true Christians will be killed shortly after Antichrist is revealed. But those who are walking in holiness, submitted to God in the good times, will be even more determined in the bad. Unafraid of death and unlike lukewarm professors of faith, they would rather die than turn against their Lord. And die they will when all the legions of Hell are unleashed against the saints during Tribulation. Even so, the elect will not fear the wicked one. To them, the man of sin is little more than the culmination of forces they have been fighting since they went all the way with God. To them, he is just another, albeit clearer, sign to their homesick hearts that the end of all things has come and their Savior must return, soon and very soon. *"… Even so, come, Lord Jesus"* (Revelation 22:20).

THE REFINER'S FIRE

As if a hostile world is not enough to deal with, the one who would be holy must also contend with a holy God. Because our Heavenly Father loves us, He chastens us when we sin (Hebrews 12:6). The same God that heals also inflicts difficult circumstances, trials of faith, even perplexity and pain *"… that we might be partakers of His holiness"* (Hebrews 12:10). God wants us all to be holy like Him, so if He must issue the rod of godly correction to beat out the chaff, He will.

God intends that we bear fruit unto Him (Galatians 5), the fruit being personality traits of His Son, the evidence of holiness. As natural branches need pruning and trimming, so do the members of the "true vine"—Jesus

Christ: *"... every branch that beareth fruit, he purgeth it ..."* (John 15:2). Without purging, we would be severed from the Vine (vs. 6) for our spiritual growth would be stunted, our flow of energy from Christ hindered. God is not static; accordingly, He expects His offspring to be ever-growing, always producing "more fruit" and then "much fruit" where once they only produced "fruit." That requires the pruning knife of God's holiness.

If the knife is not enough to cut out our carnality, then perhaps the heat that precedes Christ's coming will burn it out. It may take the heat to refine and purify most of us. We are going into hard times before our Lord returns; expect it, saints. Even as Satan rages in combat with the holy remnant, God Himself is going to turn up the heat on His own people. He's going to ignite the refiner's fire of affliction, hardship, and isolation to consume all the dross, all the dirt, all the smut, cleansing even our secret sins: *"... for he is like a refiner's fire, and like fullers' soap: And he shall sit as a refiner and purifier of silver: and he shall purify the sons of Levi, and purge them as gold and silver, that they may offer unto the LORD an offering in righteousness"* (Malachi 3:2-3).

While the refiner's fire is melting and purging God's elect, His fiery judgments will only harden the ungodly. The pure will grow stronger *"... and do exploits"* (Daniel 11:32), but the corrupt will fall further from God, stubbornly refusing to repent: *"And the rest of the men which were not killed by these plagues yet repented not of the works of their hands ..."* (Revelation. 9:20). Daniel, looking ahead to the end of time, saw the same rift between God's repentant ones and Satan's incorrigible ones: *"And some of them of understanding shall fall, to try them, and to purge, and to make them white, even to the time of the end ... Many shall be purified, and made white, and tried; but the wicked shall do wickedly: and none of the wicked shall understand; but the wise shall understand"* (Daniel 11:35; 12:10).

Part of the rebellious crowd will consist of church people, that burgeoning host of "plastic saints" who break at the slightest trial, who look for any angle, and obscure interpretation of Scripture to lift them out of tribulation, present and future. This bunch of brittle believers claims that Christians should not have to suffer, now or ever. A God of love must shield His flock from adversity, especially that greatest of all holocausts, the Great Tribulation.

If this were the case, then why have untold millions been allowed to die for God through the years? Why do they continue to die? Why will a "great multitude" of saints enter and be massacred during the Great Tribulation? (See Post Tribulation analysis in the Appendix.)

PERFECTION

No, God does not delight in our tribulations; He does not derive some sort of sadistic satisfaction at seeing us trudge through life lonely, sick, despised, bruised, and maligned. But He does see a purpose in it all—our perfection: *"But the God of all grace, who hath called us unto his eternal glory by Christ Jesus, after that ye have suffered a while, make you perfect ..."* (1 Peter 5:10).

Whether from the abuses of man or from the chastening of God, suffering is for our benefit: *"... though our outward man perish, yet the inward man is renewed day by day. For our light affliction, which is but for a moment, worketh for us a far more exceeding and eternal weight of glory"* (2 Corinthians 4:16-17). It may not seem like it at the time but God has a sovereign plan soaring high above our temporal pain. He knows that grief is sometimes needed to expose the vanity of earthly pursuits and to fill our hearts with longing for Heaven's peace. He knows that deprivation is sometimes needed to break the gravitational pull of this world's charm. He knows that afflictions are sometimes needed to weaken the vessel so that the glory goes to Him and not to self. He knows that burdens are sometimes needed to make us feel the hurt of others. He knows that a foretaste of judgment is sometimes needed to produce in us a healthy, reverential fear of the Almighty (Hebrews 12:7-9).

God also knows that calamity is sometimes needed to make us trust Him, not ourselves: *"... we had the sentence of death in ourselves, that we should not trust in ourselves, but in God ..."* (2 Corinthians 1:9). Suffering does its work if, in our trial, we turn from self and its abilities to God and His power; if, in our pain, we sense our own insufficiency, drawing instead our strength from God; if, in spite of the outcome and regardless of the circumstances, we cling to God in total dependence: *"Though He slay me, yet will I trust in Him ..."* (Job 13:15).

Those who refuse to hold onto God now likely will not rely on Him when things fall apart during the Great Trial. Addicted to their security, the mark of independence already imprinted on their hearts, they likely will accordingly wear the Beast's visible badge of ownership when he says it is the thing to do. That final, soul-damning act of self-reliance will secure them all right—a place in Hell forever (Revelation 14:9-11).

God knows that adversity is sometimes needed to mold us into the image of His Son, preserving in us a Christ-like character free of the foreign elements of flesh and worldliness: *"Always bearing about in the body the dying of the Lord Jesus, that the life also of Jesus might be made manifest in our body"* (2 Corinthians 4:10). God intends that Christ be formed in us. For that to happen, we must die. No, not literally, but we must die to every fleshly lust or sin, every selfish motive or deed, every haughty look or remark. Sanctification and its ensuing works (e.g., separation, purification, and consecration) sometimes need the added pressure of pain to thoroughly deaden our old man's flesh-driven appetite. When the flesh is sufficiently weakened by infirmities, sin at last ceases. So said Peter *"... he that hath suffered in the flesh hath ceased from sin; that he no longer should live the rest of his time in the flesh to the lusts of men, but to the will of God"* (1 Peter 4:1-2).

Not only is pain a final cure for besetting sin, but it is also good preventive medicine as well. Through suffering, our old man is denied the pleasant fields he needs to germinate and sprout afresh in our hearts. Even the mighty Paul confessed that the potential for sin in his own life was reason enough for God to permit a thorn in his flesh, *"... lest I should be exalted above measure through the abundance of the revelations ..."* (2 Corinthians 12:7). This messenger of Satan buffeted Paul, it is true, but for his good, for the continuance of revelations, for an open stream of God's Resurrection power. Paul had not sinned, and he praised God for preventing him, with pain. In fact, he gloried in it (2 Corinthians 12:9).

Strangely enough, Paul actually delighted in all his difficulties, as he stated in 2 Corinthians 12:10: *"... I take pleasure in infirmities, in reproaches, in necessities, in persecutions, in distresses for Christ's sake ..."* But he, unlike most of us, recognized and patterned his life after a precious spiritual paradox: *"... when I am weak, then am I strong."* Paul was strong in the Spirit, but he was strong through the power which is of God: *"He giveth power to the faint; and to them that have no might he increaseth strength"* (Isaiah 40:29). For that strength, even the power that raised Christ from the dead, Paul would be as the faint, he would forfeit all of life's comforts and conveniences; he would endure a lifetime of hardship and pain.

Understandably, this type of sacrifice can only be made by those who value their eternal existence more than this temporal mound of clay, whose glimpse of Christ has smothered any endearment to this present life, whose love for Him is so intense that their lives become unimportant obstacles standing between them and their Lord. If He doesn't return before their sojourn here is finished, then death becomes just a long-awaited friend who comes to usher their soul into His glorious presence. So much did Paul yearn for the Beloved that he welcomed death as a suitable means to unite his soul with the object of his affection: *"For to me to live is Christ, and to die is gain ... For I am in a strait betwixt two, having a desire to depart, and to be with Christ ..."* (Philippians 1:21, 23). Such should be our testimony as well.

And, why not—*"For we know that if our earthly house of this tabernacle were dissolved, we have a building of God, an house not made with hands, eternal in the Heavens"* (2 Corinthians 5:1). The only way any of us will endure the hardness of Christian servitude now and the anguish of Tribulation woes then is to look ahead to the supernal blessings that await us when this earthly house is dissolved: *"... For if we be dead with Him, we shall also live with Him: If we suffer, we shall also reign with Him ..."* (2 Timothy 2:11-12). The only way any of us will overcome the spirit of Antichrist now and the deceitful butcher, himself, then is to fall out of love with this present life and in love with the next: *"And they overcame him [Antichrist] by the blood of the Lamb, and by the word of their testimony; and they loved not their lives unto the death"* (Revelation 12:11 brackets added). The only way any of us will bear up under our cross now and bare our necks to the executioner's ax then is to have hope in that Heavenly city, that city not made with hands.

Through the shadow of this present trial and the Tribulation darkness that is yet to be, our hope is in that glorious future of light, love, and peace forevermore, that eternal future *"... when this corruptible shall have put on incorruption, and this mortal shall have put on immortality ..."* (1 Corinthians 15:54), that triumphant future when Christ will reign, truth will at last prevail, trials will finally fail. Praise God!

21

THE BEST OF TIMES

*S*aints of God do selflessly die for their Lord, caring not for their own blood-bought mounds of clay. They are not overly concerned for the eternal rewards of dying rather than bowing to the Antichrist or taking his mark of ownership. But there will be rewards, eternal and temporal, physical and spiritual, for end-time saints who yielded to the Refiner's fire in pursuit of a life of holiness.

To the holy, there is eternity in Heaven, and that in itself is quite a wonderful reward. Clearly, we would all be happy if that were the sum total of our rewards. But there is more in a spiritual sense for all God's elect and much more right here on earth for martyred Tribulation saints. John the Revelator shares a heretofore hidden truth:

> "... I saw the souls of them that were beheaded for the witness of Jesus, and for the word of God, and which had not worshipped the beast, neither his image, neither had received his mark upon their foreheads, or in their hands; and they lived and reigned with Christ a thousand years. But the rest of the dead lived not again until the thousand years were finished. This is the first resurrection." (Revelation 20:4-5)

According to John, only the martyred elect will rise in the "first resurrection," and then they will reign with Christ during the Millennium. Repeat: they and only they take part in the partial Rapture at the end of

Tribulation. We say partial rapture because, as John said, the rest of the dead (he means good and bad) lived not again until the Millennium is over. After they are resurrected, they stand before the Great White Throne and are judged according to their works. *"And whosoever was not found written in the book of life was cast into the lake of fire"* (Revelation 20:15). (See also Revelation 20:11-15.) The obvious implication is that some of those in the "second resurrection" are found written in the book of life, and it is all the sainted dead down through the ages, except the martyred Tribulation saints.

They are the last to be killed, but the first out of the grave. The last shall indeed be the first and shall be rewarded with one thousand years of rule over this old earth. They rule with a rod of iron; yet it is not like the dishonorable thieves who preside over our pockets today. They are part of the only God-ordained form of government, a legitimate theocracy with Christ in charge. Once slain in the street, truth and justice are resurrected, along with the martyred in Christ, and they all take their rightful positions with the Lord as righteous rulers over the remnant of unholy man. Finally, there will be peace, real and lasting peace when the Prince of Peace takes His rightful place of unquestioned authority over His creation on the very site of their creation, planet earth.

During the Millennium, roles are reversed and retributions made to saints victimized by the Beast and his followers. Christians who are tortured, starved, and killed will then rule the heathens who survive the Tribulation. God rewards those Christians in time and space while He rights the wrongs they endured for His name's sake. Think of it, a thousand years with absolute command and control over unregenerate humanity who are not immortal as you are. You will not hurt and you will not die, but you will make others wish they could, for unrighteous behavior will not be tolerated. Finally, the good folks will be in charge.

Good will be called good, and evil will be named for what it is—evil—and it will be punished by the righteous. Righteous judgment will be extended to all remaining mortals by the righteous that would have been killed in the Tribulation for their righteousness. Say goodbye to deception, back room deals, inequalities, and class warfare. Do not expect to see that blank, forlorn, and apathetic look plastered on the faces of the lost, leaderless, and couldn't-care-less masses who fall for every socio-political trick thrown at them. Not to worry, though, for during the Millennium, humanism/

liberalism and all the "ists" and "isms" will have been destroyed and their remaining adherents humbled into submission for a subservient role in the Christ-run theocracy. It just doesn't get any better than that down here, or does it? Wait, there is more.

Because of the purging brought about by the Tribulation and the subsequent return and firm rulership of Christ, the Millennium will be absent a host of nuisances and outright obnoxious torments heretofore thrown at the world, especially at freedom-loving Christians, by Satan himself. Tribulation saints can rejoice, for during the Millennium there will be:

- No more ridicule and scorn, with them as the butt of anti-Christian jokes and put downs.
- No more looking through a glass darkly. We will see clearly then. We may even understand why all the apparent contradictions in the spiritual scheme of things and realize it was all part of the supernatural plan from the beginning. We may even know why there is evil in the world.
- No more religions of the world or vast denominational networks with doctrinally impenetrable and unchangeable structures.
- No more charlatans masquerading as messengers of God promising a new way while pleading for more of your money.
- No more man-written laws or constitutions (as good as they might have been), only the laws of God administered by the Lord Himself.
- No more of the institutions of the world system now run by Satan.
- No more political parties or corrupt politicians sold to the highest bidder.
- No more democracies which always degenerate into mob rule driven by self-serving voting blocs of the oftentimes ignorant masses.
- No more dictatorships.
- No more hyphenated Americans.
- No more class warfare promoted by those in politics who prosper from the divisions they help create.
- No more national and international strife.
- No more United Nations pretending to solve the world's problems.
- No more of the "rights" activists or peace and green movements.
- No more taxation without so much as a hint of just representation.
- No more of the "isms" and ideologies that would enslave their disciples and send them to Hell.

- No more corrupt vote purchasers like ACORN and the like.
- No more ACLU to prevent or remove every vestige of Christian thought or tradition from the public square.
- No more labor unions or self-serving lobbyists.
- No more IMF, Trilateral Commission or Federal Reserve.
- No more liberal judges rewriting the laws as they jolly well please.
- Best of all, no more abortions. The Roe vs. Wade decision hatched in Hell will be finally and violently overturned for good.

I suppose we could go on *ad infinitum,* but you get the idea. After Christ returns, everything will be different in a literal and observable sense. If we must die for our Lord in the Tribulation, we can indeed anticipate seeing all the changes. Equally important, we can look forward to the Resurrection and Rapture and our immortal existence here for a thousand years, then afterward throughout eternity.

In the meantime, here on earth, there are precursors of eternity for us to enjoy. In the midst of the worst of times for our physical being, the end of time (before and during the Tribulation) could be the best of times for our spiritual condition and expressions as well.

Hardships may indeed press our hope beyond this present gloom into that celestial city of endless day, but, even so, this life is not just one big, spiritless encounter with monotony and emotional stagnation. God forbid that we should wander aimlessly through life bored and apathetic, just waiting for it all to end. No, heavens no!

As Daniel said when speaking of the end time, God's people will see miracles even as the wicked perform their own through the power of Satan. *"And such as do wickedly against the covenant shall he corrupt by flatteries: but the people that do know their God shall be strong, and do exploits"* (Daniel 11:32). However, those who know God do not need a new brand of hyper-faith to do exploits. They do not need a festival-type Pentecost that has been watered down to accommodate power-crazed Charismatics bent on saving the world from itself by their wonderful works and positive words.

All they need is an abiding relationship in Christ, crucified to self, alive unto God, free from the dominion of sin. All they need is an awareness of their own inabilities and their own insufficiency and the knowledge that, apart from God, they can do nothing: *"But we have this treasure in earthen vessels, that the excellency of the power may be of God, and not of us"* (2 Corinthians 4:7). All they need is holiness, without which there is no reproof of sin, no fear of God, no Holy Ghost impartations of power.

We may face our persecutions, we may have our share of problems, but in a spiritual sense, our sojourn here is filled with promise. For those who have replaced their rags of flesh with a robe of righteousness, there is the promise of peace, the peace of following God, of knowing His will, of worshiping in His presence. There is the promise of joy, the joy of charitable works, of new converts, of signs and wonders, of Holy Ghost outpourings. And, there is the promise of revelations, revelations of God's infinite wisdom and understanding, revelations of His vast knowledge (via the revealed Word), revelations of His immeasurable perception.

Granted, all see through a glass darkly now (1 Corinthians 13:12), but for a select few—the spiritually-minded—the scales of darkness and delusion are falling from their eyes. Their vision no longer blurred by sin and self, they are seeing things otherwise obscured to the carnal mind. Certainly, God is not divulging new truth (as some suppose); He is making these enlightened minds more aware of the old. He is not offering new revelations to supplement the Bible (as some teach); He is disclosing to these awakened minds the old doctrinal truths of His Word.

THE WORD

Even as Christ prepares for His second visit to an undiscerning world, God is opening the Scriptures to His holy remnant, giving them understanding not available to the masses of carnal Christians. With new insight into the written Word, they are lifted above the restricted, earthly plane of human reasoning into the boundless, celestial sphere of supernatural thought. They *"... ride upon the high places of the earth ..."* (Isaiah 58:14), viewing life and logic from a loftier perch and a more reliable perspective: God's. Intellect gives way to illumination, and, for the first time, they see clearly. For the first time, they understand life; the present ceases to be a muddled continuum of inexplicable cycles, and the future is no longer a murky maze through which they fear to pass.

Additionally, through an expanded consciousness of God's Word, its flaming torch of truth scorches the heart and turns to ashes all their preconceived ideas and pet doctrines, all their denominational fables, all their heretical perversions. At last, they are emancipated from institutional barriers to independent thought and free expression. Now, God's Word alone tells them what to think. Now, God's Word alone tells them what to say.

With the freedom that flows from understanding, the revealed Word becomes a wellspring of new life to spiritually-illumined minds. To them, the Word is assurance, for it alone is clear in this clouded world of confusing "isms," ideas, and ideologies. To them, the Word is authority, for it alone contains all the answers to God, the soul, and human destiny. To them, the Word is reality, for it alone is reliable in an age of error so intense it threatens to mislead even the elect. To them, the Word is holiness, for it alone is the impetus for revolutionary changes in their own character, changes patterned after Him who is from everlasting to everlasting, the Word made flesh, Jesus Christ.

With the revealed Word now open to them, enlightened saints are further transformed into the image of the incarnate Word as they gaze upon His glory and fashion their lives after His perfect life: *"But we all, with open face beholding as in a glass the glory of the Lord, are changed into the same image from glory to glory, even as by the Spirit of the Lord"* (2 Corinthians 3:18). Growing Christians look to Christ, never debating His principles; growing Christians yield to Christ, never skirting His commandments; and they are changed. All their lives, they are changed. Until life's race is run and glory's crown is won, they are letting go of moods and manners, tempers and tendencies, beliefs and behaviors that clash with those of Christ.

This they do because even those walking in holiness with every sin forgiven and every temptation challenged still have room for improvement. Until death sends the saint home, there will be a call from God's Word for additional molding into the image of Christ. There will always be pressure to surge ahead, forgetting past blunders and blessings, *"... reaching forth unto those things which are before"* (Philippians 3:13). There will forever be a challenge to *"press toward the mark"* of perfection in Christ Jesus.

Those who value the Heavenly prize of their calling will stay on their knees before God, and they will devour His Word, for nothing less than the *"... excellency of the knowledge of Christ Jesus ..."* (Philippians 3:8) will satisfy their souls. They will look unto Him, the Rock from which they were hewn (Isaiah 51:1). And they will grow, for His face is before them night and day. His sadness and sorrow, His surety, His spotless life, His sinless walk, all will beckon them ever onward, ever upward, ever attaining unto the measure of the stature of the fullness of Christ.

To New Covenant legalists, unwilling to undergo this unconditioned transformation, the Word of God is hidden. The Bible is mere words on sheets of paper to all who predetermine how they will believe and behave. They then rewrite the Scriptures to prove themselves right. To them, Christ is nothing more than a laudable historical figure, the profound biblical mysteries nothing but cold lifeless facts, and God's timeless wisdom nothing at all. They never see the soul of the text, only the letter. They never feel its fire, its unction, its dagger of conviction *"... piercing even to the dividing asunder of soul and spirit ..."* (Hebrews 4:12). They never see the mind of Christ or the heart of God transcending the words, flowing between the lines like a mighty river between two streams.

This ignorance of God's Word, prolonged and widespread in the end-time church, has evolved into a hodgepodge of confusing and conflicting doctrines. From this doctrinal madness has emerged a host of denominations and splinter groups, all claiming the same risen Savior, all basing their beliefs on the same Bible, yet all to varying degrees different from each other. Which is right?

Consider this: God will not reveal Himself through the Word (or through any other means) to unholy, worldly-minded Christians. Instead, he casts a haze over their eyes, lest they should look into the Word and behold His holiness in their impurity. God, Himself, said, *"... I will send a famine in the land, not a famine of bread, nor a thirst for water, but of hearing the words of the LORD ... they shall run to and fro to seek the word of the LORD, and shall not find it"* (Amos 8:11-12). So when impure Christians form their doctrines, they do so without God. There is only one interpretation of the Scriptures, but God allows the unsanctified to reach any number of conclusions, each with perhaps a measure of truth, yet none totally representing the mind of God.

DISCERNMENT

Sadly, many Christians who walk in spiritual darkness today will be hopelessly overcome by it during the Tribulation. For them, there will be no transformation of mind, no change of character, only deception and lies. Because they reject sanctifying truth, casting their lot instead with the unrighteous, God *"... shall send them strong delusion, that they should believe a lie"* (2 Thessalonians 2:11). Duped *"... by the means of those miracles which he [Antichrist] had power to do ..."* (Revelation 13:14 bracketed words added), they will turn to the man of sin, the world's savior, for solutions to all their problems. They will be convinced that none but he can bring calm to the volcanic eruptions of terror and turmoil, fear and violence, hostility and hatred. To the deceived, Antichrist will be the welcomed ruler for a chaotic world, a "natural" to unravel the tangled web of economic and political upheaval. And when the Beast does unite the world, whether by force or by cunning, they will worship him. They will believe his lies, take the mark, and be damned forever.

If it were possible, even the elect would be taken in during these delusory times (Matthew 24:24); but it is not possible, for saints of the Most High have discernment. The prophet Malachi rightly concluded that those whom God purifies in the fires of tribulation will emerge from the ashes with the probing power of God to *"... discern between the righteous and the wicked, between him that serveth God and him that serveth him not"* (Malachi 3:18).

This means that not only will the craftiness of Antichrist be revealed to purified hearts, but that the holy will recognize sin's paralytic presence whenever and wherever it occurs. From God's perspective, that exposure of evil must begin at His house, as does His judgment. And it must begin now!

Yet, who among us catches even a whiff of the stench that fills the house of God? Who among us is nauseated at the sight of charlatans masquerading as ministers of the gospel? Who among us is sickened by the chicanery of false prophets, their blasphemous mixture of good and evil, their tear-in-the-voice appeals for more money? Who among us is appalled at the paltry parades of flesh, the ego trippers and self worshipers, the smell of sacrilege on the very altar of God? Who? Only the pure of heart. Only those with discernment.

Only those with discernment can feel the entire religious establishment trembling, its adulterous union with the world system about to erupt into a one-world religion. Only those with discernment feel the spirit of Antichrist in nearly everything that spews out of the mouth of Laodicea. Only those with discernment will be spared deception's strong hand; only they will recognize the man of sin when he is exposed. Only those with discernment will refuse his mark; only they will break the binding spell cast over an unsuspecting, sin-riddled church.

Only those with discernment sense the gray areas of unrighteousness, not just in the church, but in the world around them as well. Among friends and associates, in routine activities, in relationships—no matter what—at times, they have a witness that something is not of God. They may not know altogether why the thing is wrong, but they know it has no spontaneity, it must be forced, it feels of death. Lacking this perception, there are times that even the godliest of souls would fail to differentiate between right and wrong, friend and phony, prophet and pretender. Tozer explains: "So skilled is error at imitating truth that the two are constantly being mistaken for each other. It takes a sharp eye these days to know which brother is Cain and which Abel … That soft-spoken companion with which we walk so comfortably and in whose company we take such delight may be an angel of Satan, whereas that rough, plain-spoken man whom we shun may be God's very prophet sent to warn us against danger and eternal loss."[64]

Lastly, it is those with discernment who are sensitive to even the subtleties of sin within their own breasts. To the spiritually alert, God discloses hidden or would-be sins, sometimes even before they blossom into open violations of the holy code. Paul said it: *"Let us therefore, as many as be perfect, be thus minded: and if in any thing ye be otherwise minded, God shall reveal even this unto you"* (Philippians 3:15). If in anything, the perfect (those who hate sin and strive to live above it) differ dispositionally or behaviorally from God, He will expose it. This, the laying bare of everything in the saint that is contentious to God, is the epitome of discernment. It is the hallmark of holiness.

THE RESURRECTION REALM

In spite of hardships and perhaps because of them, the righteous in these last days will once again move and function in the supernatural realm. For the holy, the old man of the flesh is dead, and the new man is alive unto God. His consecrated walk in the Spirit has become his consecrated worship, worship which lifts him above the physical plane to the celestial realm of spiritual communion with his Lord. So awesome is this communion that the new man gains a dynamic vision of God's grandeur; he is struck with wonder; he is filled with fear. So intimate is this communion that the new man shares common thoughts with God, he moves in concert with Him, he adores Him, he abides with Him in the Resurrection Realm.

Sadly, most Christians in this Laodicean Age know nothing of personal communion with God. Wed to the world in a defiling mixture of sacred and secular, they keep up the routines of worship, but know nothing of the spontaneity and intimacy of spiritual worship. Lacking a burning desire to know Christ, their church-going is ritualistic and dead; their service, mechanical and meaningless. So driven are they with activity that Christ is left out; so in love with precedent and process that spirituality is squeezed out.

As in Christ's day, Laodicean legalists are particularly antagonistic toward holiness. They scream foul when some hungry soul breaks out of the world's mold, then look feverishly for ways to condemn and crucify his Christ-centered life. As a smokescreen for their own divided hearts, the new breed of legalists ironically label as "legalism" all sacrifices of the one who rejects the lusts of this world, who casts off the entanglement of flesh, who gives himself wholly to the things of God, who wants holiness more than life itself. In this sense, legalism becomes a buzzword for the host of ritualistic worshipers who feel condemned by the separatist and who wish to discredit his sanctity and dispel his kind altogether from their company of conformists.

Those who would reside in the resurrection realm no longer worship God in the flesh. Instead, they worship Him in the Spirit, as their Lord commanded: *"... true worshippers shall worship the Father in spirit and in truth ... God is a Spirit: and they that worship Him must worship Him in spirit and in truth"* (John 4:23-24).

Disgusted with the apostate establishment, weary end-time saints are forsaking its fleshly worship for the solace and rest they are finding in the spiritual. In the Spirit, their religious works of the flesh are nullified and unnecessary; activities and natural knowledge give way to power and wisdom; freshness and revelations replace boredom and repetition.

In the Spirit, their worship is elevated above the plane of the earthly and the mundane into the ascended, celestial sphere of Christ Himself: *"But God ... hath raised us up together, and made us sit together in heavenly places in Christ Jesus"* (Ephesians 2:4, 6). As Christ is in Heaven and in them at the same time, they can be here and seated with Him in the Heavenlies at the same time, if they abide in Him. Christ descends from

Heaven via the Holy Ghost to inhabit the temple of their souls, and they ascend into the Heavenlies through consecration to worship continuously with Him and His angelic host.

In the Spirit, no longer is their worship confined to a particular place, for *"... the most High dwelleth not in temples made with hands"* (Acts 7:48). Nor is their worship appointed for a certain time; rather, it is all the time. It is never broken, never ending, never static, ever-expanding, ever-changing their lives into the image of Christ.

In the spirit, they are ever mindful of their potential for displeasing God, ever sorrowful when they do. There is a continual searching of the heart, comparing its contents with the character of God, scrubbing its stains, flushing its filth.

In the spirit, they are ever prayerful, ever thankful. With the four living creatures and the twenty-four elders in Heaven, they praise the Creator always: *"... Holy, holy, holy, LORD God Almighty ... Thou art worthy, O Lord, to receive glory and honour and power ..."* (Revelation 4:8, 11).

In the spirit, their walk and their worship become inseparable and indistinguishable as one continuous stream of praise, honor, and glory to His name. Their walk becomes their worship; their worship becomes their walk. Every day becomes Sunday, and Sunday becomes yet another day to fellowship with God in His majestic presence.

What hath humanism to compare with this precious gift of discernment, or, for that matter, with any of the revelations of God? Nothing! What passing pleasure, what prized possession, what prestigious position can compare with the ecstasy of peering into God's inexhaustible storehouse of *"... deep and secret things ..."* (Daniel 2:22), of gazing "... with astonished wonder upon the beauties and mysteries of things holy and eternal,"[65] of looking into an open heaven at *"... the glory of God, and Jesus standing on the right hand of God"* (Acts 7:55)? None, no not one!

Furthermore, none of this world's goods or glories can compare with just one glimpse of God's unfathomable mysteries, or just one touch of His resurrection power, or just one taste of His revealed Word. Nothing tainted by the hand of man can compare with the thrill of discovering hidden treasures of truth, of being overwhelmed by an inner radiant knowledge of Jesus Christ, of walking in the light through a world overcome by darkness.

For the best of times, end-time saints really have an easy decision to make. If they are hungry for the deeper things of God, they will choose the less-traveled road. Indeed, they must choose the only road that leads to Him, the highway of holiness. By no other means will He be revealed to man, now or ever. *"Follow peace with all men, and holiness, without which no man shall see the Lord"* (Hebrews 12:14).

CONCLUSION

As Christians, we know tough times are coming. We expect it. We accept it, but not lying down. We will prepare our hearts and minds with a holy walk before God. We will prepare to overcome the Antichrist by being overcome by Him. We will give up that which Christ purchased when He gave up His life: our own lives.

Tough times, yes, but for sure a good time for those who name the name of Christ to get back to the fervor and anticipation of the first century church. They knew the Lord. They blended as one in the upper room. Their hearts were clean, exploits were many, and minds were focused on the mission and the soon return of their Lord.

Yes, it is late, but it is not too late for us all to prepare for the dark days, to purge the temple, and to proceed on a journey into the most hopeful (the blessed hope) time in man's history, the time that those same apostles and saints through the ages have longed for, the soon return of our Lord and Savior, Jesus Christ.

The world teeters on the brink of a cataclysmic paradigm shift in the way its citizens think about and deal with: the accumulation and distribution of wealth, the isolation and extermination of the world's thorn in the flesh (Israel), the outdated and debilitating influence of Biblical Christianity, and the subjugation of the American super power.

America will fall or fold before the end of time, but "we, the people" do not have to be part of the fall and merger into the global humanist cesspool of immorality. We, as individuals, can rise from the ruins through personal reformation and a return to the roots of our beliefs—Biblical Christianity as manifested in a life of holiness.

APPENDIX A
The Post Tribulation Rapture

*A*s put forth in an earlier chapter, we believe that the Tribulation is upon us, that the end is indeed near. We also believe that, on the day it all ends, a group of saints will be raptured to meet Christ in the air on His second visit to earth. This, His one and only Second Coming, in which He takes wrathful vengeance on the Beast and his people at Armageddon, also acts as a trigger for the "catching up" of the living and the dead in Christ, that is, with certain caveats.

The wrathful portion of that day will not occur until Christ has raptured His own out. If any are alive at that time, they will be "caught up," as Paul said, *"... we who are alive and remain ... "* (1 Thessalonians 4:17). Notice that, at that point, Paul thought he would be alive, so we can assume the verse doesn't necessarily mean that any of us will be alive at the end of Tribulation (except maybe the 144,000 sealed Jewish believers).

Before the living are raptured, Paul said that the dead in Christ must rise first to join their Lord in the air (1 Thessalonians 4:16). We have always assumed this meant that all the dead in Christ would take part in the first Resurrection. According to John, that is not the case, for only the martyred Tribulation saints have that honor (Revelation 20:4-6). His view is the final and definitive look at the Rapture. All glimpses before his are partial and seen through a glass more darkly. I'll go with John on this, for he sheds the best light on the subject.

These are our beliefs, and we certainly do not take their presentation in the public domain lightly. Nor do we do so as an ego-stroking attempt to win the much debated, often divisive Rapture argument. We offer a rebuttal to the pre-Tribulation escape theory because of potentially harmful side effects and soul-damning dilemmas awaiting those who look for Christ to return and remove them before the Tribulation.

Those who are wrong on this issue simply will not be prepared for the trauma and deception that awaits them in the Great Tribulation. Too, many who are expecting a fast get-away could be in the Tribulation and not even know it. Since they are expecting Christ to come for them before the Tribulation begins, they could easily accept Antichrist as their returning Savior (particularly in the beginning). Because they are still looking for the Christ, the false Christ could deceive them into taking his mark since they think the Tribulation has not yet arrived.

Yet, many Christians in this age of relative ease find it hard to believe they could be called upon to suffer and die for their testimony, or that Antichrist could be so cunning that even they might be deceived into taking his mark. They find it easier to believe, without sound logic and Biblical proof texts, that they will escape, via a Pre-Tribulation Rapture, all the death and delusion of the Tribulation. The whole hypothesis is held together by faulty human reasoning and arbitrary interpretations of obscure passages and vague Biblical texts.

> "The Pre-Tribulation Rapture theory is built on a postulate, vicious in logic, violent in exegesis, contrary to experience, repudiated by the early church, contradicted by the testimony of eighteen hundred years, and condemned by all the standard scholars of every age."[66]

In this section, our intent is to support our belief in a post-Tribulation Rapture with careful and logical evaluation of pertinent Scriptures, dismissing our own somewhat selfish desire to also escape it all via a pre-Tribulation get away. We wish it were so, but the Biblical evidences do not, to us, support it.

In the forthcoming discussion, all we ask is that you give our thought fair play. Challenge if you must, but study what we have to say with an open mind. We, too, were of the pre-Tribulation Rapture persuasion for many years until we determined to study for ourselves, dismissing all of our pre-conceived ideas and previously taught doctrines, and then forming our own conclusions after a thorough study of God's Word. We concluded that Christians will enter the Tribulation with little or no chance of escaping it, short of death, but that their martyrdom entitles them to be raptured as part of the First Resurrection when Christ returns. The basis of our conclusion follows.

THE DAY OF THE LORD

The misunderstanding often centers on the placement of either three and one-half or seven years between the Rapture and the Day of the Lord. This is a critical move, for clearly the Day of the Lord describes Christ's triumphant return to earth after the Tribulation to take vengeance on sinners: *"Behold, the day of the LORD cometh, cruel both with wrath and fierce anger, to lay the land desolate: and he shall destroy the sinners thereof out of it"* (Isaiah 13:9); *"... Behold, the Lord cometh with ten thousands of his saints, to execute judgment upon all, and to convince all that are ungodly among them of all their ungodly deeds which they have ungodly committed ..."* (Jude 1:14-15).

Furthermore, on the Day of the Lord, He (Christ) will come *"... out of his place to punish the inhabitants of the earth for their iniquity ..."* (Isaiah 26:21), particularly the man of sin *"... whom the Lord shall consume with the spirit of His mouth, and shall destroy with the brightness of His coming"* (2 Thessalonians 2:8). And, consume He does! With a consummation of flesh akin to a nuclear holocaust, He smites the Beast and his international armies that have gathered in Israel *"... to make war against Him [Christ] that sat on the horse ..."* (Revelation 19:19 brackets added)—*"And this shall be the plague wherewith the LORD will smite all the people that have fought against Jerusalem; Their flesh shall consume away while they stand upon their feet, and their eyes shall consume away in their holes, and their tongue shall consume away in their mouth"* (Zechariah 14:12).

No matter how badly we might want to escape the horrors of Tribulation, we cannot arbitrarily slip years between the Rapture and the dreadful Day of the Lord. The Bible simply will not support that. Instead, Scripture teaches that the saints' reward (Resurrection and Rapture) and the Lord's revenge occur at the same time. The prophet Isaiah said, *"... your God will come with vengeance, even God with a recompense; He will come and save you ... Behold, the Lord GOD will come with strong hand, and His arm shall rule for Him: behold, His reward is with him, and his work before Him"* (Isaiah

35:4; 40:10). John the Revelator said essentially the same thing: *"And the nations were angry, and thy wrath is come, and the time of the dead, that they should be judged, and that thou shouldest give reward unto thy servants ... and shouldest destroy them which destroy the earth"* (Revelation 11:18).

No one knows the day and hour Christ will return with vengeance, but one thing we know for sure, on the same day He lashes out at the wicked, He airlifts the elect out beforehand. Christ symbolically confirmed the saints, same-day escape from Armageddon: *"But the same day that Lot went out of Sodom it rained fire and brimstone from heaven, and destroyed them all. Even thus shall it be in the day when the Son of man is revealed"* (Luke 17:29-30).

Paul called this last-minute evacuation the "blessed hope," an event he said would take place when Christ appears openly and visibly in judgment after the Tribulation. In a letter to Titus, Paul linked the Rapture with Christ's appearing: *"Looking for that blessed hope, and the glorious appearing of the great God and our Saviour Jesus Christ"* (Titus 2:13). Then, in his second epistle to Timothy, he again spoke of the appearing of Christ, but this time in connection with judgment: *"I charge thee therefore before God, and the Lord Jesus Christ, who shall judge the quick and the dead at his appearing and his kingdom"* (2 Timothy 4:1). Therefore, since the blessed hope occurs at Christ's appearing and since His appearance is also marked by vengeance, the Rapture must logically coincide with the Day of the Lord.

However, logic is not needed to prove that Paul made no distinction between a pre- and post-Tribulation appearing of Christ. For Him, it was just the Second Coming, with no delays, no stages, no intervals, no secret departure. For Him, the coming, the gathering, the catching up, and the Day of the Lord were all one and the same.

In his first letter to the saints at Thessalonica, Paul clearly taught this single, indivisible return of Christ. He began with the classic Rapture text: *"For the Lord himself shall descend from heaven with a shout, with the voice of the archangel, and with the trump of God: and the dead in Christ shall rise first: Then we which are alive and remain shall be caught up together with them in the clouds, to meet the Lord in the air: and so shall we ever be with the Lord"* (1 Thessalonians 4:16-17). Then, in almost the same breath, he switched from the "catching up" to the Day of the Lord as if it were a foregone conclusion that the two were interchangeable: *"But of the times and the seasons, brethren, ye have no need that I write unto you. For yourselves know perfectly that the day of the Lord so cometh as a thief in the night"* (1 Thessalonians 5:1-2). To that, Paul added a word of encouragement, the very fact of which rules out a Pre-Tribulation Rapture: *"But ye, brethren, are not in darkness, that that day should overtake you as a thief"* (1 Thessalonians 5:4). Were the brethren raptured seven years before the Day of the Lord, the possibility would not exist at all that they could be overtaken by it, were they walking in darkness.

Again, in his second epistle to the Thessalonians, Paul established that the gathering together (Rapture) of the elect is in the same time frame as the Day of the Lord. First, he described the day of vengeance, *"... when the Lord Jesus shall be revealed from Heaven with His mighty angels, in flaming fire taking vengeance on them that know not God ..."* (2 Thessalonians 1:7-8). Then, just four verses later, he said, *"Now we beseech you, brethren, by the coming of our Lord Jesus Christ, and by our gathering together unto Him, that ye be not soon shaken in mind, or be troubled, neither by spirit, nor by word, nor by letter as from us, as that the day of Christ is at hand"* (2 Thessalonians 2:1-2). Clearly, His coming (singular, not a second and a third coming) will serve a dual purpose: to take vengeance on them that know not God and to gather together the elect unto Himself. But, as Paul points out, that day of the Lord's coming for the saints of God is not yet at hand (present).

Paul gave two reasons that the Day of the Lord was not present at that time: the church had not yet fallen into apostasy, and the Antichrist had not yet been revealed. He concluded that these two calamitous events must precede the coming of our Lord Jesus Christ: *"Let no man deceive you by any means: for that day [the Day of the Lord] shall not come, except there come a falling away first, and that man of sin be revealed, the son of perdition"* (2 Thessalonians 2:3 bracketed words added). And since the gathering together takes place on the Day of the Lord, the Rapture cannot occur until after the falling away of apostate Christendom and after the revelation of the son of perdition.

As that day fast approaches, we are even now witnessing the great apostasy. So the Rapture cannot be far off. But it is still not present, for the man of sin is yet to be revealed and will not be revealed until *"... he as God sitteth in the temple of God, showing himself that he is God"* (2 Thessalonians 2:4).

That humanistic declaration of deity depicts the abomination of desolation, which occurs halfway through Daniel's seventieth week (The Great Tribulation): *"... and in the midst of the week he shall cause the sacrifice and the oblation to cease, and for the overspreading of abominations he shall make it desolate"* (Daniel 9:27). Therefore, the gathering together of God's elect, no matter how imminent, will not take place until after the midpoint of Tribulation. And, in light of already-mentioned Biblical facts, that leaves but one logical time for the Rapture: post-Tribulation.

Before the man of sin is revealed, another momentous and often misunderstood event must take place. The force that now prevents Antichrist from dominating the world must first be removed: *"For the mystery of iniquity doth already work: only he who now letteth will let, until he be taken out of the way. And then shall that Wicked be revealed ..."* (2 Thessalonians 2:7-8). Many Pre-Tribbers contend that *"he who now letteth"* is the church or the Holy Ghost operating through the church. So, Christians must of necessity be caught up and taken out of the way before the Tribulation begins. But this defies logic, for, as Paul said, the Rapture will not happen until after the son of perdition is revealed. Yet, the son of perdition is revealed after *"he who now letteth"* is taken out of the way. Therefore, the Hinderer cannot be the church for he (the Hinderer) is gone when Antichrist is exposed, and the elect are not raptured until after the man of sin is revealed. As previously stated, we believe that the Hinderer is the Holy Spirit. It makes sense that His departure would coincide with the arrival of Satan on earth.

THE ELECT

As Paul alluded in 2 Thessalonians 2, Christ plainly taught in Matthew 24 that the elect would still be here in the middle of Tribulation, for they would witness Antichrist's proclamation of deity: *"When ye therefore shall see the abomination of desolation, spoken of by Daniel the prophet, stand in the holy place ..."* (Matthew 24:15). Then the Lord went even further by disclosing when the Rapture would take place: *"Immediately after the tribulation of those days shall the sun be darkened, and the moon shall not give her light ... and then shall all the tribes of the earth mourn, and they shall see the Son of man coming in the clouds of heaven with power and great glory. And He shall send His angels with a great sound of a trumpet, and they shall gather together his elect from the four winds, from one end of Heaven to the other"* (Matthew

24:29-31). From this, the very words of Christ, there can be no doubt; the gathering of the saints of God will be "after the tribulation."

Then, after the elect are gathered together, the overwhelming wrath of God (on the Day of God's Wrath) is poured out on those who are not yet killed by Satan or the plagues from Heaven. That is why Christ could say, *"Watch ye therefore, and pray always, that ye may be accounted worthy to escape all these things that shall come to pass ... "* (Luke 21:36). Obviously, He was not here speaking of escaping the Tribulation altogether, for He had just warned that persecutions must first befall the elect. He had just said that when they see wars, famines, signs in the heaven, the abomination of desolation, etc., that their redemption draws near. Saints still alive at the end of Tribulation will be redeemed and removed before the judgments of the awful and dreadful Day of the Lord begin. They will escape from Armageddon by way of the Rapture, secured in the Lord's custody, while He punishes the earth's wicked inhabitants: *"Thy dead men shall live, together with my dead body shall they arise ... Come, my people, enter thou into thy chambers, and shut thy doors about thee: hide thyself as it were for a little moment, until the indignation be overpast"* (Isaiah 26:19-20).

At or about the same time the elect are raptured, all of Jewry finally accepts Jesus as the Son of God: *"And so all Israel shall be saved ... "* (Romans 11:26). When Christ returns for His saints, the Jews see Him and the ugly scars inflicted by their fathers on the rejected Messiah. And they repent: *"... they shall look upon me whom they have pierced, and they shall mourn for Him, as one mourneth for his only son ..."* (Zechariah 12:10). Their repentance and acceptance of Christ occurs after *"... the fullness of the Gentiles be come in"* (Romans 11:25)—at the end of Tribulation—and coincides with the Resurrection and Rapture of God's elect: *"For if the casting away of them [the Jews] be the reconciling of the world, what shall the receiving of them be, but life from the dead?"* (Romans 11:15 Bracketed words added).

To nullify the aforementioned and obvious references to a Post-Tribulation Rapture, some Pre-Tribbers allege that the elect who remain during Antichrist's reign of terror are not Christians at all, but are, rather, unregenerate Jews. All New Testament references to the elect are made to true Christians, and only true Christians. According to God's Word, the elect are Jew or Gentile who have accepted Jesus Christ as their Lord and Savior and who are sanctified and obedient to the call for holiness: *"Elect according to the foreknowledge of God the Father, through sanctification of the Spirit, unto obedience and sprinkling of the blood of Jesus Christ ... "* (1 Peter 1:2). The elect are Jew or Gentile who are called according to the purposes of God, then justified, glorified, and conformed to the image of Jesus Christ (Romans 8:28-30, 33). The elect are Jew or Gentile whose eyes are opened to the gospel of grace (Romans 11:5, 7), whose hearts are circumcised and whose service before God is in the spirit not the letter of the Law (Romans 2:29). The elect are the true body of Christ, including the holy ones of every generation from the first century right on up to the Second Advent.

Another Pre-Tribulation assumption has it that the elect mentioned in connection with the suffering and death of the last days are Tribulation saints. In other words, they are people who realize they missed the Rapture, repent, and in many cases, give their lives for Christ. This too has no backing in the Word of God. Some non-believers may indeed repent, and some callous Christians could surrender all to God after the world falls into the hands of Antichrist, but not likely.

When the Holy Spirit is removed Mid-Tribulation, it likely will be difficult, if not impossible, to be saved, for it is the Spirit that draws man to a place of repentance and acceptance of Christ as their Lord and Savior. Because of a driving, demonic force (which is already at work), widescale repentance in heretofore "Christianized" countries may not be as evident during the Tribulation as procrastinators are hoping for. The gospel of Jesus Christ will be proclaimed worldwide by an angelic force during Daniel's Seventieth Week (see Revelation 14:6-7), and those who have never heard the good news will have an opportunity to be saved, but gospel-hardened hearts who say no to Christ and His holiness now will probably only get harder then. In spite of God's judgments, lovers of unrighteousness would rather die than turn from their mediocrity and their mischief: *"And the rest of the men which were not killed by these plagues yet repented not of the works of their hands ... "* (Revelation 9:20).

APPENDIX B
The End of Time

What is meant by the "end of time"? What does time itself mean? Time, as we know it, began for us when the Alpha (Beginning) and Omega (End) created the heavens and the earth and will end when God creates new heavens and a new earth at the end of the Millennium. At that time, eternity for mankind will begin.

The Millennium is a thousand-year period on this old earth in which Christ will rule mankind (along with some of us) with a "rod of iron." During that time Satan is bound in the bottomless pit. At the end of the period, he is released, deceives man again, and together, they rise up against Christ, are defeated again, and he (Satan) is cast into the Lake of Fire where Antichrist and the False Prophet will have been since the end of Tribulation.

The end of the Millennium marks the end of time as we know it, but for purposes of discussion in this book, we have defined the end of time as that period leading up to and including the seven-year Tribulation, culminating in the return of Christ.

No one knows the day and hour Christ will return. He does not even know, so it is for sure we don't. But of the times and seasons preceding our Lord's Second Coming, we can, with a degree of certainty, feel fairly comfortable. And we are fairly comfortable that prevailing conditions and unfolding events of these harsh times do indicate that the end of time is near. We will examine a few.

- There is the well-established Christ-predicted increase in wars and rumors of wars, famines, pestilences, and earthquakes in various places (see Matthew 24). The increase in all these unsettling events is well documented by professional numbers crunchers, but with twenty-four hour news coverage, even we casual observers have noticed a world plagued by more and more natural upheavals.

- Christ also said that the love of many people would grow cold in the end of time because of the proliferation of sin. That two thousand year old prediction sure does seem to have come true with our generation. Granted, since time began, there have been wicked men on earth. But now, sin seems to be everywhere; who can deny it? Who can avoid it with all the enticements thrown at all of us day in and day out through the countless mediums available to man? Christ, again, said that end-time man would be exceedingly wicked as he was in the days of Noah and the days of Lot. I, for one, believe we are there. Christ linked sin and a lack of love; because sin abounds, love will fade away. Anyone breathing knows there isn't much love in our world, except self love. Been driving lately?

  With good reason, the religion of self-love, humanism, has spread like an aggressive cancer around the world, including America. The pandemic push for individual and group rights has played no small part in the exacerbation of sin and its consequent impact on our ability or willingness to love beyond our own selfish selves.

- Paul's prophetic look at end-time man in 2 Timothy 3:1-5 provides a mirror image reflection of modern man:

  > "This know also, that in the last days perilous times shall come. For men shall be lovers of their own selves, covetous, boasters, proud, blasphemers, disobedient to parents, unthankful, unholy, without natural affection, trucebreakers, false accusers, incontinent, fierce, despisers of those that are good, traitors, heady, highminded, lovers of pleasures more than lovers of God; Having a form of godliness, but denying the power thereof: from such turn away."

  Even so-called believers, under the influence of humanism, manifest a powerless form of godliness while they make a god out of pleasure.

Across the belief and non-belief spectrum, modern man, like Paul's vision of end-time man, is woven tightly around the present, the here and now. He is in love with himself, with no regard for others or for the truth. He is untrustworthy and unthankful. He is arrogant and mean. Sounds all too familiar to me. How about you?

- There is the phenomenal increase in general knowledge and knowledge of end-time events as the end approaches (see Daniel 12:4). The explosive amassing and conveyance of information boggles the mind. Our minds are full of "stuff," so much that we really don't know what to do with everything we know. Our intelligence and wisdom either are not there in the first place or just have not kept up. In a sense, so much knowledge of the irrelevant and trivial has helped to make us dumber in ways that really count.

- Then there is the uneasy feeling inside us that the world is in trouble. Around the clock news coverage makes us all well aware of global economic distress, expanding shortages, terrorism threats, so-called global warming (climate change), incurable diseases cropping up, growing disparities between the haves and have nots, increasing hatred within and among nations, ethnic cleansings, etc.

  With the uneasiness comes fear, fear that we just might not survive as a civilization. Then follows a compulsion to find a cure for all that ails us or, better yet, a leader who can do it. To the worldly-minded that must, of necessity, be a global world leader with the acumen, knowledge, and wherewithal to pull it off.

  Globalization, with the world already interconnected in a myriad of ways, paves the way for this the world's savior (far from a savior, this one world leader turns out to be none other than the Antichrist). But, globalization, of necessity, requires that all nations submit to global rules and international laws—yes, that includes America.

  Of late and of grave concern to patriots, America appears poised to surrender much of her sovereignty, along with her economic and military supremacy, to world organizations. Hated by much of the world, the relentless target of terrorists, on the verge of bankruptcy and severe global status reduction, the American eagle is surely falling.

But this must be before the end because all nations gather against Israel for the final battle—Armageddon. Sadly, that includes America, so she must fall before the end, and because the fall seems inevitable, we feel this is a clear indication that the end is near.

- Probably the most compelling reason for our Apocalyptic belief is the almost universal hatred of Israel and her desperate need for someone in power to confirm her right to exist (This occurs at the beginning of the Tribulation). Already, Israel is almost completely marginalized in the world. Soon she will be all alone; *"All thy lovers have forgotten thee ..."* (Jeremiah 30:14).

As suggested earlier, all nations (including America) will gather against Israel for the final battle, Armageddon. This occurs at the end of Tribulation. Our bond with Israel has been strong since her rebirth in 1948, and God blessed us (Remember God's covenant with Abraham, *"I will bless those ..."*). But in recent years the bond began cracking, and with liberals firmly in power for the foreseeable future, the break will soon be complete. Even now, the United States has many voices opposing the Jewish state. America, under our Marxist-inspired, anti-Semitic leadership (at the time of this printing), will likely abandon Israel. When she does turn on her old friend, the end cannot be far off.

As we saw in Chapter One, humanism is entrenched on a worldwide scale. With its atheistic stance, it is no wonder that Israel is the focus of so much hatred. Almost all nations hate Israel, probably because of her belief in the one true God, her birthing of the male child (Christ), and through her, the oracles of God were delivered and preserved. Through her, God spoke, and the only true religions were born—Judaism and Christianity, both of which Satan hates. Plus, Israel serves as a witness to the world that God does exist and interjects Himself in the affairs of man.

We do believe that the end of time is closing in on an unsuspecting world. Perhaps our reasons for this belief are flimsy and fanciful to the unbelieving and totally unnecessary to those who already feel as we do. In either case, all of us need to approach these times with the intent to transform our own spiritual selves as we pursue the model walk before our God—the walk of holiness.

BIBLIOGRAPHY

CHAPTER ONE

1. Humanist Manifesto II
2. Humanist Manifesto II
3. H.G. Wells, from *The Hidden Dangers of the Rainbow*, page 125
4. Claire Chambers, from *Humanism* (Lubbock, Texas: Missionary Crusader, 1981), Page 2 Preface
5. Humanist Manifesto II, page 8
6. Humanist Manifesto II, page 8
7. Humanist Manifesto II, page 3
8. Humanist Manifesto II , page 8
9. Humanist Manifesto I
10. Humanist Manifesto II
11. Humanist Manifesto II
12. Humanist Manifesto II
13. Humanist Manifesto II
14. Humanist Manifesto II
15. Humanist Manifesto I
16. Humanist Manifesto II

CHAPTER TWO

17. Humanist Manifesto II, page 9

CHAPTER FOUR

18. Humanist Manifesto II, page 4
19. A Fabian, Sidney Webb, page xxix Democracy and Liberty
20. Humanist Manifesto II, page 7
21. *Democracy and Liberty*, Volume One, page xxix
22. *Democracy and Liberty*, Volume One, page 27

CHAPTER SIX

23. William Bowen, *Globalism: America's Demise* (Shreveport, Louisiana: Huntington House, Inc., 1984), Page 123

CHAPTER SEVEN

24. Humanist Manifesto I
25. Roland Gammon, from *A Planned Deception*, page 103
26. Found in *Guide for Action* put out by the American Humanists Association, from Humanism, page 3 Preface

27 Humanist Manifesto II
28 Humanist Manifesto I
29 Kilpatrick, *Psychological Seduction*, page 179
30 A reviewer of a book promoting charismatics, from *Beyond Seduction*, page 76
31 Humanist Manifesto II
32 A.W. Tozer, *Gems From Tozer* (Camp Hill, Pennsylvania: Christian Publications, 1979), page 47
33 From *Beyond Seduction*, page 260
>   Note: David Wilkerson's sermon *Christless Pentecost* gives an excellent and detailed look at the extent to which this prophecy has been fulfilled.

CHAPTER TEN

34 Humanist Manifesto II

CHAPTER ELEVEN

35 Humanist Manifesto I

CHAPTER FOURTEEN

36 David Wilkerson, *Bearing Fruit*, sermon
37 A.W. Tozer, *That Incredible Christian*, page 55

CHAPTER FIFTEEN

38 Richard Anderson quoting Louis Berkhof in *No Holiness, No Heaven* (Carlisle, Pennsylvania: The Banner of Truth Trust, 1986), page 69
39 A.W. Tozer, *The Best of A.W. Tozer*, pages 134, 177
40 T. Austin-Sparks, *The School of Christ* (Lindale, Texas: World Challenge, Inc.), pages 42, 56, 58
41 J.B. Stoney, *The Refiner's Fire*, Volume I, pages 80, 103
42 David Wilkerson, *Bearing Fruit*, sermon

CHAPTER SIXTEEN

43 A.W. Tozer, *The Best of A.W. Tozer*, Page 150
44 Leonard Ravenhill, from *The Refiner's Fire*, Volume I, page 68
45 Dr. James Hitchcock, from *The Home Invaders* (Wheaton, Illinois: Victor books, 1985), page 12
46 George Christie, from *A Planned Deception*, page 195
47 Dr. Rose K. Goldsen, from *The Home Invaders*, page 11
48 Donald Wildmon, *The Home Invaders*, page 14
49 Dr. James Hitchcock, from *The Home Invaders*, page 12
50 C.S. Lewis, from *Beyond Seduction*, page 180

CHAPTER SEVENTEEN

51 A.W. Tozer, *The Best of A.W. Tozer*, page 192
52 George Warnock, from *The Refiner's Fire*, volume I, page 50-53
53 David Wilkerson, *The Elijah Company*, sermon
54 David Wilkerson, *Call to Grief*, sermon
55 Humanist Manifesto II
56 Mikhail Gorbachev, *Mandate For Peace* (New York, New York: Paperjacks, LTD., 1987), page 254

CHAPTER NINETEEN

57 A.W. Tozer, *That Incredible Christian*, page 19
58 Ibid., page 105

CHAPTER TWENTY

59 Humanist Manifesto II
60 William Kirk Kilpatrick, *Psychological Seduction*, page 22
61 Leonard Ravenhill, *Why Revival Tarries*, page 88
62 A.W. Tozer, *The Best of A.W. Tozer*, page 201, 202
63 William Kirk Kilpatrick, *Psychological Seduction*, page 26, 46

CHAPTER TWENTY-ONE

64 A.W. Tozer, *That Incredible Christian*, page 50
65 A.W. Tozer, *Renewed Day by Day: A Sacred Gift of Seeing*

APPENDIX A

66 Nathaniel West, from *The Great Rapture Hoax*, pages 24, 25

About The Author

Thomas G. Reed

Thomas Reed earned his degree in Mathematics and Physics at East Carolina University. After working for 16 years as a design and cost analysis engineer for the telephone company, he took a two year sabbatical to study and try to understand the true meaning of holiness, especially as contrasted to the smothering effect of humanism and liberal progressivism on all our lives. The theological side of *After Capitalism and Christianity* was written during this period, but remained unpublished for twenty years. Then in 2009, the political side of *After Capitalism and Christianity* was written in response to the sharp turn to the left in American politics and how the liberal left's agenda appears to match exactly that of religious humanism. Specifically, their common goal of a one world government necessitates the demise of our country. Thus, we are even now witnessing the demise and dismantling of the greatest nation on earth—even the fall of the once mighty American eagle. By mixing religion and politics in the same book, we hope to connect America's (and Americans') future with our willingness to choose between our current destructive course and a quest for personal holiness and national revival. At least then we would have the hope that no matter how America falls, we can be saved.

Thomas is married and a business owner in Western North Carolina.